Ecstasy, Ritual, and Alternate Reality

Felicitas D. Goodman

Ecstasy, Ritual, and Alternate Reality

Religion in a Pluralistic World

Indiana
University
Press

Bloomington and Indianapolis

Manufactured in the United States of America

Library of Congress Cataloging-in-Publication Data

Goodman, Felicitas D.
Ecstasy, ritual, and alternate reality.
Bibliography: p.
Includes index.
1. Religion.   I. Title.
BL48.G635   1988   200   87-46248
ISBN 0-253-31899-8

1 2 3 4 5 92 91 90 89 88

To my teachers, the shamans—
past and present

Contents

Acknowledgments

The initial draft for this book was written during my sabbatical leave from Denison University in the 1975–76 school year. The early formulation underwent a number of revisions as I gained experience in presenting the topic in undergraduate classes, and later in intensive courses and workshops to a more sophisticated group of adults, and as I added results from my continuing research. In its formative stages, this research was supported by Public Health Grant MH 07463 from the National Institute of Mental Health, by the Denison University Research Foundation, and by a grant-in-aid for research from the Society of the Sigma Xi. I want to express my appreciation to these agencies. I am also deeply grateful to my students and research consultants who so generously shared their observations with me.

In the cultural history of the West, interest in religion keeps waxing and waning, but even in periods of apparent inattention, the subject is seen lurking just beyond the border. No matter what attitudes prevail, each generation seems constrained to write its own version. To latter-day observers, each of these versions appears incomplete, yet their own attempts will fare no better in the eyes of their successors. So we might as well accept our limitations. In this sense the present work lays no claim to completeness or finality. It is simply an invitation to contemplate yet another configuration of facets on that glittering, mysterious, elusive sphere that we call religious experience.

Introduction

Works about religion are nearly as old as writing itself. For a history of those works, the reader will have to go elsewhere. What is presented here is not a diachronic but mainly a synchronic representation of religions around the world. The account is intended to heal an old rift, to rectify an image created by the contention still extant in the modern literature that there are two kinds of religion. They are thought to be qualitatively different, one group being "great," the other "primitive." By implication, the former are considered to be valid, possessing the Truth (usually capitalized), or at least part of it, while the latter are "a collection of superstitions," characterized by "childish fancy," as John MacQuarrie, a writer on comparative religion of the 1960s, put it. In the Western world, the distinction is an ancient one, based on the universalistic claims of the Christian denominations that their god is the only god and their path the only one to salvation. Other large religious communities have come to similar conclusions. The Japanese category "religion" includes only those faiths possessing a known founder, a "book," and a formalized body of dogma.

Mid-nineteenth-century evolutionary theory provided what appeared to be a scientifically grounded underpinning for this view. Working with pitifully inadequate ethnographic reports, social thinkers of Darwin's time applied his evolutionary theories to non-Western societies. They argued that in the same manner as there were still amoebas and reptiles and lungfish around, tokens of a distant past of the earth, there were also fossil societies that because of some innate inferiority had not been able to achieve the stage of the superior industrialist countries. Logically, then, societies with simple technologies had simple, primitive religions, while those with blast furnaces and steam engines worshipped in the most advanced way. It was not too difficult, they held, to reconstruct from the religions of existing "savage" societies the steps by which religion might have evolved. Thus, Lubbock, a late-nineteenth-century Scottish author, stipulated the following sequence of development:

atheism
fetishism
nature worship
idolatry or anthropomorphism
deities become truly "supernatural" beings
morality becomes associated with religion

The powerful paradigm of evolution remained dominant in social-science speculation for decades. Eventually, however, two other approaches also became influential. One was a simplistic kind of comparative method, still much used today, where snippets are cut from all sorts of religions, which are then assembled into a collage of doubtful value. An example of this sort of pastiche is provided by *The Golden Bough* of the late-nineteenth-century English writer J. G. Frazer. The other train of thought is the creation of Sigmund Freud, the father of psychoanalysis. Drawing his conclusions from individual psychopathology, Freud invented a myth, according to which "original man" lived in a primordial horde, in which only the father had access to all the females. Enraged, the sons finally killed and ate him. After the deed was done, they began to feel guilty, and declared their father to be their totem, instituting prohibitions against eating it. And since it was their desire to copulate with their mother and sisters that had started the tragic sequence, they introduced the rules prohibiting incest, thus initiating "religion."

The inception of modern fieldwork swept away much of this kind of speculation. We possess today a large number of excellent monographs of non-Western religions. What they demonstrate is that just as there are no "fossil" societies or languages, for that matter, there are no fossil religions, either. There is no way in which we could reconstruct the religion of beings antedating *Homo sapiens*. Scraps thrown together on the basis of superficial similarities as done by the early comparativists can teach us nothing about the early stages of religion. And Freud's myth does not stand up to the findings of modern primatology. Even nonhuman primates, for instance, have incest taboos.

One defect that the various approaches to the phenomenon of religion share is that they are very narrowly focused. Even as late as the middle years of this century, the subject was usually discussed in the rarefied atmosphere of theology alone, or in combination with some heavy-handed philosophy. For non-Western religions, the discussions did not go much beyond Frazer. But religion is a complex behavior, and a considerable number of factors have impinged on its development. If we want to gain some understanding of it that goes beyond mere acquaintance with its surface, we need to consider also insights provided by such diverse fields as ecology, psychology, neurophysiology, linguistics, and even, as mentioned above, primate studies. As we shall see, treating the topic in a more cross-disciplinary manner than hitherto attempted is going to open up truly exciting new vistas in an ancient field.

Part One

Theory

ONE

⤳

The Religious

Can It Be Defined?

Magic versus religion. In contrasting the so-called "great religions" and others, the term *magic* is often employed to describe the latter. In the past, this usage was popular because it seemingly supported the superiority of the "great religions." There, a religious ceremony, so the argument went, was designed to elevate, to praise, etc., while a magical rite of savages was thought to be able, "falsely, of course," to manipulate the objects and circumstances of the real world.

Even when a somewhat more balanced view of non-Western humanity began to dawn, the topic of magic proved to be surprisingly slippery, despite the fact that at first blush it seemed to represent an apparently neat and well-defined category. Recognizing the difficulty, social scientists tried repeatedly to re-define the difference between religion and magic. To the French sociologist Emile Durkheim, it lay in the fact that a religious rite was obligatory, while a magical one was optional. Frazer, also much quoted on the topic of magic, subdivided the category into types, such as "contagious magic," "imitative magic," etc. He considered magic "false science": Science worked, magic did not. The British social anthropologist Bronislaw Malinowski, consistent with his view that all cultural behavior was "functional," i.e., directed toward the goal of satisfying physical needs, advanced the suggestion that magic had a definite practical purpose, while religious rites were expressive without pur-pose. Harking back to Frazer's "false science," he felt that magical practices attempted to bridge the hiatus between knowledge and practical control, so that magic was applied when the practitioner felt that there was an element of uncertainty involved. In a now-famous example (1954), he described how in the Trobriand Islands, where he did fieldwork in the first decade of this century, no fishing magic was used to enhance the catch and provide protection within the lagoon. Such rituals were carried out only on the high seas.

Weston La Barre[1] attempted to stretch the phenomena of religious behavior to fit the Procrustean bed of Freudian psychoanalysis. As to the nature of magic, he makes the intriguing suggestion that "mothers make magicians; fathers, gods" (1970: 109). In an entirely Freudian vein, he points to the distinction between the father figure as instilling fear, while the infant can summon the mother simply by crying. In the same way, magic is an outcry for help: "Magic is . . . an oral context adaptation: the magic cry summons succorance, coerces reality, and the inchoate infant ego emotionally consumes the world" (1970: 95). Magic is seen as the "self-delusory fixation at the oral-anal phase of operation" (1970: 10).

Upon closer scrutiny, none of the suggestions advanced by the above writers holds up. Rites are not either elevating or manipulative, obligatory or optional, abstract or practical. They usually combine these various features, which in addition do not correlate with a religious/magical opposition. Contrasting magic as "false science" and our presumably "true" one is so ethnocentric, it hardly warrants comment. In fact, Malinowski was the one who early pointed out that non-Western societies had "true" science, or else how could they have survived? As to La Barre, he twists his own metaphor later in the same discussion. Mothers, he continues, do not "make" magicians, in the way fathers "make," i.e., become overpowering "supernatural" entities. Rather he finds that the magician, far from being the mother, is the child crying to the "supernatural."

No matter how we turn the individual arguments, the difference between magic and religion remains unclear. As Dorothy Hammond says, "Examination of the concept [magic] indicates that the distinction between magic and religion, whether phrased as dichotomy or polarity, is unwarranted. . . . That the distinction has led only to confusion supports the judgment that the abstraction is based in misinterpretation" (1970: 1355).

Definitions of Religion. With the concept of magic as a useful category within the religious realm out of the way, we now need to ask, What then is religion? How can it be defined? As can be expected, the literature abounds in suggestions. To cite a few examples, there is the famous minimal and descriptive one by the British social philosopher Edward Tylor: "It seems best . . . to claim as a minimum definition of religion the belief in Spiritual Beings" (1871: chap. 11).[2] The Austrian anthropologist Father Wilhelm Schmidt went the historical route:

> Original religion revolved around the worship of a high god. Out of this *Ur-monotheismus* there later arose, through a process of degenerative speculative thought, such concepts as spirits and ghosts, animal and plant souls, multiple gods, and wide variety in worship. (Paraphrased in Lessa and Vogt, 1965: 21)

Clifford Geertz suggests a normative formulation:

> [Religion is] a system of symbols which acts to establish powerful, pervasive, and longlasting moods and motivations in men by formulating conceptions of a general order of existence and clothing these conceptions with such an aura of factuality that the moods and motivations seem uniquely realistic. (1966: 4)

The influence of Freud can clearly be discerned in the psychological definition proposed by La Barre:

> In a sense religion is the group dream, or perhaps nightmare, that teaches men the proper stance *vis-à-vis* the parental divine, as characteristically shaped in that society, but in either case now "unreal" except psychologically. (1970: 12–13)

And then there are also structural definitions, such as this one by Melford E. Spiro:

> Every religion consists of a cognitive system, a set of explicit and implicit propositions regarding the superhuman world and man's relation to it, which it claims to be true. (1966: 96)

In addition to these carefully crafted definitions, we frequently encounter what Kroeber and Kluckhohn, in a book on definitions of culture, term "incomplete definitions" or "on-the-side stabs in passing" (1952: 141). Here, for instance, is one by Joseph Campbell, an author on comparative religion, from an article written for the educated lay reader:

> These three lower chakras[3] correspond to man's life in his naive state, turned outward upon the world. A religion that concerned itself with only these lower chakras, one that cared little for inward and mystical realization, would hardly merit the name of religion at all. (1975: 78)

Or another one, this time from the work of an anthropologist:

> Although the kumu [priest] ... officiates in a fertility ceremony, its form is far removed from the crude sexual symbolism that characterizes other ritual activities, and it is evident that what is involved is a true cult in which the problem of mere earthly existence has been sublimated. (Reichel-Dolmatoff, 1971: 139)

To take the incomplete definitions first, they demonstrate that the authors disapprove of sexual symbolism in religion, which is a Western cultural bias. Rather than enlighten us on the nature of religion, such "on-the-side stabs in passing" insinuate value judgments into the thinking of the reader by presenting them as generally valid. They are not, for they are artifacts of a particular culture, and thus their validity does not extend beyond its boundaries.

The other definitions quoted—there are, of course, innumerable more— demonstrate that each writer is intent on staking out a domain, mapping precise limits to the way in which the phenomenon "religion" is to be viewed. None of the definitions is entirely incorrect, to be sure. "Religion" includes some of everything they touch on: It speaks about "spiritual" beings; some societies have high gods, although "degenerative thought" is no longer acceptable to modern theory; it has symbols; it shows the operation of psychological mechanisms; it is a cognitive system, shaped by the culture of the respective society; there is ritual, and there are myths. But it will be noted that none of the definitions covers all these aspects, and by delineating boundaries and decreeing what belongs within the domain, those features that fall outside are necessarily classed as irrelevant, or worse, as inadmissible. Clearly, the many facets of the phenomenon can simply not be accommodated in a single, concise definition. What we need instead to do justice to religious behavior and to the complexity of the religions that humans profess is to formulate a sort of megadefinition, or, since that will most likely be unworkable, a theory of religion consisting of a number of interrelated tenets. The question, then, is, What might these tenets be?

Universals of Religion. Much discussion in textbooks of comparative religion is devoted to the diversity of human faiths. What is often overlooked is that beyond their undoubtedly great differences, all religions share some "universals," a certain rather limited number of striking traits. These traits are as follows:

1) *Ritual.* One of the most visible manifestations of any religion is its ritual. Some anthropologists have gone so far as to use the term *ritual behavior* as synonymous with religion. This is an unfortunate choice, because all habitual human behavior is ritualized (see, e.g., Goffman, 1967). Religious ritual, properly viewed, has a special task, namely, expressing all or part of the complete drama of human life, from birth to procreation, and to death.

2) *Altered states of consciousness.* A religion can be described using ordinary language, but a religious *experience* can take place only if there are radical changes in the way the body functions, initiating an alteration in consciousness, in the perceptual state. In religious contexts, there are in the main two altered states of consciousness that are institutionalized: *lucid dreams* occurring in sleep, and the religious altered state of consciousness, the *religious trance*, leading to the experience of ecstasy. Both provide entrance into the *alternate reality*.

3) *The alternate reality.* This aspect of reality is often described as being "supernatural." The term will be avoided here except in quotations. The argument in favor of such an omission is that if a phenomenon were *super-*

natural, humans, being part of nature, would be unable to perceive it. Instead, we will assume the stance, shared by religious specialists the world over, that the alternate reality is another part or dimension of reality as a whole. Ethnographers innocent of the experience of this reality often contend that it is identical with images perceived during ordinary dream states. This is an error that has haunted modern writings ever since Tylor first proposed it in the last century. Ordinary dreams, however, are very different from experiences in the alternate reality. They are strongly idiosyncratic; their components are usually one-dimensional, dissolve easily, and are difficult to remember.

By contrast, the alternate reality entered with the help of the religious trance or the lucid dream is patterned by the specific culture that the religious practitioner belongs to. Such experiences or visions have great internal consistency. The objects of a vision can be examined from all sides, and the details of a visit to the alternate reality are easily recalled, often being remembered as long as a person lives.

4) *Good fortune, misfortune, and the rituals of divination.* Unaccountable changes in life, be they good or bad, are usually attributed to nonhuman agencies, and there are numerous rituals by which humans try to wrest their secrets from them. This leads us into the intriguing topic of divination.

5) *Ethics.* Humans have a basic need to live harmoniously with each other and to safeguard a dynamic balance between ordinary and alternate reality in their lives. This is accomplished by obeying certain principles of conduct, incorporated into a system of ethics.

6) *The semantics of the term for "religion."* All societies have a word for religion: It is a named category. Unfortunately, this term is often mistranslated or misinterpreted, and may even go unreported. Linguistic fieldwork indicates that it is a composite category, consisting of three distinct parts: two refer immutably to the religious trance and the attendant ecstatic experience, on the one hand, and to the alternate reality, on the other, while the third one varies with the respective culture.

The six traits outlined above that all religions share, offer a convenient framework for a systematic comparison. However, as we try to compare religions cross-culturally using these characteristics, we discover a curious discontinuity. While in some instances, religious systems appear to be closely related, in other cases the differences with respect to a certain trait are so thoroughgoing, they cut so sharply, that we intuit the action of a powerful disruptive force. I propose that this disruption resulted in a change in interaction with the habitat, leading to an important modification in lifestyle. The introduction of domesticated plants, for instance, altered among other things the settlement patterns, tools, clothing, and social structure, as well as the position of women, the bringing up of children, and population dynamics. It stands to reason that it should also affect religious behavior. That is, the interaction with the habitat represents to my mind the pivot, the "independent variable," as it is called in experimental science. It is the ratchet wheel in the complicated system that is culture. The components of culture are its dependent variables, including the universals of religion listed above.

Independent variable: The interaction with the habitat. I have chosen to speak of "habitat" rather than "nature" in order to indicate that in the context of human experience, nature is a "cultural fact." Humans do not perceive nature directly, in the raw, as it were, or in its entirety. As Marshall D. Sahlins says, "[At issue is not] the reality of the world; [what is at issue is] which worldly dimension becomes pertinent, and in what way, to a given human group by virtue of a meaningful constitution of the objectivity of objects" (1976: 145). This "meaningful constitution of the objectivity of objects" changes as humans adopt a new and different subsistence activity, which in turn changes their manner of interaction with the habitat.

In the course of human history, fundamental changes of this nature did not occur all that frequently. One such change was mentioned above: the introduction of the domestication of plants. There was also the domestication of animals, and finally urbanization. In anthropology, we distinguish the following societal types as the result of changes in adaptation to the habitat: hunting and gathering; horticulture; three different forms of nomadic pastoralism; full-blown agriculture; and urbanism. To paraphrase Sahlins, each new adaptation causes a different worldly dimension to become pertinent.

The sophistication of the religions of the hunter-gatherers and their extensive cross-cultural agreement suggest that religion must have been a part of human culture at least from the time when our herbivorous and/or scavenging ancestors became hunter-gatherers. In other words, it must be unimaginably old. Elaborate burials and traces of shamanistic activity go back sixty thousand years or more. To the eyes of the prehistorian, such evidence of religious activity is quite advanced. It is to be assumed that it was preceded by even earlier forms not detectable in the sites of still more ancient human activity. The beginnings of religion, in other words, are lost in the misty reaches of our past.

In summary, we may then say:

> *Religion is an ancient part of human culture. It shares cross-culturally a set of universals, namely, ritual, the religious trance and its attendant ecstasy, the alternate reality, ascription to the alternate reality of changes in fortune and rituals of divination, a system of ethics, and a tripartite named category. These universals are dependent variables of the interaction with the habitat. Religions vary systematically with societal type, that is, in correlation with modifications in the interaction with the habitat.*

The above concise theory provides the general outline of this work. In chapter 2 I am going to provide some "maybe" answers to the question concerning the process of emergence of religious behavior. I will do that by combining in an admittedly speculative manner results from archeology with ideas derived from linguistic research on the same topic. In chapters 3 and 4, I will present further details on the independent variable and the six dependent variables touched on above. Chapters 5 to 9 contain ethnographic examples of religions in correlation to societal type. In the Conclusion, finally, I will develop some conjectures on the future role of religion in urban societies.

TWO

Human Evolution and the Origins and Evolution of Religious Behavior

In 1866, the Société de Linguistique of Paris banned all discussion of the origin and evolution of human language and speech. The argument was that nothing could be known about the topic, and thus its treatment was sheer conjecture and idle speculation. No such interdict was ever issued with respect to religion, although the disquisitions on its origins have equally been plagued with "sheer conjecture and idle speculation." Take the French author Ch. R. de Brosses. He suggested in 1760 that humans first invented fetishism, that is, the worship of inanimate objects and of animals. Egypt, he thought, showed traces of such practices, which had also been reported by casual visitors to the West African coast. Fetishism gave rise to polytheism, and that in turn to monotheism. Subsequent speculation ran along similar totally unsupported and fanciful lines. Gradually, however, ethnography, archeology, prehistory, primatology, and even neurophysiology have greatly added to our knowledge about the cognitive evolution of humans, emboldening even the linguists to take a second look, more than a hundred years after the above quoted Paris decision.[1] As we shall see, some of the suggestions that emerged from their renewed consideration of the topic supported the idea that there might possibly be some parallels in the emergence of language and religion. To understand this train of thought, let us take a brief look at the course of human evolution as reconstructed by modern science.

Fossils unearthed at Olduvai, at Afar in Ethiopia, at Omo, at Lake Turkana (formerly Lake Rudolf), and at Laetolil or on the Potwar Plateau in Pakistan all contain faint traces of an elusive being evidencing recognizable differences that set it off from the nonhuman, pongid population. Its "hands, feet, pelvis, the trunk, jaws, etc. ... [were] all used somewhat differently than in other primates" (Holloway, 1976: 344). This creature—let us call it early *Homo* in order to avoid the acrimonious debate raging about its exact nature and descent—in all probability lived in the late Pliocene and early Pleistocene, that is, from several million to about one million years ago. During an exceedingly long transitional period, antedating the above time span, this early *Homo* had acquired grasping hands, bipedal locomotion, and upright stance, as well as a complex middle ear and stereoscopic vision. These changes had gone hand in hand with a reorganization of the brain, resulting especially in an increase of its auditory and visual areas.

Early *Homo* lived in hordes and subsisted on a mixed diet. It is to be assumed that even that early there was a division of labor. The men, with their heavier muscles, did the scavenging—not hunting yet, according to Pat Shipman (*Science* 224 (1984): 861)—while gathering was left to the women. The latter is a sophisticated task, as we know from modern gatherers. Vegetal food must be sought out and remembered, its location and seasonal variation noted; it must be harvested, arguing for a very ancient use of the digging stick, and carrying implements must be fashioned. There are no traces left of these perishable goods, but there certainly are vestiges of the foods brought to the living floors. These floors have also yielded stone tools, indication of a brain activity more developed than that of nonhuman primates.

We may assume that an important complex of social rules was further elaborated on the substrate of nonhuman tradition, namely, that of regulating sexual behavior. Modern humans and modern nonhuman primates share some of its features, suggesting that they may have derived from habits instituted in a common ancestral group. Its minimal form proscribes sexual relations between mother and son, a stricture, for example, observed by Jane Goodall in chimps (1971: 188). It is equally respected by baboons, and is also reported among vervet monkeys and other types of mammals. The second rule, observed in many mammals, is exogamy, that is, mating outside the natal group. Since it is found in baboons, but not in chimps, it may have been specific to an ancestor common to baboons and humans, but not to chimps, as argued by Robin Fox (1972). For humans, Owen Lovejoy (1981) suggests another line of reasoning. Our "reproductive success" (a concept of sociobiology) may have made exogamy necessary. This success came about because our ancestors overcame the long time gap between births, which still hampers reproduction of present-day nonhuman primates. Chimpanzees, for example, give birth on the average only once every 5.6 years. A closer succession of births for humans would have brought about a faster increase in population. Our similarity to the baboons accordingly may be only the result of an accidental convergence of traits. Both the incest rules and those governing the endogamy/exogamy complex have undergone extensive cultural elaboration. But only rarely are they tied to the religious complex, as a cross-cultural comparison readily reveals.

Prehistory and a better understanding of nonhuman primate and other mammal behavior effectively invalidate Freud's hypothesis about the origin of religion. The latter had nothing to do with the incest rule and must have had its roots elsewhere. The question is, where?

Going back to a point made earlier, I argued that one should not use "ritual behavior" as synonymous with religion. The fact that such usage could even come up, though, calls our attention to the fact that ritual is a visible part of religious behavior and that in this sense religion is involved with communication. So we may be able to get a handle on the riddle of the origin of religion if we look at the evolution of communication.

The intense contact between the members of a horde of early *Homo*, among the men during scavenging and among the women during gathering and home-making, could hardly have taken place without using some type of communication system. Research on human development in infancy allows some conjecture as to the nature and evolution of this communication.

Without going into the complex reasoning of the so-called recapitulationists, we can summarize their ideas by saying that ancient physical characteristics of long-forgotten ancestors can still show up in their descendants a million or more years later. A favorite example is the watery lifeway of the human embryo in its mother's womb. Some linguists, such as John T. Lamendella (1976: 397), contend that the same can be postulated about cognitive development. For instance, nonhuman primates and very young infants share the characteristic that their vocalization is limbically mediated. This means that it originates in brain structures located in the limbic system, an ancient part of the brain from an evolutionary perspective. Extremely ancient *Homo*, we may assume, used some such vocalization, perhaps what the linguist R. J. Andrew (1976: 673) calls "humanoid grunts." As long as *Homo*'s brain remained relatively simple, with only a rudimentary neocortex, vocalization did not progress any further than that. This period must have been immensely long, because at the same time the tools humans used remained virtually unchanged also. As the arche-ologist Glynn Isaac points out, "Early stages of material culture were by our standards incredibly long-lasting and static" (1976: 276; references below to toolmaking and the accompanying conceptual abilities are taken from Isaac's article). Our chuckles, shrieks, and laughter are part of a general human genetic endowment and go back to that ancient period in our evolution.

The assumption that the neocortex in early *Homo* must have been developed quite poorly can be deduced from the way humans made tools at the time. The tools found in Plio-Pleistocene sites show definite purposive activity, but hardly any imposition of design. This may have been a result of the target form's not being thought out clearly, the execution's being imprecise, or both. Either would indicate that the physical and neurophysiological preconditions for preparing tools had not yet developed significantly beyond those of con-temporary pongids. The basic range of tool forms was available, but at the time in question they occurred in "anarchic combinations with other variables of object forms" (Isaac, 1976: 281).

Returning to human infants, we find another "layer" of communication being added during the first year of their development to the limbically mediated vocalization, namely, gestures. Nonhuman primates use gestures also, an ability that was first explored by Gardner and Gardner (1969), who taught a chimpanzee to sign. We are therefore on pretty safe ground when we stipulate that the next step in the evolutionary sequence of *Homo* with respect to communication was also gesturing. As Lamendella argues, "More recently encoded genetic information generally tends to unfold later in ontogeny so as to preserve the temporal sequence in which new components of the genetic code were laid down" (1976: 398).

Whether the emergence of gestures as communication coincides with the evolving of grammar cannot be stated with certainty. Workers with nonhuman primates cannot tell for sure whether their subjects are indeed using grammar or not when arranging their signals into phrases. There is evidence, however, that infants using gestures possess a grammar, albeit a simple one. And as for early *Homo*, it is quite easy to show that a "grammar," that is, a body of rules, was indeed beginning to arise. Tools of the early Pleistocene demonstrate the increasing sophistication of the intellectual capabilities of early *Homo*. The total range of tools is not what changes, but rather what is developing is "the degree to which there were distinct target forms in the mind of the craftsman . . . , and the degree to which the craftsman could control his production, so that an orderly series of replicating forms resulted" (Isaac, 1976: 279–280). It stands to reason that this newly arising capacity was also expressed in communication, producing an increasing complexity of the gesture system.

The evolution of the neocortex, which mediated the gesture system, as it still does in infants and in nonhuman primates, was powerfully stimulated by a thoroughgoing change in the environment of early *Homo*, which started about the same time. Humans lost their sheltering, heavily forested habitat. As the result of a shift in climate, the dense forests gave way to a mixed landscape consisting of savanna, woodland, and open islands of space. Only those populations survived that had the plasticity to adapt to the new demands arising from this alteration, and to reorganize their social interaction in an efficient manner. This kind of challenge would select for the most intelligent in a given group, brutally favoring only those with a larger brain. Eventually, the change became measurable. While in the distant depths of our past, the ratio between brain and body weight, termed encephalization, had edged up only minimally, and brain size hovered between 350 and 400 cc, there was a sudden jump about two million years ago. Brains grew to 600 cc, and in another million years to close to 1,000 cc. Encephalization was augmented simultaneously. As the American neurophysiologist Harry J. Jerison remarks: "The rate of encephalization in hominids is particularly noticeable [at this time]. Its rapidity and extent were unique among Plio-Pleistocene vertebrates and must have resulted from extraordinary selection pressures for enlarged brains" (1975a: 403). And Henry M. McHenry, an American paleontologist, adds, "Not much before two million years ago . . . the stabilizing selection maintaining smaller brain size was transformed into directional selection favoring larger brains" (1975: 430).

By one million years ago, the stone toolmakers were producing very refined objects indeed, and particular forms were being picked out by custom and replicated in series, with an accent on symmetry. Several hundred thousand years later, there are deliberate and highly organized techniques of core preparation. What we see, in other words, is the emergence of a more and more complex grammar, which must have been accompanied by equally sophisticated conceptual thinking and the arising of a symbolic system.

The question is whether a sign-based communication could bear the burden of such increasing sophistication. After all, isn't sign language mostly "iconic," picture talk, unable to transmit abstract ideas? Gordon Hewes argues that experimentation with pictorial representation proves this idea to be wrong. He cites the example of Catholic missionaries who in the sixteenth century developed highly ingenious pictorial catechisms, which survived as the so-called Testerian manuscripts (1976: 495).

Observations in the laboratory lend further support to the hypothesis that humans used sign language first and developed speech later:

> Kendon (1975) can show, from frame-by-frame analysis of films, that the gestures either precede or are made at the same time as the relevant vocal signs, but never follow them. Normally, they anticipate the spoken words by several milliseconds. This priority is not what we might expect, were the manual movements merely some kind of subconscious spillover or leakage from the primary vocal message; moreover, if the voice is interrupted, the gesticulatory sequence usually is not disturbed. Here, as in the case of the apparent gestural communication priority in infants, we seem to have a suggestion that gesture is more fundamental and thus perhaps may be phylogenetically antecedent as well. (Hewes, 1976: 495)

Eventually, speech did enter the picture, and with that, we forever left the nonhuman primates behind. While human infants babble, for instance, nonhuman primate infants do not. We may want to ask, What sort of evolutionary factor or change in the brain may have led up to this new behavior? Logically, we may want to look once more to events in the neocortex. In doing so, we find that even when nonhuman primates do vocalize, the neocortex is not involved, while in young humans it is. There are brain connections there, in other words, that our nearest cousins in the animal kingdom do not possess. Yet that is probably not the entire story. Oscar S. M. Marin, a linguist, believes that the new trait had its point of origin in the auditory system. This assemblage, he says,

> served principally as an alerting system for rather indiscriminant recognition and detection of location of visually hidden targets; cognitively, it was the secluded cradle in which a symbolic system could operate independently of the environment. (1976: 907)

If we accept this line of reasoning, then we can say that speech entered the scene initially as an "auditory sign language." It surely must have evolved slowly, facilitated by a certain preadaptation that early *Homo* possessed. Perhaps as a result of their early upright stance, humans had a vocal apparatus different from that of their nonhuman primate cousins.[2] In addition, while being able to recognize holistic patterns, something that animals can do also, humans were early on capable of indentifying components in sequence, as evidenced by their tools. This is important for speech recognition, and is apparently limited to humans.

According to Hewes, holistic processing favored by signing and the sequential, analytic mode entering with speech may have been mingled:

> Professional sign-language interpreters for the deaf, who are hearing individuals, characteristically speak while signing, even though word order and syntax of the two languages [American Sign Language and English] may differ significantly. This suggests a capacity to communicate simultaneously in two languages, and . . . productively in both. . . . Such an accomplishment could have been the standard form of language during the hypothetical stage of its transition from gesture to speech. (1976: 495)

What pushed sign communication to the periphery was probably the fact that speech is a more pliant instrument for the needs of everyday communication than signing is. The latter has what amounts to a rather bothersome limitation. As the linguist William C. Stokoe points out,

> The sign language phrase puts its elements, not in the order in which they come out in writing, but in the natural order of events themselves and of the ideas to which these correspond. (1976: 507)

But humans do not usually want to stick to the "natural order of events." With greater sophistication of the brain, such constraints must have become increasingly irksome. What humans want to do is to exert control, mixing and scrambling the sequence of elements. In linguistics, this procedure is called "embedding." For example, in the sentence "The man who came to dinner was my boss," the phrase "who came to dinner" is embedded in the main clause, "the man was my boss." It is a grammatical strategy learned relatively late by children and so, we may assume, also came late in human cognitive development. Once more, the assumption is supported by what can be observed in tool assemblages. According to Isaac, it shows up in objects such as hafted axes, where the handle is subordinate to the head of the ax.

Yet, as we have seen, gesture as part of our genetic endowment has remained the companion of human speech, underlining and amplifying the message, and there are situations where it has continued to hold on to its dominant position. Imagine a love scene without the gesture of touching, for instance. Obviously, the spoken word is of secondary importance there, and we all feel sorry for Romeo, with Juliet confined to the balcony. And in ritual of any kind, gesture always takes precedence over the spoken word. A man cannot be knighted without the sword of his sovereign touching his shoulder. It is the gesture that imbues the ritual with its awe-inspiring quality. This process is even more pronounced in the religious ritual. A baptism cannot be performed by a spoken message from a tape recorder. A few years ago, a Catholic baptism was declared invalid by German church authorities because the requisite gestures, including the sprinkling of the water, had not been carried out, although all the necessary formulas had been spoken. It was the opinion of the priest from whom I have the story that a baptism performed only with the prescribed gestures would have been acceptable.

In ritual, in other words, we are once more back at the point of evolution where gesture reigned and speech as the newcomer had a mere subsidiary role. Given the overriding importance of ritual in religious observances, we can posit by extension that religious behavior must be at least as old as this point in our evolution. The linguistic argument neatly buttresses that of the archeologist, who as mentioned earlier has long pointed to intricate prehistoric burial customs as evidence for the antiquity of religious behavior.

THREE

~❦~

The Independent Variable
Interaction with the Habitat

In the course of the history of our species, a number of different adaptations have appeared vis-à-vis the habitat. Athough transition between them is fluid, anthropologists have been able to recognize five principal lifeways: hunter-gatherers, horticulturalists, agriculturalists, nomadic pastoralists, and city dwellers. As an ideal type, each one of these adaptations correlates with a different religious behavior. It is important, therefore, to outline their special characteristics.

The hunter-gatherers.[1] As we know, the exact time at which modern humans appeared is still a matter of debate. Most recently (see *Science* 237 (1987): 1292–1295) it has been suggested on the basis of new fossil evidence and molecular biological research that they arrived on the scene no earlier than 200,000 years ago. It appears pretty certain that their point of origin was Africa, and by 10,000 before our era they had succeeded in covering the earth.

In a very real way, the hunters and gatherers open the first chapter of our human history. And fittingly, this dawning was as close to paradise as humans have ever been able to achieve. The men did the hunting and scavenging, working for about three hours a week, and the women took care of daily sustenance by gathering vegetal food and small animals. It was such a harmonious existence, such a successful adaptation, that it did not materially alter for many thousands of years. This view is not romanticizing matters. Those hunter-gatherer societies that have survived into the present still pursue the same lifestyle, and we are quite familiar with it from contemporary anthropological observation. Despite the unavoidable privations of human existence, despite occasional hunger, illness, and other trials, what makes their lifeway so enviable is the fact that knowing every nook and cranny of their home territory and all that grows and lives in it, the bands make their regular rounds and take only what they need. By modern calculations, that amounts to only about 10 percent of the yield, easily recoverable under undisturbed conditions. They live a life of total balance, because *they do not aspire to controlling their habitat, they are a part of it*.

Nowhere is the harmony of their existence more evident than in their attitudes toward death. Myths of the hunters speak of a time when humans were immortal. That, of course, could not last. According to a Kiowa myth, their culture hero Saynday met Ant one day. This was some time after Saynday had guided the people up from the lower world through a hollow cottonwood tree, and some of them were beginning to get old. Saynday thought that humans should die and after four days should come back to life again, but Ant suggested that death should be permanent. People should die to make room for new people. Saynday agreed, and although Ant later repented of his suggestion when his own child prematurely sickened and died, Saynday did not change his mind. For the harmonious balance of the world to continue, humans had to start dying. But still, a death brings sadness, not only to the bereaved but also to the habitat, of which the deceased is an integral part. Therefore, when a hunter dies, such as a Pygmy of the Ituri rainforest in Africa (see Turnbull, 1962), the Forest, representing the habitat, needs to be consoled with a feast.

The horticulturalists. About twelve to ten thousand years before the present, in some instances even earlier, the stable picture we sketched above began to change. Almost simultaneously in many parts of the world, archeologists detect traces of humans beginning to work the soil and to domesticate plants. While the fact is clear, the reasons are less so. This was demonstrated by papers presented at a conference on the topic in 1973,[2] where a considerable number of mutually incompatible hypotheses were offered as to what might have happened and how. The most plausible one was published in 1977 by Mark Nathan Cohen, who argued that by about the tenth millennium before our era, humans had simply run out of space into which to migrate. Slowly and inexorably, their numbers increased everywhere. "Therefore," he writes, "it is not unreasonable to find a roughly synchronous building up of population pressure over very large portions of the globe, with the result that agriculture was 'invented' or adopted by most of the world's population within the same fairly brief time span" (1977: 16).

The cultivation of plants, Cohen points out, is actually not easier than hunting and gathering and does not provide a higher-quality, more palatable, or more secure food base. Its advantage is that it provides more calories per unit of land and time, and thus can support denser populations. Understandably, people did not go over to the cultivation of plants everywhere to the same extent. Where game and palatable plants continued in relative abundance, cultivation was kept to a minumum, while in other regions, more cultivation was needed. What we see is something like a sliding scale of traditional "horticulturalist" societies even today, with some working small gardens and doing a great deal of hunting and gathering, while the situation is reversed in other areas.

The role of women as gatherers in prehistory suggests that they must have been at the forefront of this cultural change, because of their superior knowledge of plants. After all, it is Eve in the biblical story who proffers the apple to Adam. This historical fact is clearly reflected also in horticulturalist mythology. In a story of the Creek Indians, a woman invited a number of neighbors and friends, and she offered them a delicious drink that they were not acquainted with. They were curious, of course, and finally observed that she kept washing her feet in water, and kernels of corn would come from her feet. That was what they had been served. Eventually, she taught them how to grow corn (Jackson Lewis, 1929: 10).

In another Creek variant, the grandmother and the corn are the same person. According to this legend, a boy was living with his grandmother. She always had corn and beans for him but would not tell him how she obtained such food. So one day he said he would go hunting, but he spied on her instead. His grandmother placed a riddle on the floor, stood with one foot on either side of it, and scratched the front of one of her thighs, whereupon corn poured down into the riddle. Then she scratched her other thigh, and beans came pouring out. That was how he found out how she obtained the food. Later he married and left home. When he returned to visit her, she was gone, but where the house had been, there grew all sorts of Indian corn and beans. "So the corn was a person, that old woman," the tale concludes (Big Jack of Hilibi, 1929: 11, 13).

And according to a story from Cochiti, a Rio Grande Indian pueblo, the people brought corn with them as they emerged into the present world, and once more, corn was associated with a woman: "The people were coming up from Shipap, Masewa led them, and after him his brother Oyoyewa. After them came our mother Iareku, the corn fetish" (Benedict, 1931: 13).

The change of culture ushered in by the horticulturalists was profound. Humans distanced themselves from the habitat. Burial customs reveal no trace that the habitat needed to be consoled when someone died. The same, by the way, was true of all subsequent adaptations. Instead, attention focused on healing the rent in the social fabric. Even more important, *humans began aggressively asserting control over the habitat*. By working the soil, they forced Mother Earth to yield what she did not have readily available. This represented a fundamental break with hunter-gatherer attitudes. While no doubt the cultivation of plants was a solution in a period of great need, what was experienced as a rape of the Mother still produced a massive feeling of guilt. It is with the horticulturalists that we encounter for the first time a prediction about the end of the world as ultimate retribution for this sacrilege. Of such horticulturalist prophecies, the Hopi one is the one known best in this country. It has been interpreted as referring to the destruction of the earth by World War III, and the emergence of humankind into the fifth world from this, our fourth one. "That time is not far off. It will come when the Saquaschuh [Blue Star]

Kachina dances in the plaza. He represents a blue star, far off and yet invisible, which will make its appearance soon" (Waters, 1963: 334). A prophecy recorded early this century from another horticulturalist society, this time from Brazil, is even starker, not holding out the promise of a fifth world. This is how the Apapocuva-Guaraní put it:

> When Ñanderuvuçu [First Man] decides on the end of the world, to put an end to the suffering of the earth, he will awaken the bat demons that hang from the rafters of his house and will send them out to devour the sun and the moon.
>
> Then he will order the blue tiger lying under his hammock to attack humanity. Singing, the blue tiger will descend from the heavens, and no one will escape his voraciousness. Finally, Ñanderuvuçu will pull away to the east the eternal wooden cross that supports the earth. Simultaneously, starting at the western edge of the earth, the world will burn below the surface. Farther ahead, the flames will break through the surface, and the piece behind them will crash into the precipice with a thunderous noise. Slowly at first, then ever faster, the destruction will progress, until the earth sinks down into the eternal night. (Curt Nimuendajú, 1914: 400; translation by me)

Ethnographic accounts of horticulturalist societies attest to the durability of this tradition over time and to its wide distribution. Recently (1984) Gerhard Baer, a Swiss anthropologist, described an extensive body of beliefs about the destruction of the world among the Matsigenka Indians of eastern Peru. Robert Dentan (1968) tells of a blood sacrifice offered to Thunder and his allies by the avowedly nonaggressive Semai of Malaysia, apparently to ward off this retribution by the habitat. As they explain, if they did not perform this ritual, "this whole place would be flat to the ground, covered with mud—we'd be underneath it" (p. 23). And in his book about the Japanese mind, Robert C. Christopher (1983) contends that every Japanese achievement is shaped by a sense of impending catastrophe and the overwhelming need to survive. Japan is our only example of a large, stratified, industrialized society that, in Shinto, its folk religion, retained a horticulturalist system of beliefs and rituals.

While the dominant cultural idea of the hunter-gatherers is balance, that of the horticulturalists is metamorphosis. In essence, this theme is already presaged in hunter-gatherer initiation rites: Via the ritual, the youth turns into an adult. But it comes to full fruition with the horticulturalists. Seeds, after all, become plants, only to yield seeds once more. The plant is merely another aspect of the seed. For the seeds to reveal their alternate aspect, they need to undergo the ritual of being planted in the ground. All other objects of ordinary reality have alternate aspects also, insects, stones, mountains, the wind, the heavenly bodies, and of course also humans, and in the ritual of metamorphosis, alternate between these aspects. The point is made beautifully clear by the

Plate 1. Olmec shaman metamorphosing into jaguar. From Furst and Furst, 1981: 22, 23.

two Olmec statues shown in plate 1, where in the same body posture the man has a human head in the first one, and that of a jaguar in the next one.

The agriculturalists. In many regions of the world, horticulture remained dominant as the most suitable adaptation for the particular ecological niche it occupied. In other areas it represented only a short interlude between hunting and gathering and full blown, open-field agriculture. In Central Europe, for example, it lasted very briefly, as demonstrated by excavations carried out at Lepenski Vir, a site near the Iron Gate gorge on the Danube. The hunting and gathering phase, with its fishing and the utilization of wild vegetal foods, lasted from the time of the occupation of the site at about 5,600 before our era until six hundred years later. By contrast, the horticulturalist phase, with the introduction of domesticated grasses and amaranth being added to fishing and hunt-

Plate 2. Façade of the sanctuary of house no. XLIV (Lepenski Vir II) with
two sculptures in their original position. After Srejović, 1981: 85, pl. 30.

ing, came to florescence and then declined in a scant hundred years. Even
though fleeting, the era produced some hauntingly beautiful monumental
sculptures of humans metamorphosing into fish, such as those seen in plates
2 and 3.

Because the transition from horticulture to another phase happened so early
in Europe, and also possibly because the phase itself did not last very long, as
demonstrated by Lepenski Vir, there is only a shadowy memory of it in legend.
Many Western social scientists hardly even make a distinction between the
two types of societies, lumping them together under cultivators. This creates
the illusion that the tradition was practically imperceptible, a gradual increase
in the size of the fields out of demographic or economic necessity, until we
arrive at the permanent villages and open fields of more recent times. However,
people are always reluctant to give up a cherished lifestyle, and this must have
been especially harsh when what was being lost was as rich and satisfying as
the culture of the ancient hunter-planters.

Plate 3. Sculpture no. 5 (Lepenski Vir II). After Srejović, 1981: 95, pl. 51.

That the contest between horticulture and agriculture was a wrenching, brutal struggle becomes clear when we examine the epic literature of societies closer in history to these events than those in Europe, such as the *Popol Vuh* or "Book of Counsel" of the Highland Maya, written before the middle of the sixteenth century in Quiché Maya, but using the Latin alphabet.[3]

In my view, the story deals with the conflict between the world view of horticulture and that of agriculture and is played out in the border region between ordinary and alternate reality, that is, in history and in myth. From the start, the aggressors are the Sky Spirits. Interestingly, the comments to the text by the translators are all in favor of these "Spirits of Light." Caught in our common Western linguistic trap, where "light" and "white" and "above" are equated with "good," and "dark" and "below" are "bad," and doubtless also because they themselves are shaped by Christian agriculturalist tradition, the commentators never realize that these beings of light are anything but benevolent. In fact, as the story unfolds, they show themselves to be vain, power hungry, and treacherous, lying murderers.

At the outset, the Spirits of the Sky set about creating people for the express purpose that they should praise their creators. They make them of wood, but forget to provide them with mouths, so they callously destroy them, for mouth-less people cannot utter any praise.

Their next undertaking is directed against beings already on the earth. Why? Because these personages are proud, and so are presumably unsuited for ut-tering docile, mindless praise. In the shorthand of the narrative, it is entirely clear who these men are. The first one murdered—possibly a stand-in for his entire society—is Chief *Macaw*, that is, a shaman who in metamorphosis is a bird. In other words, we are dealing with adversaries of the Sky Spirits who are horticulturalists. In agriculture, there is no ritual of metamorphosis. The next one who arouses the anger of the Spirits of the Sky is the "son" of Chief Macaw, that is, a member of a similar society. He is *Sage Fish-Land*, someone whose metamorphosed identity is a fish, but being a human, he is a "fish on land," reminiscent of the shamans of Lepenski Vir (pl. 2 and 3). Other victims of a similar nature soon follow suit.

The next part of the campaign of the Sky Spirits against the horticulturalists is a war of propaganda, directed against that warm and sheltering womb of humankind, the lower world, beautiful home of the spirits of the dead, but also of spirits wearing animal masks and ready to make friends with humans and to help them, especially in healing, if they come to call. A party of intended murder victims is lured there, and they find that it is not at all what they had been taught to expect. Instead, it is a frightening world ruled by Chief Death. His companions are Chief Crippler, Chief Blood Flux, Chief Abscess, Chief Jaundice, and Chief Tumors on Legs. Their weapons are skulls and crossbones. There is also a Chief Betrayal and Misfortune and a Chief Blood Hawk, who fells travelers so that they die with blood gushing from their mouths. And the list goes on. There are a number of mansions: one has eternal fog, another one greets sojourners with bone-chilling cold and hail, a third one is inhabited by jaguars gnashing their teeth, and a fourth one is filled with killer bats.

After the Sky Spirits have done away with their enemies, they once more try their hands at creating submissive humans. This time they make sure that they are properly humble by creating them entirely out of maize. But they make one mistake: They endow them with miraculous eyes that can see far into the distance. That, of course, must not be. With such visionary qualities, commonplace among the horticulturalists, these humans would be like their creators. So they take that gift away from them, giving them weak, nearsighted eyes instead.

Of course, these thoroughly domesticated, ignorant humans have no idea where maize came from. So they are easy prey to the lies of the Sky Spirits, who tell them that maize and other good things were actually created in the "Houses on Top of Pyramids," that is, in their temples. The humans do have fire, but the Spirits of the Sky take it away from them, so they have to beg for it or else freeze to death. Where people are recalcitrant, not wanting to give up their fire, the Sky Spirits send rain and hail and extinguish it. As a final indignity, these maize humans do not even have any gods and need to go to the "cities" of the Sky Spirits to beg for some. We shall see in chapter 7 how successful the Sky Spirits of the world were in gutting horticulturalist religion.

In Lepenski Vir and elsewhere in the Old World, the horticulturalist phase was terminated by the introduction of new cultigens and of domesticated animals. In the earth layer covering up the remains of the Lepenski Vir horticulturalists, there is a grave in which a man's head rests on the skull of a steer.

The raising of animals brought with it the emphasis on the significance of male generative power, initiating in art the representation of the phallus. This is seen in the headless male figure from Central Europe, of the fifth millennium before our era, pictured in plate 4. With both his hands, the man is holding his erect penis, which in many contemporary pieces is painted red.

The demise of horticulture, however, could also come about without the advent of animal husbandry. For instance, except for the dog, and the cameloids on the high plateaus of South America, there were no domesticated animals in the Western hemisphere. Yet horticulture still declined early in Central America, although it remained prevalent north and south of that area. Concomitantly, the phallic complex is absent in the region's classical art. This was noted with puzzlement by nineteenth-century European explorers. Contemplating the Aztec ruins, the German traveler Alexander von Humboldt is supposed to have lamented "the absence of erotic imagination."

What all agriculturalists have in common is the illusion of power, of being able to exert control over the habitat. It is an illusion, for with the advent of a lifestyle where domesticated animals and plants provided the major or only sustenance, humans unwittingly bent their necks to the yoke. No longer could they freely roam, for they could not leave their fields behind, which represented many years of work in clearing away vegetation and stones and leveling the ground. Where paddy rice is grown, to mention an exaggerated example, some irrigation dams required as much as nine hundred years to construct. People needed to tend and guard their fields, so they constructed permanent shelters nearby. Both their fields and their homes tied them to a certain locality. In this manner, agricultural activity also restricted a group's interaction with the habitat at large: The scope of life became narrower, more specialized in outlook than that of either the hunter-gatherers or the horticulturalists. The habitat was still there, powerful, but also distant. As we shall see in modern agriculturalists, the features of the habitat are viewed in a utilitarian fashion. The British social anthropologist Gunter Wagner tells of the Abaluyia (Bantus) of Kavirondo in Kenya that the moon is praised because it shines upon the people at night and helps them to make love. The same attitude prevails with regard to the landscape:

Plate 4. Man holding erect penis.
Sesklo, Thessaly, fifth millennium B.C.
After Gimbutas, 1982: 221, pl. 228.

[Its features] command interest only in as much as they directly affect the well-being of the individual or the tribal community. Such striking sights as the broad massif of Mount Elgon, which extends over the northern horizon and is seen from every point of the district, or the Kavirondo Gulf of Lake Victoria, which is clearly visible from many hills in the southern part of the district, seem to arouse little interest. . . . The only exception is that among the Logoli the waters of Lake Victoria serve as a dumping-ground for witch-craft medicine. (1954: 33–34)

The earth is seen mainly as a docile partner; no feeling of guilt attends to despoiling it. In a Hindu myth, the *sha-ligrams*, perfect beings floating in an ocean of light, are getting bored and ask their Lord Shiva for permission to go traveling. They find a beautiful planet and colonize it, and assuming human shape, they live in great happiness. Eventually, however, conflicts arise, there is a frightful war that engulfs the entire planet, which is ravaged and destroyed. With never a thought given to what they leave behind, the *sha-ligrams* divest themselves of their human bodies and fly home, only to set out later on another onslaught on some distant shore, repeating the entire cycle once more.

Instead of being plagued by guilt feelings toward the earth, agriculturalists are beset by paranoia toward "bad" plants—weeds—and toward equally "bad" animals that intrude into their fields, all of which are to be exterminated in order to protect the harvest. These attitudes are part of a hidden, more abstract complex. In the agricultural adaptation, humans have drawn a magic circle around themselves, their homes and fields. They are confined within their fences, but also protected against what lies beyond. Any intrusion is experienced as threatening in the extreme. The intruder brings with it danger, sickness, pollution, the curse. (See Gehrts, 1967, who analyzes the story of Romulus and Remus using this cultural model; also Duerr, 1985, whose entire work *Dreamtime* is an elaboration of this premise.)

The presence of this complex makes intelligible the shift we see in agriculturalist apocalyptic prophecies away from horticulturalist notions of a ravished earth toward a more socially informed basis. This is evident even in stories where the cataclysm is displaced into the past, as in the myths about the flood. A catastrophe, a kind of ultimate exorcism, will rid the world of all evil people, and the good will survive and carry on undisturbed in their pure and sacred confines.

The nomadic pastoralists. In regions of the earth where there were animals capable of being tamed, and other ecological conditions were suitable, the innovation of animal domestication, leading to various forms of pastoralism, appeared regardless of the existing societal type. In all instances, of course, it significantly altered human interaction with the habitat.

In northern Europe, and in north and central Asia, hunter-gatherers followed already existing herds, such as reindeer, eventually exerting multiple control over the animals. The complexity of the root causes involved is illustrated by the fact that the same evolution did not take place between caribou herds and the surrounding Eskimo population. In other instances, hunters created herds of animals which they initially came to know as pets, as most likely happened with the horse. There is archeological evidence of the domestication of the horse on the plains of Eurasia going back five thousand years. Although the herds provide the principal part of subsistence, bands still follow the wildlife, going on extensive hunting and fishing trips, with the women providing vegetal foods by gathering berries, field onions, and wild garlic in the taiga.

Horticulturalists also became associated with herds. Animals capable of domestication began congregating around plantings, eventually to be captured and become subject to selective breeding. Or, as happened in Lepenski Vir, they were brought in, already tamed, by migrants: A more gracile physical type appears together with the first cattle skeletons. When animal husbandry combined with horticulture in Africa, on the other hand, a division of labor evolved along sexual lines, with the men taking on the herds, and the women concentrating on the gardens. The Nilotic societies of sub-Saharan Africa show this pattern, as do the many groups in Papua-New Guinea, the former with cattle, the latter with pigs. Such a sequence of events can often be traced in legend. The British social anthropologist E. E. Evans-Pritchard (1956) tells that according to the African Nuer, humans in the mythological state were "simple," having neither sex organs nor stomachs and being able to make a meal of a single grain of millet. It was not until they acquired a stomach, and with it hunger, sex organs, fire, and spears, that the men started killing. Their first victim was the mother of cow and buffalo, that is, of animals associated on the one hand with the outside, the bush, in the form of the buffalo, and on the other hand with the home, the inside, i.e., cattle. Pigs assume the same double role in Papua-New Guinea, for there are both wild and domesticated pigs.

Finally, there are many instances, for example, in the Near East, where domesticated animals did not become important until the cultivation of the soil had evolved into full-scale, open-field agriculture. Herds made it possible to exploit marginal areas by grazing, at the same time providing a livelihood and eventually a distinct lifestyle for the surplus population. Mainly because they needed agricultural products for subsistence, such herders retained strong ties to the agricultural parent society.

Herders are continually prompted by considerations for the safety and well-being of their herds to gather information from the whole of their territory. This makes them acutely aware of the unitary aspect of the area that they view as their own, the arena in which they structure their cyclical migrations. Within it, however, there is usually one particular region, outstanding possibly because of lush pasture, an exceptionally reliable source of water, or other features, which the respective society considers more essentially homeland than all others traversed during the year. Only if the villages are permanent settlements and the jungle accessible with year-round vegetation, so that the herds need not be moved, as with the pigs in Papua-New Guinea, is this unitary aspect no longer apparent.

However, what all herders have in common is that although they do not actively modify their natural environment, they are not part of it, either. Instead, they exploit their habitat by interposing their animals. Culturally, the animals occupy center stage, although only part of the herders' subsistence derives from them. Other sources of food, although often of considerable importance, are ideologically deemphasized, because the animals represent the bridge between humans and the all-encompassing habitat, both in subsistence and also psychologically. With the habitat also possessing a sacred aspect, the animals thereby assume the role of the mediator, the bridge or messenger between the habitat and its alienated children.

The sacrifice and messenger complexes are central to the herder's religious experience. "It is the role and destiny of the cattle to be slaughtered in sacrifice," say the Nuer (Evans-Pritchard, 1956: 269). The point is supported by the observation that herders who hunt do not consider game as "sacrifice." In fact, the respective traditions are quite specific, excluding also domestic animals. They may historically have been latecomers, or never had the aspect of deriving from the "outside," the sacred ranges of the habitat. In the early Middle Ages, Christian missionaries, bent on destroying the pagan culture of Central Europe, dealt a severe blow to traditional religion when they forbade the sacrifice of horses: No substitution could be made.

For the ancient Mayas, although they were never herders, turkeys may have played a similar mediating role. Subliminally, at least, killing them even in secular context, such as for a wedding feast, has retained its numinous quality into the present. The slaughtering of cattle or pigs elicits no such emotion in the Maya villages. But there is a sudden change of mood, a hush that descends when at a fiesta someone asks, "Have they killed the turkeys yet?"

It is within the logic of the cultural situation of nomadic herders that they should have no tradition of end-of-the-world, apocalyptic prophecies. Any conflicts between humans and their habitat can be mediated by the sacrifice.

The city dwellers. Permanent settlements of quite large population aggregates arose almost as early as agricultural villages. Urban life was made possible by predictable and abundant food supplies located close by. Typically, ancient cities were built along river banks, facilitating the transportation of foodstuffs. For urbanites do not work the soil themselves, relying on the tillers to feed them instead. They are dependent on a subsystem of producers, who must work more than would be necessary in the absence of such institutions (i.e., the city).

Urbanites are divorced from the habitat. The earth, the sky, the rain, the plants, and the animals are not their partners in the struggle for subsistence. This alienation became even more pronounced with the advent of industrialization, eventually causing the destruction of traditional peasantries and the takeover by agribusiness. The latter has no direct tie with the habitat at all. Rather, it exploits it by the interposition of machinery. The earth, the land, is nothing but the site, the location of manufacture, commerce, and services.

Typically, therefore, the urbanites have no guilt feelings toward the habitat. The motivation of many environmentalists instead is more that of an antiquarian who wants to preserve rare books. People, in their view, have no place in pristine "nature." In the conflict a few years ago between the Forest Service and the Havasupai Indians over the latter's settlements on the rim of the Grand Canyon, the prestigious Sierra Club took the side of the Forest Service.

Yet the urbanites evince a morbid curiosity about cataclysmic prophecies, such as in our country for that of the Hopis, and have also produced some of their own. In urban predictions there is typically a tremendous natural catastrophe, with some extraterrestrial agency rescuing individuals of superior quality. The habitat, distant, incomprehensible, and blind, the ultimate outside force, will one day ineluctably strike. This view of the world may account psychologically for why it is so difficult to create a truly massive opposition against the threat of nuclear annihilation: The total, irreversible nuclear winter "fits in." The social side of this complex gave rise in Europe to Marxism and anarchism, which have exorcistic aspects as well as millennial expectations.

FOUR

~◆~

Dependent Variables

RITUAL BEHAVIOR

A ritual is a social encounter in which each participant has a well-rehearsed role to act out. It takes place within a set time span and in a limited space, and involves a predetermined set of events. Once initiated, it has to run its course to completion. In interaction with others, humans perform many rituals in everyday life. In our present context, however, we will concern ourselves only with those rituals that touch on the nonordinary, the religious aspect of human existence.

The number of religious rituals is legion, and social scientists have tried to categorize them in a number of different ways. The most successful attempt to date was made by the Dutch social scientist Arnold van Gennep. His slender volume, first published in 1909, went through many editions. His popularity resulted from the fact that he put forth a scheme that made a complex task appear deceptively simple. He proposed that the multitude of rituals reported from around the world notwithstanding, they all could be ranged into three types: those of separation, of transition, and of incorporation. Rituals, he pointed out, accompanied people throughout their lives. They marked situations of crisis, such as birth, puberty, marriage, and death, with proper solemnity, functioning to facilitate the passage from one social condition to the next. He coined the term *rites of passage*, without which hardly a writer could authoritatively discuss Johnny's Bar Mitzvah or the president's inauguration.

Through the intervening years, no one had much to quarrel with van Gennep's scheme. It is so general that any ritual can conveniently be placed into one or the other of his categories. Those who later gave the matter some thought wrote instead about the nature of ritual, as did Freud, for instance. In his essay "Obsessive Acts and Religious Practices" (1948–50), interpolating from his patients to the world at large, Freud propounded the hypothesis that the repetitiousness of ritual was the expression of compulsive neurosis. Since humans engage in repetitious rituals month by month and year by year on a

large number of occasions, Freud was obviously quite pessimistic about the
general mental health and stability of humankind.

A cheerier view was put forth by the Dutch cultural historian Johan Huizinga
(1939), who considered all ritual to be play. Religious ritual was to him the
most formalized variety of play. More recently, Victor Turner (1967) proposed
that the elements of ritual clustered around two poles: the pole of the moral
and social order, and the sensory pole. In his scheme, people engaged in a
ritual were using elements of the sensory pole in order to express something
located at the pole of the moral and social order. To make clear what Turner
is trying to do, let us apply his analysis to a ritual most of us are familiar with,
the Christian baptism. In that case the water would belong to the sensory pole,
and washing away the sins would be its counterpart at the other pole. The
mode of analysis is obviously an application of structuralism as formulated by
the French anthropologist Claude Lévi-Strauss. The problem that Turner ran
into when studying more complex rituals, such as those of the African Ndembu
society that he studied, was that there were so many elements clustering
around his hypothetical poles that any semblance of structure was totally ob-
scured. No wonder that he titled his book on the topic *The Forest of Symbols*.

Because of such difficulties, one is tempted to try a different approach.
Comparing many different rituals, it was my impression that instead of elements
simply crowding haphazardly around two opposite poles, there might possibly
exist an underlying structure ordering these elements. Given the tendency of
humans to preserve such structures, a phenomenon well known from historical
linguistics, such a structure might indeed be very ancient. The problem was
how to get at that hidden matrix.

Taking my inspiration from generative semantics (for details, see my essay
"Touching Behavior: The Application of Semantic Theory to a Problem of
Anthropological Analysis," 1976), I proceeded by first familiarizing myself with
the rituals of one particular culture area, namely, those collected in Julian
Steward's *Handbook of South American Indians*. I then asked myself: What
exactly are people *doing* in these rituals? Surely, those many different acts of
touching, the many distinct segments of their performance, were not arbitrary.
As I dissected the rituals and began ordering their constituent parts into logical
sequences, I suddenly saw the underlying structure revealed. I think the reason
that its nature had not occurred to anyone else before was that all previous
seminal analyses had been done by men. For what I perceived, and what made
marvelous sense, was that the underlying matrix of these rituals was the grip-
ping drama of birth. What the rituals spelled out, clearly and for everyone to
see, was a ritual transmutation of the mother's labor pain, the newborn's issuing
from her womb, its being welcomed, attended, and finally placed at the mother's breast to draw nourishment.

While the birth act was clearly the center of the ritual event, this was not
a drama of woman alone. For the spirits of the dead, both men and women,

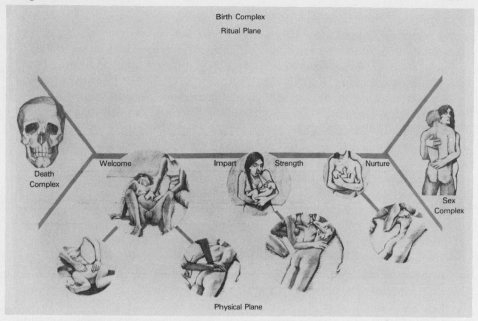

Figure 1. The human drama. Original drawing by Reed Campbell.

stood in attendance as invited guests as the act of birth started. And the men concluded the drama and simultaneously started the cycle over again in a ritual allusion to the act of procreation. Figure 1 is an attempt to make this basic outline understandable in a pictorial manner, making visible the underlying flesh-and-blood experience, the physical plane that is thought to act as the deep structure underlying the events on the ritual plane.

The religious ritual, it seems to me, is the most exalted form of human communication, and recognizing this kind of deep structure restores to it that dignity that is lost in the desiccated categorizations of earlier years. One might use the comparison that what humans compose in their rituals is something like a huge canvas of what makes them human, a celebration of humanness, as it were. What made it so difficult to recognize this was the fact that the artists, the creators of the canvas, had less in common with the realism of a Michelangelo Buonarotti than with the surrealism of a Salvador Dali. For although ever-mindful of the general plan of the composition, they made light of details. In an Australian ritual, for example, a man is a male at one point, and at another he represents a girl; and then again, a yam may take his place. Or in something like ritual shorthand, the story of the Last Supper and the salvation myth are compressed into the brief span of a mass, and the sumptuous meal into a thin wafer and a sip of wine. To put it more simply, with the onset of the ritual, we are transported wholesale into another plane of reality. It is an orderly world, just as is the ordinary one, but its rules are different, and the modes of ordinary reality do not apply. The babe may turn into the initiate, and he/she is the one who has to suffer pain, the pangs of birth; or the babe is the patient, guided through the drama of being born again, this time to renewed health; then again, the infant is the guest, welcomed, attended, and fed; the guest, in turn, may have arrived from the alternate reality to accept the sacrifice of respectful care, food, and drink. No matter, the basic outline remains the same, and the record of human rituals is replete with exuberant variations on the basic complex theme of life.

As *a dependent variable*, ritual changes as humans modify their interaction with the habitat. The hunter-gatherer ritual occupies the full expanse of the ritual canvas. Alterations of the interaction with the habitat, a departure from the hunter-gatherer lifestyle, invariably produce a shrinkage. With the horti-culturalists, as we shall see, this involves initially a mere shift in emphasis, with the agriculturalist villagers, there is a concern principally with the shared meal to the neglect of other features. In the cities, finally, we see an inversion of the ritual, not ingesting but disgorging: Mass sporting events resemble huge exorcistic convulsions. The canvas, once so brightly lit, darkens through the ages, until only a segment or two is picked out by the narrowing shaft of light.

Ritual has one feature that is occulted even more thoroughly than the gen-erating deep structure described above. That feature is the religious trance and the attendant ecstatic experience, to be discussed in detail in the next section. It is the vehicle that does not just transfer the participants to another plane of emotion, but rather propels them to an altogether different aspect of reality, or, as others see it, to an alternate one. A careful look at rituals reveals that without exception they contain a signal to the participants indicating that this is the point where they should make the switch to this different mode of perception. To mention a few examples, the ethnomusicologist Morton Marks identified a brief segment of "noise" in the music of the Santería sect, a move-ment well known in New York and on the Caribbean islands. The noise is produced by percussion instruments. Before it, the ordinary state prevails; after it, the other one takes over. In the Apostolic (Pentecostal) churches in Yucatán (Mexico), where I did fieldwork, the shift is invited by a special *corito*, a brief hymn that asks the Lord for his fire, an allusion to the feeling of heat that comes with the trance. Among the Wolof of West Africa, a change in the rate of drumming marks that spot of the ritual.

Descriptions of religious rituals rarely call attention to this important feature. One reason is that until quite recently, Western observers were unaware of even the availability and pervasive institutionalization of the trance in most rites, let alone able to identify its occurrence during an actual event. Neither did they realize that the strenuous initiation rituals that most non-Western societies subject their young people to, were designed to confer a lifelong control over the ability to enter a trance. Non-Western practitioners, on the other hand, in early contacts most likely had no inkling that their Western guests were ignorant of this fact. So they did not volunteer the information, as banal to them as if to say, "You need to open your eyes if you want to see." Later, of course, they did not remain ignorant of Western prejudices against the trance, which would cause them to hide whatever signals might betray its presence.

If the invitation to enter the trance is built into rituals generally, then it should of course also be present in those that we are familiar with from our own culture. And indeed, the ringing of the church bells is probably an ancient reminder. In the Catholic churches, there is an abundance of such signals. There is the semidarkness of the older buildings, the flickering candlelight, the fragrance of the incense, the hymns, the repetitious prayers, and the kneeling. Even the telltale break is there, preceding the "transformation" of the bread and the wine into the true body and blood of Christ, a step into the alternate reality that should by rights be experienced in trance. However, a number of changes were wrought in the Catholic church by the Second Ecumenical Council and by other innovations that make the institution of the trance difficult, if not impossible. The modern churches are light; candles either are encased in plastic, so they do not flicker, or are replaced by electric lights; and incense is rarely burned. In some of the most recently built churches, the worshippers cannot even kneel. The Latin formulas that allowed the slipping into trance because they made no demands on the intellect are now presented in the vernacular.

Most important, the experience is no longer expected. An Austrian friend and former priest told me that as a seminarian, he and a few of his friends would stay in the church after mass and attempt to achieve something that they vaguely thought of as a *mystic* experience, by contemplatimg some religious symbol or content. There is an extensive Catholic tradition about this kind of meditative introspection, and in the so-called Dorpat school of religious psychology, three generations of predominantly Protestant psychologists were equally interested in this path to religious experience. It is not nearly as effective as sensory stimulation, as we shall see in the next section, and at any rate, the attempt by the young Austrian seminarians was actively discouraged by their teachers and superiors. Since the onset of the Age of Enlightenment nearly three hundred years ago, and even earlier, there has been a trend away from religious experience in all Christian denominations and toward a *thinking about* religion instead.

THE RELIGIOUS TRANCE

The religious trance is one of a large number of changed perceptual states,[1] such as daydreaming, REM (rapid eye movement) sleep and lucid dreaming, the meditative states, hypnosis, the Indonesian *latah*, and others. Owing to some rather striking features, the religious trance has until recently had the rather dubious distinction of being the only one singled out by Western psychiatry as being abnormal and hence insane. Yet reports that this behavior formed an important part of numerous religious observances kept cropping up in the ethnographic literature. So in 1963, years before the topic became a burning issue in this country because of the burgeoning drug culture, Erika Bourguignon of Ohio State University decided that it might be useful to determine just how widespread such supposed insanity actually was. Funded by the National Institute of Mental Health, she and her students embarked on a five-year project designed to produce a statistical survey.[2] They found eventually that, for instance, in a sample of 488 small societies, the kind of groups of interest to anthropology, 92 percent showed evidence of religious trance behavior. Unless one wanted to maintain that the overwhelming majority of humanity was insane at least some of the time and regularly, the conclusion was inescapable that the religious trance was a perfectly normal human experience. We need to add an important qualifier here, however. *Institutionalized* religious trances are normal. That is, when and if the trance represents controlled behavior, when it is a *ritualized action*, capable of being called forth and terminated on a given cue or signal, *then* it is a perfectly normal phenomenon. Some brain diseases or biochemical disturbances of the body occasionally manifest themselves in a loss or change of consciousness, hallucinations, convulsions, and the like. This alteration is an illness. The religious trance is not.

The distinction is not always easy to make, for switching into the religious trance state is relatively easy. It is part of our genetic endowment, in the same way as knowing how to walk or to sleep. It always lurks someplace just around the corner, and sometimes a person may stray into it quite by accident, like a traveler who has lost his way. That is what happened to an elderly woman, a member of an Apostolic congregation in Yucatán, whom I knew quite well. As I described in my essay (1973a), her two sons told her about the "new religion," the Apostolic faith, that they had become interested in and had converted to. Possibly because of the excitement over their decision, she woke up one morning and shook so severely that she was unable to walk. In the hospital where her concerned sons took her, they could find nothing wrong with her, and so they sent her home. She told of having seen white angels holding white flags and galloping by on white horses. She had also seen a huge Bible suspended above the door of the hospital. Eventually her shaking became less pronounced, and she was able to eat again; and when about forty days later she consented to being baptized into the sect, all her complaints vanished and never recurred. During the worship service she spoke in tongues regularly, a religious behavior that utilizes the religious trance. In other words, she was able to fit her newly won ability into an institutionalized framework, calling it forth at will and terminating it at the ritually proper point during the religious observances.

The nature of the religious trance. The religious altered state of consciousness, or trance, causes a number of changes in the body. Some are readily observable. The individuals involved may start breathing more deeply. Some perspire profusely, they may blush, tremble, or twitch. Occasionally muscles tense, especially around the neck. Were a person to speak in this state, there would be a switch to a beautifully rhythmic vocalization, pulsing like poetry, and rising in intonation until the end of the first third of the utterance unit, then steadily dropping toward the end. A careful observation of subjects experiencing a religious trance indicates that a single occurrence, an episode, has a clearly discernible start, a certain duration, and an end or dissolution. To understand the phenomenon better, it will be useful to look at these phases in more detail.[3]

The individual trance episode. The start. All religious communities where the religious trance is institutionalized have rituals to induce it, and those participating learn to react to them. The singing of a certain hymn or chant may do it; so will clapping, dancing, drumming, rattling, turning around one's own axis, reciting a certain formula or prayer, glancing at a flickering candle or moving water, even smelling a certain fragrance, such as incense. There is hardly any limit to the types of stimuli that are suitable for induction. The reason for this great variety lies in part in the fact that it is not so much the stimulus in and of itself that produces the switch from one state of consciousness to another, but rather the expectation that it will happen. This, together with the associated ritual situation, produces an intense concentration, which is in turn aided by the stimulus. It is concentration that is taught as a preliminary, an introductory, strategy. In the Apostolic congregations in Mexico where I learned many of the details about this religious behavior, the worshippers are admonished to forget their daily worries. The men should not fret about where in the jungle to cut the vegetation to make room for their next cornfield, and the women about what to serve with the daily tortillas. Instead they should direct their thoughts exclusively to the Holy Ghost descending into them and taking control over their speech, which is what these congregations experience while in the religious trance. Speaking in tongues communicates to themselves and to the congregation that the hoped-for event actually did take place.

The onset of the changed perceptual state is experienced in a number of ways. A participant in an experiment involving this kind of trance said, "At first you feel that you have come to a barrier, and you are afraid. All of a sudden you are beyond it and everything is different." Such barriers are often described. "One more river, and that is the river of Jordan," says a Negro spiritual, and crossing a river is mentioned by Christians, but also by the non-Christian

African Pygmies. An Australian medicine man related how his passage was barred by a stone door, which he succeeded in opening with his magic darts.

Sojourn. During this phase, the body works hard, exhibiting those features described above. The observer notes pallor to perspiration, trembling, twitching, extremely rapid motion, sometimes even what looks like a swoon, a catatonialike rigidity. The latter is actually the sign of tremendous excitation, so intense that movement is no longer possible. It is during this sojourn phase of the religious trance, so similar for all humans as far as physical manifestations are concerned, that differences occur in the ecstatic experience. For while we are one species, sharing the same nervous system, we are very diverse culturally. The physiological changes of the religious trance are our common gateway, but they admit us to our own, distinctive alternate reality. The Pygmy will find himself in the Forest, a transposed reality of his rainforest home, while the Sufi, an Islamic mystic, will see, as Idries Shah (1964) tells, "a golden bird in the sky and the demons in the earth."

Most people return to ordinary consciousness after this phase. A select few, however, undergo a tremendous peak experience, an enlightenment, most probably only once or a very few times in their lives. Christians call it the *unio mystica*, but it is known from other religious communities as well, under such names as *samadhi* among Yoga practitioners, *satori* among Zen masters, and many others. A person having gone through such an experience is never quite the same again. An old Maya peasant whom I came to know quite well had this happen to him. Ever since then, he maintained, the entire Bible seemed to him as if made of glass, and if he heard a verse quoted, he instantly knew what it meant and how it related to everything else in the Bible.

Dissolution. Eventually, the trancers awaken. This may happen as a response to a signal in the ritual. The drumming ceases; the rattle falls silent; a sharp bell sounds the conclusion. Novices occasionally have problems obeying such cues, and an experienced fellow participant or someone from the audience will come to their aid. But in time, simply because the biological process has run its course, all participants in the ritual will return to ordinary consciousness.

Aftereffects. The trancers are rewarded with a feeling of an overwhelmingly sweet joy, an intense euphoria, that comes upon them after the conclusion of the trance. Especially during an early experience, this tends to linger. Later on it becomes less pronounced. Together with the perception of heat during the trance, it is this euphoria that is most often mentioned by participants in a religious trance ritual.

Only guesses and tentative observational deductions were available until recently about what internal physical changes might be expressed in such nonordinary behavior. Thus, Barbara W. Lex, a medical anthropologist, conjectured (1979) that in trance the body is engaged in an alternating ergotropic and trophotropic arousal of the autonomic nervous system, something that I had also noted earlier (see my table 1, 1972: 78). But since then, laboratory experiments carried out in cooperation between Ingrid Mueller, a German medical student, and me at the Neurophysiological Clinic of the University of Munich in 1983 have given us a clearer notion of the complex processes involved. Using a trance-induction technique I had developed with student volunteers since 1972 (see Goodman, 1976a, 1977, and 1986), we tested the reactions of four volunteers. We found the trance to be accompanied by a considerable increase in the heart rate and, surprisingly, a simultaneous drop in blood pressure, a finding known otherwise only from life-threatening situations, such as when a person is close to death from an infectious disease or bleeding. This reaction was accompanied in the blood serum by a drop in the so-called stressors (adrenaline, noradrenaline, and cortisol), while the beta endorphines, the body's own painkillers, began to appear and stayed high even after the end of the trance. That endorphines might be involved in the religious trance experience had been suspected for some time, but this was the first time that their presence was confirmed by an actual laboratory experiment. The EEG (electroencephalogram) tracings showed an electrical brain activity in the theta range (6–7 cps), not seen in normal adults during an awake state, which the religious trance is phenomenologically, i.e., from the point of view of experience. In addition, there was little activity in the other frequency bands.

The paradoxical nature of these neurophysiological processes during the religious trance was further stressed by experiments in the spring of 1987 at the Institute of Psychology of the University of Vienna, Austria. Its director, Professor Giselher Guttmann, supervised some preliminary research there using not the ordinary clinical EEGs, but one utilizing direct-current measurements of the negative charge of the brain. Such charges, amounting to at most 250 microvolts, are present during learning. Negative charges measured in some of our trancers, however, reached an astounding 1,000 to 2,000 microvolts. The presence of the slow theta waves was also confirmed, once again characterizing the activities of the body during the religious trance as puzzlingly paradoxical. Professor Guttmann is planning further research on these extraordinary findings.

Because of their thorough training and the support offered by their group, many practitioners can keep the trance behavior going from the time of their initiation until old age. Others, however, especially in Christian denominations, lose the capacity, as is known, for example, of children reporting visions of the Virgin Mary. Such loss is also part of the lore among Pentecostals. "Four of us started speaking in tongues together," a young woman of the Mérida (Yucatán) Apostolic congregation told me. "That was three years ago. Now I am the only one left. One wonders how the others may have angered the Holy Spirit."

Whether people remember the content of the ecstasy is not left to individual choice, but rather depends on what is expected in their religious community.

In other words, amnesia, i.e., forgetting, is not an inherent quality of the religious trance. Amnesia will set in only if there is an express instruction demanding it. In some Mexican Apostolic congregations, people say that they
remember nothing about what they experienced while speaking in tongues,
and so no one does. In other congregations, the opposite is the case, although
no one says, "You have to remember."

Millennial movements. There are occasions when an entire group enters a
religious trance more or less simultaneously and then finds itself unable readily
to escape from it. Such episodes occur most probably as a result of a cumulative
shock experienced by all members more or less at the same time. I had occasion
to record such a crisis cult in Yucatán (see Goodman, 1974). In that case the
precipitating event was the rejection that the congregation suffered at the
hands of its own very popular minister. In a preliminary phase, some members
had visions, and there arose the prediction that the end of the world and the
start of the millennium would occur at the beginning of September, 1970.
During the subsequent highly excited stage, there were no longer any regular
worship services. Prayer sessions were held day and night; most people spoke
in tongues; some had convulsions and screaming fits. The men left their jobs;
many sold and more often burned some of their possessions. The women and
children started living communally in the temple, while the men went to the
neighboring villages to try and convert as many people as possible before the
end came. This agitated phase was over in about forty days. The painful episode
nearly caused the dissolution of the congregation, which had a hard time coping
with the fact that the Kingdom of God had not arrived on the projected date,—
in other words, that prophecy had failed.

Communal trance events of this nature are not at all rare. A few years after
the above occurrence, another one started in a Mayan village southwest of
Mérida (see Goodman, 1980). It was aborted by the resolute intervention of
the ministers who had experienced the failure of the 1970 prophecy. The
cargo cults of Melanesia early in this century come under this heading also,
as do the student uprisings on American campuses in the late sixties and early
seventies. On occasion, one or the other of these events finds its way into the
history books, because they mark the start of important social or religious
movements. A careful analysis indicates, however, that nothing new is invented
during such outbreaks. Rather, ideas already available at the time achieve a
new form on such occasions and eventually coalesce in a revitalization movement. Christianity did not begin during the forty days following the death of
Jesus, when the apostles were obviously in a continuous religious trance, and
during the events of the Pentecost: Jesus had preached his ideas for three years
before then.

Controlled Dreaming. The usual entrance into the religious trance is from
the ordinary waking state. There are, however, practitioners who can pass into

it using sleep as a port of entry, so to speak, as George Appel reports from Indonesia (personal communication). The information about this phenomenon is confusing, however, possibly for linguistic reasons. In many languages, it is only by context that dreams can be distinguished from visions. It is not clear, for example, what an Australian father experiences when in sleep he "dreams" the souls of his future children, finding them in the country of his mother's lineage. Is this a "lucid dream," now being explored by American sleep researchers, where a trained subject can at will change certain elements of the dream sequence? Or does he use sleep as a vehicle to slip into the religious trance in order to undertake a spirit journey? Or is this, in fact, what the lucid dreamer is also doing? Are the Australian father and the American lucid dreamer doing the same thing or something different? We do not know. And although controlled dreaming is fairly often reported by anthropologists, we have no record of how the skill is learned.

Drugs and the religious trance. During the heyday of the American drug culture a decade or so ago, avid drug users were wont to proclaim that the psychedelics provided them with a "transcendent" experience. "There is something to that," a thoughtful student told me. "You do pass beyond the limits of ordinary experience, and you get to some region or place that is like nothing here and now. But when you get there, you ask yourself: Now what? I tried to find a guru to tell me, but there was nobody around. That is why I stopped taking all that mind-altering stuff. I was getting nowhere."

Very astutely, this comment points up the difference between taking drugs out of individual motivation, whatever that might be, and the ritual, communal use of psychedelics, reported from many areas of the world. In a specific religious context, once you "get there," you know what to expect and why you are there. In other words, there is always a reason why you are going, and there is a guide to show you around in your society's alternate reality into which the drug provided an entrance.

The sophistication that many non-Western religious specialists demonstrate when preparing hallucinogens, as well as the detailed botanical knowledge necessary, suggest the presence of a science and related cult activity of great antiquity. It is thought that in Eurasia, this tradition may date back to the Upper Paleolithic, to the Old Stone Age, and to the hunter-gatherers of northeast Asia. From there it passed on to India, and then southwest to the Near East and the Mediterranean region. In the New World, the profusion of psychoactive plants, which outstrip those of Eurasia ten to one, makes it intelligible that a large number of societies institutionalized their use.

During a religious ritual, the psychedelic drug acts as the stimulus that induces the trance, acting on the nervous system much like a drum signal or a certain dance step. Religious communities that use drugs to this end, teach their members how to switch from the intoxication to the religious trance. For instance, the Colombian anthropologist Gerardo Reichel-Dolmatoff reports of the Desana (1971), an American Indian society of Amazonia, that while the participants in the ceremony lie in a drug-induced stupor in their hammocks, their shaman recites what they are to see. The Desana report finding themselves initially in a dense fog. Out of it, they enter upon the Milky Way, the road to the realm where the beings of their alternate reality live. They meet animal spirits or masks that counsel them, and they converse with some of the Holy Ones, such as the Sun, the Daughter of the Sun, or the Beings of the Days, until eventually they return once more to their bodies in the hammock.

The religious trance as a dependent variable. As the interaction with the habitat changes, the use to which the religious trance is put varies also. As examples in the ethnographic section will illustrate, the hunter-gatherers use the trance not only for curing, which is done in all types of societies, but especially to undertake a spirit journey.

As the horticulturalists enter upon the scene, the spirit journey becomes greatly elaborated. It may be embarked on as an adjunct to another alternate-reality adventure, as when the Amazonian Akwē-Shavante encounter a departed spirit who invites them to come along. Spirit journeys may be undertaken vicariously, which is the case when the Yąnomamö living farther north send out spirit beings that they had invited to live in their chests, to fight the spirit helpers of enemy shamans. Some societies, such as the Apapocuva-Guaraní, feel that they have lost the ability "to make their bodies light enough," and so they can no longer visit First Woman in her magic corn garden. As an innovation in this type of society, the trance is used to achieve metamorphosis, an experience not carried over into agriculture, where possession predominates instead: A being of the alternate reality enters into the body of the practitioner and assumes control over it.

In accordance with their evolutionary history, the nomadic pastoralists utilize the religious trance for a number of different purposes. Those who combine hunting with herding engage in spirit journeys as well as in minimal possession. Where only the women are cultivators and the men occupy themselves with the animals, we find that the women are the ones who have the possession rituals, and the men are the diviners. (See more about divining later in this chapter.)

In agreement with its independence of the habitat, the modern city is a marketplace for the various utilizations of the religious trance. In addition, it may have evolved a special adaptation, stripping it of its religious character and making use of the burst of creativity that goes along with this type of trance. These are those special "flashes of insight," a sudden ability to integrate previously disjointed details that those especially gifted can call up by dint of tremendous concentration.[4]

Controlled dreaming as an institutionalized behavior is reported only from the hunter-gatherers and the horticulturalists. It is rarely mentioned among the pastoralists, and full-fledged agriculturalists seem to have lost the ability altogether, although it is attested for Tibetan monastic spiritualism. In the latter case, it may be a holdover from the ancient Tibetan Bön tradition, a shamanistic religious system.

As mentioned at the outset of this section, Western psychiatry used to consider the religious trance behavior to be psychotic. One of the arguments was that in ecstasy, people reported having "seen things." In psychiatry, seeing things not perceivable to the outside observer is termed *hallucination*, and it is considered an important symptom of insanity. Yet not only the religious specialists of uncounted small societies, but also through history the known founders of religions such as Buddha, Jesus, or Mohammed, were certainly not insane, and in addition left no doubt that they considered what they saw in trance not an illusion but simply another reality. It is this alternate dimension that we will turn to next.

THE ALTERNATE REALITY

A great deal of tedious discussion has been wasted on the question of the "objective" existence of the alternate reality. The religious practitioners argue for it, either because it is part of their dogma or because, as they affirm, they have "been there," they have experienced it. The hard scientists take the opposite position, again as a matter of conviction, for lack of "scientific evidence," although some of them are not so sure anymore. As social scientists, our situation is a happier one: At least we can state that without any doubt, the alternate reality is a social fact. During the times and at the places that we have information about, societies have always indicated by their actions that they took the existence of the alternate reality and the dual nature of reality for granted. Frequently, the understanding of this duality has been veiled, becoming "esoteric" knowledge, hidden by a special vocabulary. Thus the Sufis speak of "shining" versus "concealment." By shining they mean the "breaking through of the sun of the reality of God from the clouds of humanity" (Idries Shah, 1964: 312). In this view, the "reality of God" is the perception gained upon entering the alternate reality, and "clouds of humanity" stands for the ordinary one.

The easiest way to understand this perceived dual nature of reality is to try and grasp that both aspects of reality are in this view experienced as existing simultaneously, as being present at the same time and in the same space. Paraphrasing the German folklorist W.-E. Peuckert, for example, in the case of ordinary seeing there is merely a stump in the forest, but during *seeing*, i.e., during the religious trance, we realize that it is a gnome. Or think of the familiar toy, sometimes shaped like a card, or a little television set: If you hold it one way, you see Mickey Mouse, but at a slightly different angle, Donald Duck appears. The effect is produced by cutting both pictures into very thin strips and gluing them to the base in an alternating fashion. The surface is then covered with a ridged sheet of plastic. Both images are on the toy surface, but they cannot be seen simultaneously. Just as it depends on the angle at which the toy is held which picture the viewer perceives, in the same way it is a matter of which state of consciousness is present whether the ordinary or the separate reality appears.

That *seeing* is the central issue is illustrated by the following example. In the collections of the Museum of History and Anthropology in Mexico City, there is a small terra-cotta statuette, created about thirty-three hundred years ago in what today is Tlatilco (see pl. 5). It represents a delicate woman with tiny breasts, a slender waist, heavy, curved thighs—and two faces, two finely shaped mouths, two pronounced noses, and three large eyes, for the two faces share one eye. The work is not titled, of course, and so various suggestions have been offered about what the artist might have intended to express. Calling attention to the curved thighs of the little lady, the author of a book on Mexican art speculates that we are dealing with an example of a "fertility goddess," voluptuous figurines of which from Cro-Magnon times (ten thousand to forty thousand years ago) are encountered in several European excavation sites. There is an important difference, however. The European figurines have no faces. Besides, both male and female Tlatilco sculptures of that period had wide thighs. Another author suggests that we might be dealing with a representation of day and night. But it seems to me that that is not a weighty enough subject. It is more likely, I think, that the artist had something more important to say: She is one integrated person, but turning one way, she looks into ordinary reality; turning the other way, she contemplates its alternate aspect. That is what humans are about.

While the message about perceiving the alternate reality is artistically veiled in the Tlatilco figurine, references to *seeing* in ecstasy are entirely explicit in the literature. When Siddhartha, on his way to becoming Buddha (Enlightened), sat under the fig tree, he remembered all his previous existences; then he *saw* the previous lives, deaths, and rebirths of all beings, perceiving the universe as if in a mirror. This is how he understood how freedom from this worldly web would be possible.

Similarly, the prophets of the Old Testament knew how to *see*. Thus, Isaiah told,

> In the year King Uzziah died, I saw the Lord seated on a high and lofty throne, with the train of his garment filling the temple. Seraphim were stationed above; each of them had six wings; with two of them they veiled their faces, with two they veiled their feet, and with two they hovered above. (6:1–2)

Jesus *saw* the devil after fasting for forty days in the wilderness. And Mohammed *saw* the angel Gabriel, and it is told that he stood quite still, turning his face

Plate 5. Ceramic figure from Tlatilco, Mexico, ca. 1,300 B.C. Courtesy of Museum of History and Anthropology, Mexico City, Mexico.

away from the brightness of the vision; but no matter where he turned, there always stood the angel confronting him.

In order to be a religious practitioner, therefore, one of the most important things to learn is how to see the alternate reality. Among the Mentaweians of Sumatra, Mircea Eliade relates, the master seer takes his initiate into the forest to gather magic plants. Once there, he implores the spirits to make clear the eyes of the body so that the initiate can see the spirits. This invocation is repeated after they return to the seer's house. Then the seer rubs the herbs on the eyes of his student, and for seven days and nights, deprived of sleep, they sit opposite each other, singing and ringing their bells. "If at the end of seven days the boy sees the wood-spirits, the ceremony is at an end. Otherwise the entire seven-day ceremony must be repeated" (1964: 87).

If reality in this sense is a dual phenomenon, the question is, How are its two aspects related to each other? In an explanation recalling Plato's ideal forms, Black Elk, an Oglala Sioux holy man, told his interviewer:

> [Chief] Crazy Horse dreamed and went into the world where there is nothing but the spirits of all things. That is the real world that is behind this one, and everything we see here is something like a shadow from that world. He was on his horse in that world, and the horse and himself on it and the trees and the grass and the stones and everything were made of spirit, and nothing was hard, and everything seemed to float. His horse was standing still there, and yet it danced around like a horse made only of shadow, and that is how he got his name, which does not mean that his horse was crazy or wild, but that in his vision it danced around in a queer way. (Neihardt, 1961: 85)

The next question would then logically be, What would happen if one or the other aspect would disappear or be killed or destroyed? After all, if there is no body, would there be no shadow either? The answer that the Yanomamö Indians give is that people have a certain inherited soul portion, called a *noreshi*. In the jungle, there lives an animal that belongs to it, and which duplicates the behavior of the person to which it corresponds. The *noreshi* animal and the person never appear at the same spot, for if they should see each other, they would both die. One lives only as long as the other (Chagnon, 1968: 48–49). However, in Yanomamö tradition, as well as all others, some portion or segment of the personality survives and passes into an independent, preexistent alternate reality upon death, either temporarily or permanently.

The alternate reality as a dependent variable. The alternate reality into which the soul or a portion of it passes either in vision or in death differs considerably according to cultural type. It is here that it most clearly reveals its nature as a dependent variable. As we shall see in the ethnographic section, the hunter-gatherers meet the spirit counterparts or aspects of the animals of ordinary reality, and upon death, they hunt and love just as they did when still alive. The horticulturalists see villages identical to their earthly ones. For desert nomads, the home of the spirits of the dead is lush and green. The tillers who were good kneel in adoration before their rulers, while the evil ones are forever banished to their various hells. Finally, the urbanites are united with a few relatives and friends in a realm of light.

However, the alternate reality is not merely a neutral dimension, a landscape one perceives or passes into. Rather, it has an effect on humans by virtue of the fact that it is a realm where power hovers. Contact with it can invest a person with new abilities; it can afford protection, award blessings and good fortune. Yet it is also dangerous, like fire, which can burn if not handled properly. Under certain circumstances, therefore, it may be the source of misfortune. In order to discover what is in store for them, humans turn to divination.

GOOD FORTUNE, MISFORTUNE, AND THE RITUALS OF DIVINATION

According to a Hungarian folk belief, passed on within the "continuing community of children at play," to borrow the lovely phrase of the linguist Otto Jespersen, a person will have a lucky day if, when dressing in the morning, he will inadvertently put on one of his garments inside-out. The tradition is easy to interpret: Inside-out, the opposite of the ordinary, stands for, or is the signature of, the alternate reality, and contact with it is what brings good luck. The belief neatly condenses both the neutrality of that radiating power source and its effect on human life.

Good fortune. It stands to reason that as soon as humans had discovered that the alternate reality represented a force field, they would try to harness it to their own advantage. Expectably, such attempts once more vary according to societal type. In their trance rituals, such as a medicine dance, African hunter-gatherers, for instance, are usually content simply to brush against it, as it were, when they are trying to gain power to heal or to hunt. When they are seeking good fortune, horticulturalists are more inclined to trust in objects, because in the way they have been tinted or shaped, they contain a portion of the power of some animal spirit.[5] Nomadic pastoralists use amulets for the same reason, or attempt with their outstretched palms to absorb a ray of the power emanating, for instance, from the grave of a holy man. For a similar purpose, agriculturalists encase relics in richly adorned containers or even buildings. The ultimate in contact is provided by the greatly elaborated possession complex among the latter societies, with a being of the alternate reality taking up its abode in the body of the worshipper itself, instead of in an object. However, the spirit so conjured, summoned, brought in, is of overpowering might and

will take control of such a borrowed body. The mediums, humans undergoing
a possession experience, turn into the spirit's tabernacle, its canoe, or its horse.
It will shake them, make them dance; it might take over their tongues and
speak through their mouths. Only the termination of the ritual can break its
hold over the human host. Possession, however, also brings with it a number
of blessings, well-being as well as prestige for the medium. Urbanites, finally,
rarely attribute good fortune to the agency of the alternate reality, pointing
instead to the random effect of chance.

Misfortune. While women went about gathering for uncounted thousands
of years, the men hunted the game. Hunting, that is, weapons' penetrating the
bodies of animals and thus causing their deaths was a central experience. We
might imagine that it served as a model for the conceptualization of illness
and of misfortune as something penetrating the victim from the outside.

The elaboration of this model is modified in a systematic fashion as a *dependent variable* of the interaction with the habitat. The hunters, in whose
world society and habitat are intertwined in friendship and cooperation, look
to the alternate reality as the source of misfortune. The horticulturalists, as we
have seen, live in a climate of anxiety over having violated the habitat. The
less hunting and the more cultivation they do, the more the alternate-reality
source of misfortune moves into their midst, usually in the form of sorcery,
until in open-field agriculture we see the witchcraft complex in full bloom.
Among the pastoral nomads, in agreement with their several origins, there is
once more a sliding scale concerning the conceptualization of the source of
misfortune. Those that are also hunters, for instance, might erect a magic fence
against enemy spirit beings mounting an attack from without. Those with horticulturalist roots feel themselves threatened mainly from within their own
society. Pastoral nomads with close ties to agriculture see the danger arising
entirely from within. City dwellers, finally, perceive themselves to be the victims of impersonal agencies or phenomena, such as the constellation of the
stars or statistical probablity.

Systems and rituals of divination. The distribution of good fortune and
misfortune often appears erratic, the future uncertain, and the events of life
puzzling, rendering the decision-making process difficult. Humans have come
up with an appealing remedy for this state of affairs, namely, divination, which
is a type of ritual all societies practice to varying degrees, representing an
integral and important part of the respective religious systems. We should note
here that divination is not necessarily foretelling the future, but as often as not
is an interpretation of the social situation at hand. Western attitudes toward
this strategy have ranged from contempt to active hostility. Colonial rulers
have typically suppressed the practice, contending that it was irrational, an-
tirational, a fraud perpetrated on the ignorant and superstitious population.

This approach was inherited by generations of anthropologists, and consequently there are few satisfactory descriptions of divinatory sessions or systems in the respective literature, with such laudable exceptions as Richard P. Werbner's report on an African Kalanga divination ritual (1973), or more recently, an account by Barbara Tedlock of Quiché Maya divining (1982).

Despite this near-total lack of reliable and detailed material, anthropologists regrettably have taken it upon themselves to produce a number of complicated models attempting to elucidate how and why divination works. They suggest, for instance, that divination is akin to "primitive" science, used for want of the "real" thing. The structuralists maintain that divination is so popular because it reinforces traditional social structures by symbolizing their values. The functionalists are sure that these rituals endured because they made people feel better; they alleviated anxiety about the unknown and legitimized decisions.

As so often happens in theory building, most of these analytic schemes are based on valid observations, except that they are usually fragmented, paying attention only to some particular detail, so that the entire picture could not possibly be comprehended. In addition, what is overlooked, and what knowledgeable descriptions such as those by Werbner and Tedlock make eminently clear, is the fact that divination is a religious ritual in which the practitioner enters the religious trance. Diviners do not, as some anthropologists have suggested, work with methods similar to a Rorschach test, or apply a simple variant of game theory for randomizing results.

Since the basis for divining is a religious experience, in the sense that the diviner contacts the alternate reality in trance, it makes good sense instead of theory building, to use a novel method and explore the experience experimentally. To this end, my subjects used the posture of a *mallam* (for further details, see Goodman, 1986), a diviner of the sub-Saharan Nupe society (see pl. 6), and the trance was induced by a monotonous rattle sound. According to the reports of the experimental subjects, the trance in this posture frequently leads to the experience of the body, and thus perception, undergoing a V-shaped split, which we might understand as being necessary to comprehend the social situation in its entirety rather than only the details. Subsequently, there may be a sensation of seeing or turning into a whirlwind, which acts almost like cranking up an old-fashioned car: It provides the energy apparently necessary for the holistic processing of memory data. As one participant in such an experiment said, she heard the injunction, "Don't look so hard: Understand!"

A regular rattle sound is, of course, not the only method for inducing the religious trance necessary for divining. There are many other strategies, as well. Diviners are highly trained specialists, whose apprenticeship often lasts for years, and they may be able to switch into the trance state by using behavioral cues and intense concentration, difficult to discover by the outsider. Among the Quiché Maya, as Tedlock reports, the trance, perceived as "body

Plate 6. Nupe *mallam* divining. After Mair, 1969: 94.

lightning," is induced by prayer; it is kept going by prayers spoken during the course of divination, and the signal to come out of it is still another prayer. During the trance, diviners receive "signals from remote mountains, lakes, and sheet-lightning," and they interpret these according to a highly organized cognitive map, giving due consideration to the social configuration and the interests and needs of their clients. The trance produces a sudden coalescing of all this disparate information, so that the diviners are then able to *understand*. "Among the Quiché [Mayas]," Tedlock tells us, "the term for the divinatory process . . . is *ch'obonic*, 'to understand' " (1981: 169).

Since the dimension of time does not exist in the alternate reality, or is only minimally indicated, it is entirely possible, of course, that diviners will on occasion also mention a future event, so that the pronouncements become highly complex, and most of the time, the diviner also functions as a social and psychological counselor. He/she thus plays an important role in contributing to the mental health and well-being of the respective populations. Quoting Tedlock, diviners "instruct thousands of people [the world over] concerning past, present, and future events and guide them in the crucial decision-making process" (1981: 26–27).

Examining the divinatory ritual as a *dependent variable*, we find that hunter-gatherers divine by going on a spirit journey. They also use scapulomancy, the reading of cracks caused by fire in the scapulas of game animals, which is interpreted as a map. Among American Indian horticulturalists, divining is frequently a part of a session during which hallucinogens are ingested. Baer (1984: 274–287) gives a detailed protocol of such an event. With nomadic pastoralists, divination is usually a part of animal sacrifice. In agriculturalism, the role of the diviner is often assumed by the medium, as, for instance, in Japan[6] and reported by Carmen Blacker (1975). For the urbanite, astrology represents a favorite system of divination.

Some agriculturalist societies have developed extremely intricate divinatory systems. Examples include in our hemisphere the Maya tradition alluded to briefly above and preserved apparently intact by the Quiché Mayas; in East Asia the Chinese I Ching; and in Africa the Ifa divination of the Yoruba. These we want to consider in a bit more detail below.

Quiché Maya divination. In the late 1970s, Dennis and Barbara Tedlock were accepted as apprentices by a Quiché Maya diviner. The practice they became proficient in involves essentially, as mentioned above, the receiving of signals from distant features of the habitat, possible only, of course, in trance. The "blood" registers these signals, which are mapped by the diviner on his own body by location, on his arm, his right shoulder, etc., and are perceived as "lightning" that travels in the blood. The traditional Maya calendar serves as a second reference system. To quote Barbara Tedlock:

> The counting out of the day names . . . is conceived as the speaking of the calendar [i.e., the calendar itself does the speaking] by Quiché diviners, which is tied by way of the year-bearers and their secretaries [both spirit beings] to the mountains of the directions. In a given count, the calendar is questioned through the medium of the starting day, which is addressed as a being, no less than a "lord." Divinatory understanding in highland Guatemala comes though the interweaving . . . of the counting of the calendar, the speaking of the blood, the facts of the case, and the rapport of the diviner and the client. (1981: 24–25)

The extremely complex divining session (for details, see Tedlock, 1982, chap. 7) begins with the client inquiring whether the day is suitable, and if it is, stating his/her question. The diviner will then set up a small table and place the bag containing the divining paraphernalia on it, next to the small gift of money brought by the client. After "opening" his/her body to the cosmos, the diviner will address various deities in a framing prayer and then ask the pardon of both God and the earth, and will "borrow" the "breath" of the particular day. Once the diviner feels the "blood moving," the question will be framed in a formal way. The question is answered on the basis of a complex arrangement of corn, beans, and crystals.

Among the Quiché, the diviners are called *ajk'ij*, "day keeper." They represent a large group of practitioners of the indigenous religion who are initiated calendar diviners and act as dream interpreters and healers as well. They also make prayers to the gods and the ancestors on behalf of the people. They are recruited through illness, dreams, and ecstatic experiences or through inheritance, and are initiated after intensive training and tests in a lengthy ritual. (For extensive details, see Tedlock, 1982, chap. 3.)

The I Ching. According to Chinese tradition, the I Ching, the "Book of Changes," originated with a legendary figure, a deity representing hunting and fishing. It actually goes back to an earlier diviner's manual, possibly of the second millennium before our era, and preserves a written record of divinatory signs and their interpretation. Each one of the signs is called up by a hexagram, and there are sixty-four of these. The signs, as Arthur Waley, a British translator,[7] conjectures, record the oracular import of commonly observed events of nature, such as, "When the wild goose skims the rock ledge, you may eat and drink in peace" (Waley, 1933: 123). Later commentators, reportedly even Confucius himself (ca. 515–ca. 478 B.C.), added to this body of text, often obscuring the original meaning of the verses. Because of the written tradition, the system can be used without the help of a trained practitioner.

In the I Ching, each hexagram is accompanied by two commentaries, one called the Judgment, the other the Image. The latter, thought to be the most archaic of the system, consists of two sections, the Image proper and an elucidation, quite probably added on in the century preceding Confucius. It explains how "the kings of former times" or "the superior man" acted or would act under the circumstances. Here are two examples:

The Judgment
Contemplation. The ablution has been made,
but not yet the offering.
Full of trust they look up to him.

The Image
The wind blows over the earth:
The image of *Contemplation.*
Thus the kings of old visited the regions of the world,
And gave them instructions. (Wilhelm/Baynes, 1967: 82, 83)

Or:

The Judgment
The Creative works sublime success,
Furthering through perseverance.

The Image
The movement of heaven is full of power.
Thus the superior man makes himself strong and untiring. (Ibid., pp. 4, 6)

The hexagrams are obtained in traditional usage by throwing yarrow stalks. If they fall one way, it means "yes," if another way, "no." For a yes answer, an unbroken line is drawn, for a no a broken one; six lines give one hexagram. The yarrow stalks are considered sacred, so the understanding is that they are intermediaries between the diviner and the beings of the alternate reality, who provide the answer in the way the stalks fall. Just as in the case of Quiché divination, the answers are applied to a cognitive map, in the Chinese case the Judgment and the Image, that is, the explanatory text. It represents the accretion of millennia of thought, speculation, editing, and revision.

The Ifa divination of the Yoruba. The Ifa system, used by Yoruba religious specialists in Nigeria (see Bascom, 1969a), is equally a storehouse of rich folk tradition. In this divination (details are given in the Ethnographic Section, chap. 7), the diviner holds sixteen palm nuts in his left hand, then grasps them with his right hand in such a way that some remain in his left hand. If two nuts remain, a single mark is made on the divining tray. If there is only one, a double line is drawn. The procedure is repeated four times, and in this manner, one of the sixteen basic tetragrams is obtained (see fig. 2). Repeating the procedure eight times with the divining chain made of palm nuts, a combination of the basic figures results, namely, one of the 256 derivative figures.

All the figures have names, which the diviners know by heart. In addition, each figure is associated with memorized material. Clients asking a diviner—who is called a *babalawo*, meaning "father has secrets"—for his services, do not tell him their problems. Instead, the *babalawo* casts the figure and then begins reciting those figures that are associated with it. The client then chooses whichever figure he/she thinks is most applicable in the particular situation.

According to William Bascom, who did extensive fieldwork on Ifa divination, the system is a "sophisticated projective method approaching a Rorschach test." The native view is different, of course, and quite consistently follows the outline of the model we encountered above, especially in the case of the divinatory system of the Quiché. According to that understanding, the palm nuts and also the *babalawo* are possessed by Ifa, the god of divination. The signals, then, i.e., the figures that are cast, originate with that spirit being, and

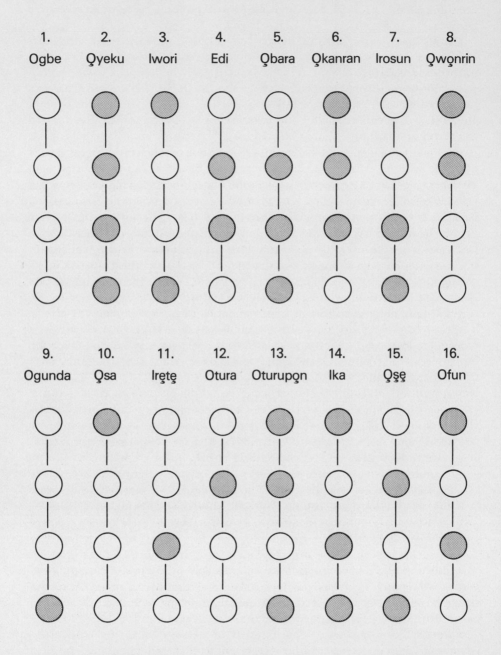

Figure 2. The sixteen basic figures of Ifa, obtained by casting the divining chain. After Bascom, 1969a: 4, table 1, B.

are subsequently processed through the formal tradition, the Yoruba cognitive map.

The Ifa case is a remarkable illustration of how a preconceived, culturally inculcated notion can blind a field observer to certain aspects of a behavior, in this case the role that the religious trance plays in divining. I had the opportunity to consult a Yoruba colleague[8] on this topic, who as an actor was interested in the performance aspect of Ifa divination and therefore made a study of it. It seems that after the *babalawo* has cast the chain, has recited the verses and stories, etc., and has discussed the matter with the client, there is a second brief part to the ritual that Bascom does not report. During this part, the *babalawo* begins to recite a formula, which is known as "knocking on the door of Ifa." It apparently induces the trance, for the *babalawo* switches into glossolalia, and he can no longer be addressed. He becomes "stiff, rolling back his eyes until only the white shows." This is the point when he appears before the face of Ifa and asks for advice about the concerns of his client. Not until this has been done does he tell what sacrifice needs to be brought in order to resolve the situation, and the trance is still so intense that he often speaks in falsetto, caused by the tenseness of the vocal apparatus during this altered state of consciousness. None of this appears in Bascom's reports.

Yoruba diviners begin to learn their art at an early age, often as young as five to seven years, some from their fathers, but most as apprentices to another *babalawo*. By the time they approach thirteen, they have usually attained the bottom rank as a diviner, having memorized the essential parts of the oral tradition, and are allowed to begin to divine. Most of them do not stop here, however, but go on studying in order to enter the higher ranks. In the course of his career, a *babalawo* may attain four of these, each one involving an elaborate ceremony of initiation and great cost. The reason for this lengthy course of study is the rich complexity of the lore associated with the system and incorporated in the verses. According to Bascom, these verses

> form an important corpus of verbal art, including myths, folktales, praise names, and even riddles; but to the Yoruba their "literary" or aesthetic merit is secondary to their religious significance. In effect, these verses constitute their unwritten scriptures. (Bascom, 1969a: 11)

In this divinatory opus, each individual verse has the same structure. First comes what might be called an image, such as, "Thin fire on the side of the sky, thin evening star in the crescent of the moon" (ibid., 149, 1–6), or "Ejinrin [a creeping vine] spreads and spreads until it enters the town" (ibid, 159, 1–11). Then follows the interpretation, story, or riddle. Finally, there is a suggestion of what kind of sacrifice ought to be made by the client.

Yoruba tradition holds that Ifa divination originated in the city of Ifę. With regional differences, it occurs exclusively in the Yoruba settlement areas. Slaves later carried it to Cuba and Brazil. The structural similarities to the I Ching are so striking that the thought suggests itself that the system may have diffused from China. We might speculate on structural grounds that it reached Ifẹ sometime after the fifth century before our era, because according to some traditions, that was the period in China when the part about the "superior man" or "former kings" was added to the older Image. It seems to correspond in Ifa to the instructions about sacrifice, a central concern in Yoruba religious life.

The prehistory of the region also supports such a conjecture. The city of Ifẹ is located in an area that has always been open to both traders and invaders. It occupies an old settlement site (Willett, 1971), going back to at least the fourth or fifth century before our era. Terra-cotta sculpture and very fine lost-wax bronze castings were made there from early in the present millennium. Chinese trading expeditions ranged far and wide and would have found in Ifẹ raw materials brought in from the countryside and a good market for their products, as well as a city population receptive to new ideas. In an urban environment, the basic outline of the I Ching could easily have found interested learners who then elaborated it and adjusted the new system to Yoruba culture.

A diffusion of this sort of course underlines the importance attached to divinatory systems, and it may not have been all that rare even in very early times. There is, for instance, another system that bears an interesting resemblance to both the I Ching and Ifa divination, namely, *Bwe*. Considered of mythological origin, it is practiced in various parts of Micronesia, and William A. Lessa wrote a summary of it. It involves divining from random knots tied in coconut pinnas. As in Ifa, the sixteen basic figures are tetragrams. They are personified and considered of divine provenience:

> Supunemen was a god, who understood the art of divination. On his body he bore the signs of destiny, the *mesanepwe*. Then he took them all and put them on the floor, and they grew to be as large as human beings; there were sixteen of them. Supunemen said to them, "Go into the forest, chop wood, and make a canoe." They did so, and in two days, they completed the canoe without a keel. On this boat, they came down to earth. (Lessa, 1959: 190)

There are also 256 derivative figures, tetragrams assembled from yes/no answers, and as in Ifa, the order of the basic figures (see fig. 2) is important. In the boat, these personages sat in a defined order, but when they reached harbor, the boat capsized, and the figure that had originally sat in the front now came to sit in the back. The tradition seems to say that not only did the system arrive from someplace else, it also suffered some modification in transfer.

In agreement with both the I Ching and Ifa, each of the derivative figures has a text attached to it, and again, this text always starts out with an image.

However, as is evident in the only complete list of *Bwe* available, published in 1912 by the German government physician Max Girschner, the images are shorter and in many ways more concrete than those of either Ifa or the I Ching. As an example, here are the first five (the numbers given are ordinals, referring to the combination of the two basic tetragrams that form the derived figure, e.g., 1 + 5 would be a combination of the first and the fifth teragrams):

1 + 1 Under the urukoia tree
1 + 2 Behind the wall of the house
1 + 3 Eating the flower wreath
1 + 4 Nearby
1 + 5 Sleeping below

Some of the figures have stories attached to them, but all these stories do is to demonstrate the veracity of the oracles. A surprising number of the 256 oracles, 80 in all, are ominous in content, predicting storms, accidents at sea or on land, suicides, and death, reflecting the perilous environment of the early settlers of this part of the Pacific.

In Micronesia, *Bwe* is encountered from Ngulu to Namoluk in the Carolines, on Palau and Ponape, and in the east as far as the Marshall Islands, but not beyond any of these points. A glance at the map demonstrates that this island world is within the range of the ancient Chinese mariners. Although *Bwe* shares a number of features with the I Ching, it has a decidedly archaic cast. Its simplicity may be a sign either of very early radiation, or possibly of the lower social class of those who carried it to the island world of the Pacific with them, emigrants who were familiar with the basic outline of the divinatory system, but not with the erudite accretions of the I Ching.

Cross-culturally, as we have seen, divination shares the feature of serving as a basis for the decision-making process. Humans, though, have still another structure that serves a similar function, and that is their ethical system.

ETHICS AND ITS RELATION TO RELIGIOUS BEHAVIOR

An often-quoted dictionary of philosophy (Runes, 1960) defines ethics as:

a study or discipline which concerns itself with judgments of approval and disapproval, judgments as to the rightness or wrongness, goodness or badness, virtue or vice, desirability or wisdom of actions, disposition, ends, or states of affairs. (p. 98)

The author outlines two possibilities for approaching the subject:
1) Why do we approve or disapprove what we or others are doing? and
2) Establishing or recommending certain courses of action, ends, or ways

of life to be taken or pursued as right, good, virtuous, or wise, as against wrong, bad, vicious, or foolish.

Anthropologists have been mainly interested in the first of these topics. How do people learn how to behave, how to function in their society? A great deal of work has been done on "enculturation," the process by which the behavior of children is shaped during the period when they are most malleable. Actually, all mammals "enculturate" their young, for being not solitary but social animals, their survival depends on the care of and cooperation with the group. This is especially true of humans, who are born immature and pass through a long period of dependency before reaching adulthood. During this period, the young learn to adjust their behavior to the behavioral norms demonstrated by their peers and by the adults.

Judging from the way the second topic cited above is formulated, the philosopher is apparently of the conviction that humans are at liberty to "establish or recommend" norms or rules of behavior. Actually, our present study suggests that basic norms of behavior are not amenable to manipulation and are instead part of a dependent variable.

How the system of norms works was investigated by Francesca Cancian, an American sociologist, who did fieldwork in a Guatemalan Maya community. She shows that "norms affect behavior by specifying what action will cause others to validate a particular identity" (1975: 135). In other words, individuals will behave in such a way that their actions will identify them as members of a particular group.

In addition to actions, a group also teaches its behavioral norms by transmitting a body of stories, and these are especially instructive when we are trying to discover in what way the norms are dependent on cultural type.

The hunter-gatherers, for instance, base their decisions and judge behavior on an *ethic of appropriateness toward the habitat*. The Indian hunters told many stories about Coyote or Raven, who kept acting inappropriately toward humans and animals alike, and ended up looking foolish or getting hurt. Sometimes, things came even to a worse end, as we learn from a myth of the Lakota Indians (LaPointe, 1976). It seems that at the beginning of time, when humans and animals were still able to talk to each other, First Man decided that animals' killing humans and humans' hunting animals was a pretty chaotic state of affairs. So he sent out a call to all the animals; a large powwow was held, and it was decided to organize a great race. It was to sort the animals into orderly species by the smell of their bodies. So birds were sent to all the directions of the wind to spread the word, and in the meantime, other animals laid out a vast racetrack on the prairie, at the spot where the broken and jagged rocks of the sacred Black Hills are encountered today. Only at that time, it was all one flat prairie.

All the animals agreed to the rules of the race. They were to run around in an enormous circle. None was to stop running or flying, not even for food or water, for one hundred days. All animals started out enthusiastically; all wanted to be winners. But soon, things started going wrong. The weaker animals were trampled to death by the larger ones. Birds began falling from the sky, exhausted or victims of accidents. After many days, a continuous ring of the strongest animals had formed, and the racers, crazed from hunger and fatigue, fell into a wild, rhythmic stomping as they raced round and round the circle.

Suddenly, the earth shook, quivered, and groaned. The path of the racers began to sink. Within the circle, a bulge appeared; it rose higher and higher, until with a thunderous roar, it burst, spewing flames, rocks, and ashes. All the animals were killed in their tracks; the race had ended in a curse of the Great Spirit. Their bones can still be found under the rocks of what is today the Black Hills.

The story tells us nothing about what happened to First Man, the perpetrator of the inappropriate action that caused the earth to erupt in pain. But many legends talk eloquently about human responsibility, as does this one of the Oregon Washo.[9]

According to this tale, there was once a young hunter who had a spirit elk for a friend. This guardian spirit helped him with the hunt, but always admonished him not to kill more than he needed or too many of any animal. The young man became a great hunter, and his family always had enough to eat. But his father kept after him, saying that he was not doing enough. "At your age, I used to do much more." This was a lie, but the young man did not know that. He was sad about his father's scolding and tried to please him by killing more and more animals. The spirit elk became angry with the father, but at last helped his young friend to kill five whole herds of elk.

During this hunt, the young hunter came to a lake and saw what he thought was a dead elk. But it was really his guardian spirit, and as soon as he tried to draw it out, they both sank. After touching bottom, the young man awoke as if from a long sleep, and he saw many wounded animals. They groaned, and he saw that they were persons. The Elk Spirit came up to him and told him that they were those animals that he had killed needlessly. His father had lied to him, he said, but because he had gone beyond what he had commanded, he could no longer be his guardian spirit.

So the young man was cast out of the lake. He went home and asked his two wives to fix a bed for him. He lay there for five days and nights. Then he asked to be washed, and for his friends to come. He told them about his father's lies and what had happened. "The spirit has left me," he concluded, "and I die." As we notice, the Elk Spirit reacts to the inappropriate action of the young man simply by withdrawal. Yet without the friendship of the spirit world, life cannot continue, and the young hunter ceremonially commits suicide.

The women play no role in this story, but in other hunter-gatherer story cycles they are very much in evidence (see, e.g., Grinnel, 1901 [1982]), and their position and the moral code governing their behavior vary decisively with cultural type. Among the hunters, the male and the female sides are pretty much balanced. In Grinnel's cover story, "The Punishment of the Stingy," for example, the men who hunt only for themselves and do not give a share of the meat to the women, are punished by the women and the children permanently leaving them. The women turn into killer whales, and the children into birds with red bills.

In the horticulturalist world, the interest of the storytellers seems to shift away from animal spirits and more to the interaction between humans. However, appropriateness is still the guiding ethical principle. In a story from Cochiti, a Rio Grande pueblo,[10] known in a number of variants, a man was dissatisfied with his wife, because she did not help him in his hunt by praying or remaining continent. So after asking her if she would do what he wanted, he punished her—with inappropriate cruelty—by cutting off her hair, so it no longer had the characteristic Rio Grande bangs, painted her face red, and put a buckskin robe on her. Then he sent her to get water. When she came back, he called a warning to the pueblo about raiders coming. When they saw the woman in her strange outfit, they all pulled up their ladders, so she had no place to go. She wandered away, eventually coming to a waterfall. The water impregnated her, and in the course of years, she bore many children. When these grew up, she told them what had happened to her, and they attacked the pueblo and killed everyone.

Yet total revenge would also be inappropriate: One baby girl survived the massacre and was raised by a pet parrot—Parrot Mother—and when she found out what had happened in the pueblo, she left and, carrying Parrot Mother on her shoulder, joined a village far enough away that she no longer needed to be afraid of the killers. In this pueblo story, the autonomy of the woman is once more quite striking. This feature remained intact in the horticulturalist world, except in the case where such societies had a war complex.

Appropriateness of actions and the equality of women clearly distinguish the horticulturalist ethical system from that of the nomadic pastoralists, where behavior is guided by obedience to the absolute power of the father. This is strikingly illustrated by a ballad of the Mordvinians, a Finno-Ugrian society from the central Volga valley with a nomadic-pastoralist tradition, and very popular all over Eastern Europe.[11] On what is the city of Kazan to be built? the ballad asks. They try to build it successively on the head of a fish, of a cow, of a dog, of a pig, and of a snake. Each one would give the planned city a different character, none of them desirable. Besides, "They build it one day, it collapses the next; they pile up the walls, but they all break down." One day the city begins to speak in a human tongue and demands a human head, the head of a beautiful girl. So the authorities call a meeting, and by design at that gathering an old man, father of the lovely Marjusa, is given much red wine and white brandy, which takes away his reasoning powers. Then they make him promise to give up his daughter. Her father will not go back on his word, her mother cannot oppose him and so is unable to save her either, and eventually she is buried alive, "to make the city as fair as she was." Her last words are a curse on her parents:

> My dear father, may you be full of maggots,
> may my mother be eaten alive by worms.
> Because I am being buried here,
> because the soil of the city is covering me,
> may you receive no tribute for seven evil years,
> may you receive no spoils for seven evil years.
>
> (Bereczki, 1982: 331)

With the agriculturalists, finally, we encounter the dichotomy of absolute good versus absolute evil, light against darkness, white against black, something that many moralists consider the only possible basis for an ethical system. Much of the material collected by the Grimm Brothers revolves around the struggle between these two forces. Curiously, however, the contest is frequently fought out between women, and just as in a peasant household, the father, the male authority figure, in the end rewards the good woman and punishes the bad one.

One story among many similar ones in the Grimm Brothers' collection makes this point clear. It is entitled "The White Bride and the Black Bride."[12] In that tale, a woman had a daughter and a stepdaughter. Once, when they were cutting fodder on the meadow, the Lord in the disguise of an old man came by and asked for directions. The mother and her daughter gave rude answers, but the stepdaughter was kind and offered to guide him. So the Lord punished the two evil women by making them "black as the night and ugly as sin." But he rewarded the good girl by granting her three wishes. She asked to be fair and pure like the sun, and to have a purse that would never be empty, and after death, she wanted to be in heaven forever. She was so beautiful that her brother asked to paint her and hung her picture in his room. He was the coachman of the king, and that is where the king, who was a widower, came to see the picture. He became enamored of the maid, and ordered the coachman to bring her to court. The evil stepmother, however, was a witch, and she blinded the coachman, while making her stepdaughter deaf. By such machinations, she caused the stepdaughter to give her ugly sister her golden robes and cap, and when they drove over a bridge, she and her daughter pushed the good and fair sister into the water. They did not notice that as the good girl sank below the surface, a snow-white duck appeared and swam down the river. The king was naturally disappointed to find his bride to be so black and ugly, and punished the coachman by having him thrown into a snakepit. But the evil mother bewitched the king, so he no longer saw how ugly his bride was, and he even married her. One evening, the white duck came into the kitchen and asked the scullery boy what had happened to her brother, and what the black witch was doing in the house. When this happened three times in a row, the scullery boy became suspicious and told the king. The king came to the kitchen, and when the duck appeared, he cut off her head. Instantly, she changed into the lovely maiden he knew from the coachman's picture. When she told him what had happened, the king freed her brother from the snakepit and then asked the evil stepmother what punishment a person deserved who had done such and such a thing, telling her her own wicked deeds. She was so deceived that she noticed nothing and said, "She deserves to be stripped naked and placed into a barrel with nails in it. The barrel should be hitched to a horse, and that should be driven out into the world." This the king ordered to be done with her and her black daughter, and then he married the white, beautiful bride and lived happily ever after.

The end of the above story brings up the question of "supernatural sanction," made much of in the anthropological literature. In simple terms, what is meant is that should a certain behavioral norm be violated, retribution originating with some being in the alternate reality will be visited upon the offender. It is fear of this punishment, it is argued, that keeps people "in line." As demonstrated by the above stories, however, there is usually no such being around that would take this task upon itself. Inappropriate action, instead, carries within it the seeds of disaster, as during the Lakota animal race. In the Cochiti story, the infraction of the social order brings along revenge by the children of the injured party, that is, within the society. At most, there is withdrawal, as in the case of the stingy hunters, or of the Elk Spirit, where the young hunter actually punishes himself.

To those societies outside of the agriculturalist orbit, the latter's faith in supernatural sanctions appears somewhat naive, as we see in a Hungarian story that I heard as a child, and which with gentle irony, born of the horse-nomad's tradition, caricatures this world view. It seems that a shoemaker accidentally strayed into heaven. He found his way to God's throne, and sitting on it, he discovered that he could see everything that went on on earth. As he watched, he noticed that a thief was breaking into his poor neighbor's sty, making away with her piglet. So he grabbed one of the angels' footstools from around the throne and threw it at the malefactor. Startled by the heavenly missile, the robber dropped his loot and took to his heels. Encouraged by his success, the shoemaker started throwing footstools at all manner of evildoers, so that by the time God arrived back at his throne, quite a number of footstools were gone. "Stop, my son," God said, "and go back to earth. If I were to do the same thing, I would soon run out of footstools."

Finally, in the case of urbanites, the last of the human adaptations to come along, there is consideration neither of the habitat nor of the community, and so individual appropriateness appears as the pivotal concern. Since societies cannot successfully operate without some general consensus on how actions are to be judged, the situation sketched by the philosopher at the outset of this chapter appears to become the norm: People get together and arbitrarily decide on what the ethical stance should be in some particular situation. In the cities of the West, this leads, for instance, to corporations' hiring an expert to formulate rules for their conduct, which is good for unemployed philosophers.

THE SEMANTICS OF "RELIGION"

All societies that we know about have a religious system, and also a word for religion. That is, we are dealing with a named category. Unfortunately, the term often goes unreported. Only the exceptional ethnographer will take the trouble to investigate what exactly the native speaker means, what semantic content is covered by the particular word. Is it, for instance, something like the "Way of the Spirits," which is a translation of *Shinto*, the name of the Japanese folk religion, or some other descriptive term? We cannot know unless we ask, that is, unless we do some linguistic fieldwork.

Research of this nature was done by Lorna Marshall[13] in 1952–53 and in 1955 with the !Kung Bushmen of the Kalahari Desert. During her fieldwork she noted, for instance, that the Bushmen often have two different terms for the same semantic content, the "real" word and the "respect" word. Thus, their word *n/um*, usually translated as "medicine," was not used during a medicine dance, when, as they maintained, there was a great deal of *n/um* around; a respect word of the same denotation, *shibi*, was used. Words, that is, might act as conductors, and if the meaning of a word was too powerful, harm could come to the person using it.

Investigating further, Marshall began to understand that *n/um* was what she called a "supernatural potency" that medicine men had in them and that enabled them to cure. It also existed in medicine songs and medicinal plants. There were a number of different forms, with a particular group possessing the *n/um* of the medicine songs called Giraffe, but not that of the songs called Honey, for example. Their great god ≠Gao N!a created it and gave it its own power, so that it would work autonomously and automatically.

Eventually, Marshall discovered many other properties of this mysterious *n/um*. For instance, it was not personified, and it was not invoked. It was strong, powerful, and invisible, and dangerous to humans if too strong. To the medicine men, it was transmitted by a lesser god. He placed it into a medicine man through his back, and it stayed with that man all through his life. Some men, however, eventually lost it, and then they could no longer cure. Old people, long dead, used to have a much stronger *n/um* than that possessed by people alive today.

Although permanently available, *n/um* needed to be activated so that the medicine men could use it to cure. This was done by singing medicine songs or by dancing, but also by heating it. For that purpose, the medicine men rolled glowing coals between their hands, they tramped in the fire, or they threw hot coals over themselves. *N/um*, they explained, would then boil up through their spinal cords into their heads, becoming so strong that they might lose their senses. But people needed to avoid making loud popping noises when *n/um* was present, because that would cause it to disappear.

The god also possessed a *n/um* that he had not shared with humans. He used it when cooking the souls as they came out of the people when they died and tranforming them into immortal spirits of the dead. He placed *n/um* into the sun, the falling stars, the rain, the bees, and many other animals and birds, and even into fire made under special, ritual circumstances.

The above list that Lorna Marshall assembled reflected a lot of painstaking fieldwork, but it seemed without structure. Working with the intuition that it might hide a complex category meaning "religion," I proceeded to put each individual item on a separate card and ranged them in a number of different ways. Eventually three distinct columns emerged (see fig. 3). On the left side, I placed all the bits of information that I recognized as concerning the religious trance. On the right side, I put those hints that referred to the alternate reality. Then there were a number of items left over, all of which had in common what the medicine man stood to gain when he entered the trance, and through its agency came in contact with the alternate reality. In other words, Marshall had actually provided all the details of the Bushman category "religion," which subsumed under one word the religious trance, aspects of the alternate reality, and the result for the group if in the trance ritual, contact was made with that other dimension of reality.

This analysis explains something that Lorna Marshall seems to have been puzzled by. When she asked about *n/um*, she could discover no myth that might explain it. To her it seemed an agglomeration of ancient beliefs, not transmitted systematically. *N/um* was this, she was told, but it was also that, and come to think of it, there was also something else that needed to be mentioned. We would run into a similar situation if we asked some English speakers what they thought of upon hearing the word *religion*, an experiment I used to carry out with my students. It made them recall something "super-natural," heaven, Jesus, God. Some of them even mentioned the "mystic state," although they had vague notions about what that might be. But many came up with "symbols," such as the altar, and especially the cross. Not one of them knew any legend telling them about how the term *religion* might have arisen. So *n/um* and *religion* linguistically act in a similar fashion. They are both composite categories, continually retaught by such remarks as "It is this," "It is that," and "It is also something else."

A cross-cultural comparison later demonstrated that the various terms for

Trance	Power	Alternate Reality
—needs to be induced	—Awards curing power	—from god
—works automatically	—medicine men have it	—good, dangerous
—has rules (rituals)	—medicinal plants have it	—Giraffe *n/um*
—can be dangerous	—medicine songs have it	—Honey *n/um*
—experienced as state or condition	—provides curative power	—god has *n/um* for changing soul to spirit of the dead
—not personified	—varies with medicine song [Giraffe, Honey]	—during spirit journey, medicine man talks to god
—not invoked	—can also have bad effect	
—not diffuse in air	—no curing without *n/um*	
—not diffuse in universe	—handling fire increases power	
—invisible		
—capacity can weaken unaccountably or in old age		
—special state for spirit journey		
—intensity increases with handling fire		
—passes from spinal column into head		
—blocks out consciousness		
—loud noise terminates it		

Figure 3. *N/um*, named category of the !Kung Bushmen.

"religion" for which there were data available in the anthropological literature were composites of this nature. However, there was also evidence that even a linguistic category of this nature could be a *dependent variable*. Linguists are familiar with this observation, speaking of an "incomplete overlap" between categories. "Animal," for instance, does not include all the same members of the animal kingdom in various languages. In the present case, we find that cross-culturally the category has a right and a left side, speaking in visual terms; that is, there is the religious trance on one side and the alternate reality on the other, but the central column changes in a systematic fashion. For hunter-gatherers such as the !Kung Bushmen, what the medicine man gains when in trance he touches the alternate reality is power, especially power to heal.

As an added bonus, the above analysis may provide an answer to the riddle much pondered by fieldworkers, namely the nature of *mana*, reported from the South Pacific, from Melanesia, and especially from Polynesia. *Mana* is said to be an impersonal, nonanthropomorphized "supernatural" power, a force not having any human shape. It can be the property of a spirit or of a person, or of inanimate objects, often sticks or stones. In our terms, this might then be a category where only the central column, that of power, is expressed. The other two columns, those concerning the religious trance and the alternate reality, are so "self-evident" that they are not picked up by the outsider, or they are eroded, no longer available because of culture change.

The discussion of the semantic content of the named category of religious behavior concludes the theory section, and we are now ready to proceed with the ethnographic examples. As we do so, a few preliminary remarks are in order. First of all, this is not a historical study, and so references to the religions of classical antiquity, often discussed in comparative religion texts, are absent. Second, all comparative data are taken from ethnographies, even when reference is made to the so-called world religions. This choice shifts the focus of the discussion from academic theology to folk religion. Third, in agreement with anthropological tradition, we will accept as given that *within a societal type*, individual societies have more in common with representatives of the same type, even if a continent away, than with groups of a *different type* within the same political boundaries. A Maya peasant has attitudes more like those of a Hungarian peasant than those of his contemporaries living and working in his capital city of Mérida, Yucatán. Fourth, every effort has been made to select examples not yet affected too radically by worldwide missionizing and other communicative intrusions, but we should realize that this is getting increasingly more difficult, and so seeming counterexamples to the "ideal" types presented here are not too difficult to find.

Part Two

Ethnography

FIVE

The Hunter-Gatherers

The bands, hordes, or groups of the hunter-gatherer type of society are usually small.[1] Each one is associated with a particular geographic area, but they do not claim exclusive rights to it. The institution of chiefly power is minimal to nonexistent, and personal property is of modest proportions. Despite the geographic distance between bands, there is communication between them for the exchange of resources and women, and for passing on new religious material, such as songs or stories. Women are equal partners. There is sexual freedom and sexual variety, in addition to permanent marriages. A man is allowed to have several wives. He also has access to potential wives, that is, women whom he would be allowed to marry without violating incest rules, as well as to his brothers' wives. Women in polygenous households may choose lovers among "permissible" men, as well as from among the husband's brothers. In addition, a woman can expect to live with a series of husbands during her lifetime, for the marriage rules usually provide that the first husband be considerably older than his wife. Most adult men and also the women are "medicine" people, that is, religious specialists. Older women are especially valued for their knowledge of ritual and may function as advisers during important rites.

Hunting bands constitute effective work units, so that the burden of labor never becomes onerous. It has been estimated that men get along with about three hours of effort a week. Also for the women, although their work involves more time, procuring of food is a pleasurable social activity. Conflicts between members, arising, for example, from personal differences or from quarrels over women, are resolved by fissioning: The dissatisfied section simply walks away.

Depending on ecological conditions, hunting bands have evolved in a number of ways, but in order to make the comparison rigorous, I have chosen societies where the local band averages fifty members or under, and where there are no factions, and no power differences between men. Subsistence is from gathering, hunting, and/or fishing. What varies is mainly geographic location, and thus the nature of the habitat.

The sample. The sample treated here includes the following societies: the Pygmies and Bushmen of Africa; the Tiwi of Bathurst and the Melville Islands north of Australia, as well as some of the desert inhabitants of that continent; the Andamanese Islanders; and the Northern and Southern Athapaskans and the Washo, Indian societies of North America.

The Pygmies living in the Ituri rainforest, where Colin M. Turnbull studied them in the 1950s, offer a good starting point. In contrast to many hunter-gatherers, who have been pushed around a great deal, the Pygmies have been in the Ituri for thousands of years, and are possibly its original inhabitants. The Bushmen, on the other hand, show the trauma resulting from being in the way of the ebb and flow of war parties of other, neighboring societies, and from being located in a harsh, marginal area. In Australia, the contrast between various aboriginal groups is more geographic than historical. The Tiwi live in the lush vegetation of the islands, while other groups, such as the ones the Australian ethnographer A. P. Elkin came to know during the first part of this century, are scattered over the open expanse of the interior deserts. The tiny villages of the Andamanese, occupying a chain of islands between Cape Negrais in Burma and Achin Head in Sumatra, have been in permanent contact with British administrators since 1788, when a penal colony for offenders from India was established there, but they had not been displaced at the time the British social anthropologist A. R. Radcliffe-Brown did fieldwork with them from 1906 to 1908. As to North America, the Northern Athapaskans remained hunter-gatherers, although living for centuries under the pressure of Western society. The same may be said of the Kiowa Apaches farther south, who used to roam the great plains in association with the Kiowa, as well as of the Hokan-speaking Washo of the Great Basin. The Navajos of the Southwest, also Athapaskans, whom I am including only as a secondary reference, became herders, horti-culturalists, and weavers. Yet their religion preserved many traits that tie them to the hunter-gatherers. This is what they were for the longest time of their history. They are thought to have entered the Southwest in the fifteenth century, about a hundred years before the arrival of the Spaniards there. Other historians place the date earlier.

A hunter-gatherer ritual. Extensive descriptions of rituals are available for all the societies listed in our sample. As an example, I have chosen the *kulama* ceremony of the Tiwi. This ritual is the major part of a sequence of rites by which men and women become fully initiated members of Tiwi society. As an annual event, it is held at a predetermined time and place, and is organized by a group of fully initiated men. All residents of a certain area participate.

As discussed in chapter 4, the hunter-gatherers compose a marvelously complete picture of human life in their rituals. This is, however, not at all clear to Jane Goodale (1971), the ethnographer. Although she describes it in great detail, as a thoughtful observer she agonizes at length over what the intent of the ritual might be beyond that of initiation. As she writes,

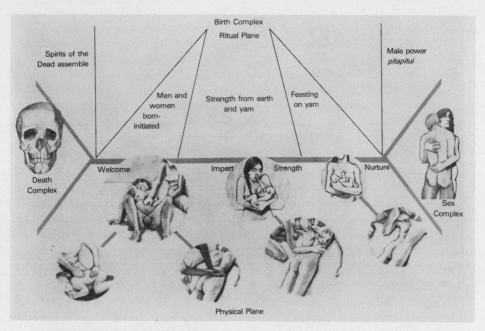

Figure 4. Hunter-gatherer ritual.

> The problem . . . of discussing the meaning and significance of the *kulama* cere-
> mony, is compounded by the lack of adequate data to describe the nature of
> the ceremony and the nature of the underlying world view and philosophy of
> the Tiwi. (pp. 219–220)

This problem, however, can be solved by using a truly adequate model to
interpret such rituals, not one that is foisted on the ritual from the outside,
but one that naturally arises from the totality of the performance, as I proposed
in chapter 4. Once we do that, everything falls into place, and instead of the
mere description that Goodale has to offer, we are awed by the grandiose
vision of the Birth Complex, flanked by those of Death and Procreation, that
opens up before us (see fig. 4).

Summary of the kulama rite. As we learn from a song at the outset, the
spirits of the dead have been hovering around the camp and have been invited
to attend the celebration. The sequence of ritual action begins with a man
throwing a fire stick into the air, the collective penis of the group. Where it
lands, that is, where its procreative power comes into action, is the "lying-
down-place" of the men, who, lying on their backs, are now fetuses in the
womb.

After a night's sojourn in the womb, birth takes place, and the infants, represented by the men, are welcomed with water and white clay. These newborn

are female. In an instant, in the shorthand of the ritual, they grow into wom-
anhood, and as women they go out and "wake up," that is, give birth to male
infants, in the form of yams, patting and gently caring for them. These "mothers"
now carry the yam-boys to the blood-wood tree, where they become initiates.
Their "mothers" wish them well, pulling the grass so they will have a long life.
From there, the yam-boy initiates are taken to the pool, a different ambient,
where their initiation will be completed as they are subjected to the aggression
of the men, whose songs now express conflict. The voice of thunder, the male
aspect of the habitat, arches over the scene.

In the meantime, a new stage setting has been prepared, consisting of a
ceremonial ring, and in it a navel. All is female within this ring. The navel is
the mother-in-law, the provider of female infants for marriage. Yams brought
into this circle are daughters. They are equally initiated, but in contrast to the
pool where the boys are prepared for adulthood, the girls' initiation takes place
in an oven, built over the navel. Their transformation is guarded by the female
aspect of the habitat, the animals, whose dances are performed at this point.

In order to understand the next scene of the ceremony, let us recall here
that in the drama of human birth, the infant is first welcomed, then wrapped
to keep it warm, and finally placed at its mother's breast for its first feeding.
The ritual traverses the same path. All participants get their bodies touched
by warm sand and by crushed baked yams. Then the yams are peeled, while
the participants sing songs about eating, about having a bountiful harvest.

The stage is now set for the final act in the drama of the life of the society,
dealing with its renewal and continuance, with procreation. The men, who
have been daubed red, proceed to put on a striking design of brilliant colors,
followed by the singing of the *apa* songs that treat of power objects.

Under the protection of the night and its bird, the owl, the men change
from female to male. Aggressively, they take the basket containing the yams.
With loud shouts, they carry it to the pond and and dump the yams on a
"marriage bed" of soft grasses. Three themes are touched on in the accompanying songs: penetration—as in the sex act; the *pitapitui*, that is, the souls
of unborn children; and the soul of the individual that walks about at night.
The meaning is clear from what Goodale tells us about the Tiwi notions concerning the nature of a newborn child. There is no ignorance concerning
conception, but for the infant to be a Tiwi child, the soul of the father must
"in dreaming" walk about and find its soul.

The *kulama* grounds, the ring, and the camping area cannot later be used
for mundane activity. The entire complex has become dangerous because of
its involvement in the ritual activity, and thus with alternate reality.

Briefly, then, the *kulama* ceremony, when analyzed with the aid of the
scheme shown in figure 4, is an internally consistent, cohesive statement of
what life, the life of the society, is about for the Tiwi. There is an ever-renewed
flow from death to birth, from providing strength to the living to sharing

sustenance, and then on to procreation and birth once more, balanced and unending. This is what is being celebrated. It thus makes eminently good sense that the *kulama* ritual should be a ceremony of initiation.

Goodale says nothing about the participants' being in trance during the *kulama* ritual. But evidence of its occurrence can be spotted in her description. Especially, there are the repeated references during the rites to something called *tarni*. For instance, when at one point the fire flames too high, there is a warning: It should be lowered, or *tarni* could result. According to Goodale's consultants, *tarni* is a sickness, but they could not describe it to her, only that it is much feared, and she intuits a connection to "magic." It is said to be under the control of Mosquito, a spirit being, and during Tiwi funeral rites, a high, trilling mosquitolike call is produced to ward off danger threatening from this being. *Tarni* thus comes under a larger complex, namely, that of culture-specific illnesses. Specifically during *kulama*, it becomes clear that it can be caught because of some mistake made in the ritual. If people are in trance, this can indeed produce a severe shock reaction. In this respect, *tarni* parallels the Bushman "star sickness," the "ghost sickness" of the Navajos, and other similar afflictions to be mentioned later.

The religious trance. The use of the religious trance by the hunter-gatherers is most clearly observable during curing. Richard B. Lee describes a !Kung[2] Bushman curing rite during a dance:

> Several of the dancers appear to be concentrating intently; they look down at their feet or stare ahead without orienting to distractions about them. The body is tense and rigid. Footfalls are heavy, and the shock waves can be seen rippling through the body. The chest is heaving, veins are standing out on the neck and forehead, and there is profuse sweating. (1968: 40)

Once "the medicine is boiling," that is, the trance is fully established, the trancers begin curing by laying on of hands. They stagger occasionally, but never lose control. Occasionally, they will dance a little in order to keep the trance going or to prevent it from dissolving prematurely. They touch everyone in the group to keep them well, and if someone is ill, they all eventually concentrate on the patient, sometimes spending ten or more minutes in treatment.

Among the hunter-gatherers, the religious trance is also used in order to accomplish a spirit journey. It takes the trancer either over the surface of the earth or up to the sky. We were able to experience the latter by assuming the posture of the well-known "stick figure" from Lascaux Cave (pl. 7). It was created in the Old Stone Age, about fifteen thousand years ago, demonstrating that the knowledge about spirit journeys must be immensely old. The man, who characteristically is wearing a bird mask, is lying supine at an angle of thirty-seven degrees, possibly on a hillock. His right arm is relaxed, bent at

Plate 7. Rock painting from Lascaux Cave, Montignac Grotto, Old Stone Age.
After Gilardoni, 1948: table 11.

the elbow, which in a natural way causes his thumb to point upward. His left
arm is tense, his thumb positioned downward, which makes it necessary to
turn the palm outward, away from the body. Participants tend to experience
the energy beginning to collect in their abdomens, pass upward into their
chests, and then seek an exit, usually through their heads. Some experience
this exiting as giving birth to themselves. Once emerged, either they feel that
they are flying, they see spirit birds, or they turn into birds themselves. Descriptions of what they see during such flights are quite elaborate, of mountain
ranges, the ocean, a river, the sun, the moon, and the stars.

Turning to our ethnographic sample, Turnbull mentions no spirit journey
in his account of the Pygmies, the BaMbuti of the Ituri. But in a letter to me
he wrote, "There *is* a sort of spirit journey in that sense, in which they believe
that they can, voluntarily or involuntarily, cross over into the 'other' world,
which is simultaneous in time and space. It is a sort of shadow world." In a
later telephone interview (31 Oct. 1977), he added some additional information. The spirit journey is conceptualized by this African society of hunters
and gatherers as "crossing over water," and it can happen to anyone. In the
Ituri, there are usually enough fallen trees to act as bridges over rivers, but

occasionally a person may have to get into the water to cross. If people do not concentrate on what they are doing, they may arrive in the alternate reality instead of on the other shore. This is sometimes referred to in jesting, as when a person acts erratically and is then asked, "What river have you crossed?"

In a later work (1978), Turnbull notes that the Pygmies contend that if a person acts violently, he might reach the edge of the personal sphere before it has time to catch up, and so disorientation results. In extreme cases, one might pierce it and pass into the other world. Some Pygmies, Turnbull related in the above interview, cross over into that world and return changed, having incorporated both worlds into themselves. They become "medial," loners, and have the ability to move through the forest all by themselves, which is dangerous for the ordinary person.

The !Kung Bushmen equally have a tradition of spirit journey. Elizabeth Marshall Thomas gives this account:

> When the medicine in a medicine man becomes stimulated by a dance, warmed by the fire and by the heat of the man's body, the man's spirit may leave him, causing his body to fall because there is nothing there to hold it up, and fly into the veld, where it seeks out the evil that is troubling people. Some medicine men in this way have seen the spirits of the dead, some have seen the great god. At another dance that we once attended, one man's spirit rushed out into the veld, where it came upon a pride of lions that had been troubling the people by their deafening roar at night. The man's spirit spoke with the lions, defied them, and ordered them away, and the lions did go; they troubled the people no longer. (1959: 133–134)

In a variant of the spirit journey complex, the Tiwi recognize a condition they call soul loss, classed by anthropologists as an illness, an important culture-bound syndrome, also known elsewhere. The Tiwi say that it results from an unprovoked spirit attack, taking place without reason. The victim of such an assault becomes deaf and cannot speak. During the attack, the spirits of the dead may abduct the soul and take it to their camping site, where life goes on pretty much as it does among the living. To treat a person so afflicted, hot paper bark is placed on his ears, eyes, face, and throat. This treatment makes him feel better, and he remembers people and friends.

While among the Tiwi, a spirit journey happens accidentally, the skill is taught by the shamans to their apprentices on the Australian mainland. Thus, Elkin reports that men preparing to become shamans are taken by their teachers to the sky, and the story is enchanting:

> In the Forest River region of northwestern Australia, for example, the medicine-man takes the postulant up to the sky in the following manner: he assumes the form of a skeleton and fastens onto himself a pouch into which he places the postulant who has been reduced to the size of a very small child; then sitting

astride the rainbow, he pulls himself up with an arm over arm action. When near the top he throws the young man out onto the sky thus making him "dead." (1964: 304)

In another type of spirit journey, there is in Australia a kind of trip that involves an entire group. The ritual is called *kadaitja (kurdaitcha)* magic. According to Elkin, it was known at the end of the last century in central, as well as in western, South Australia. His own observations were made in the latter area in 1930. According to his consultants, men make a shoe (*kadaitja*) of marsupial-fur string and emu feathers and put in it the sacred blood from the vein of their forearm. Those intent on carrying out this magic, which is undertaken to murder someone, are put through a painful ordeal during which their little toe is treated with a hot stone and is dislocated. The toe acts as an eye and prevents a man from slipping or stumbling while he is on his *kadaitja* errand. The person making the request for the murder must go along, and two or three others are also included in the party. When they reach the place where the intended vicitim is staying, one of the group sneaks up to him and spears him in the middle of his back. The victim, however, is unaware that this has happened. Neither does he realize that a white, heated stone is then applied to his wound, making it invisible. A spirit snake might also be inserted, giving the victim temporary life. He is then restored to consciousness and started off toward his camp, where he will die a few days later (1964: 288–289).

That the Andamanese equally possess a spirit-journey complex can be deduced from the following observation by Radcliffe-Brown:

> A man who died a few years ago was believed by the natives to have once met with some spirits in the jungle.... He used to go into the jungle by himself at intervals and hold communication with the spirits with whom he had made friends. From such a visit he returned with his head decorated with shredded palm fibre [a tabooed substance] which had, so he said, been placed on him by the spirits. This man had a reputation as a powerful oko-jumu [shaman]. (1964: 177)

Spirit journeys are also well known to the hunter-gatherers of North America. The Northern Athapaskan shaman either sends his spirit helper to retrieve the strayed soul whose absence makes its owner sick, or he goes after it himself. Among some Salish groups (neighbors to the Athapaskans), a dramatization of the journey in the spirit canoe in quest of a lost soul was a most spectacular performance.

Journeys of this nature are always undertaken for a purpose: to discover the reason for some misfortune; to affect a part of ordinary reality, such as above, chasing away lions or committing murder; to restore a patient's health by locating his lost soul; or to encounter helpful familiars, a tradition very much alive in North American Indian groups with a hunter past. The latter is known in the anthropological literature as the vision quest, or the quest for a guardian spirit.

Controlled (lucid) dreaming. Controlled (lucid) dreaming is not utilized uniformly among all hunter-gatherers, although traces of it are present everywhere. Thus, Lorna Marshall (1962: 238) tells that a !Kung medicine woman described vividly how in a dream the god taught her a medicine song, standing beside her and insisting that she repeat it over and over, until she could sing it perfectly. In Australia, medicine men "dream" the spirit of the culprit near the grave of his victim (Elkin, 1964: 310). Its most important elaboration, however, both for the Tiwi and among the societies on the Australian mainland, is to be found in connection with beliefs about conception. As mentioned above, a Tiwi father must obtain the spirit of a child and bring it to the mother by "dreaming" it.

According to Tiwi belief, the *pitapitui*, or unborn children, live in their own particular locality, playing and waiting for their father. The region belongs to the father's matrilineal *sib*, a unilineal kin group, tracing the descent of a person only through the mother, in the country where the father is a land owner within the aboriginal traditional legal system. It is to this region that the father goes in search of a child's soul in *dreaming*.

Whether the Andamanese are familiar with controlled dreaming is not clear from Radcliffe-Brown's data. There is always the possibility of mistranslation. Is the reference to "dreaming" or to trance when the word for the Andamanese shaman (*oko-jumu*) is translated as "dreamer"? It could easily be trance, for it is reported that in their "dreams," these shamans were able to communicate with the spirits of the dead, and especially, they could cause illness, but could also cure. We encounter similar problems of translation and/or interpretation with reports from North America. Jim Whitewolf, a Kiowa Apache, recalls the medicine man sending out Owl to discover the fate of a missing man. Since Owl is the shaman, but also the shaman's soul, this may indeed be a spirit journey, and not "dreaming," as Charles S. Brant, the editor of Whitewolf's autobiogarphy, suggests (1969).

The alternate reality. The habitat. Westerners noted early that hunter-gatherer societies had no pantheon, but rather seemed to profess belief in a single god, exhibiting a faith that the Austrian priest-ethnographer Father Wilhelm Schmidt called *ur*-monotheism. However, modern research indicates that these societies do not conceive of a universal, all-powerful, all-knowing yet personal deity, such as is familiar from Judeo-Christian tradition. What inhabits their alternate reality instead is a "power," an all-encompassing spiritual essence, the alternate-reality counterpart of the all-encompassing habitat.

For the Pygmies, for instance, the forest is the habitat. But the forest is also present as an all-pervasive essence in the alternate reality. Turnbull seeks to express this visually by referring to the forest as ordinary habitat by "forest," lower-case, and to the alternate-reality essence by "Forest," capitalizing the word. The forest is the Pygmies' home. It is the provider of their subsistence, they hunt and gather in it. A father rocks his small son on his lap and softly sings into his ear, "The forest is good, the forest is good." The forest is available to everyone, and just being in its presence can induce a trance. But the Forest is more. It is a caring entity, to which the Pygmies owe as much respect and consideration as they owe their parents, and from which they can expect the same in return. The Forest, however, is not the subject of supplication for aid and favors; it cannot be manipulated. Yet, it has a palpable presence; it can be sad, as when there is a death in the band, and a great feast needs to be given to make it glad once more. At the feast, the Forest is represented by the *molimo*, a blow instrument, which is accorded the same respect as the Forest itself. In the same way as the Forest is "hidden" in the forest, the *molimo* is also kept hidden there. In its forest aspect, the *molimo* amplifies the animal sounds produced by the singers, until they turn into the Animal Voices of the Forest.

For the Bushmen, the habitat is the desert. Its embodiment is the great god of the east, ≠Gao!na, who is less abstract than the Forest, but still shares many of the latter's attributes. "He created himself," the Bushmen say about him. And "≠Gao!na said, when he praised himself, 'I take my own way and no one can command me. I am a stranger, unknowable'" (Marshall, 1962: 244). ≠Gao!na is also "wild," as an animal is wild, meaning, "keeping his own distance." Yet he is involved with people's lives. It is difficult to think of a more cogent way to express the dual character of the habitat as "nature," out there, unfathomable, unapproachable, yet also nurturing of humans.

There is also a lesser god, the god of the west, but he was created by the great god and is his namesake. The namesake relationship is an important one in the !Kung kinship system, since one shares in some mystical way the essence of the person for whom one is named. He may therefore be viewed as another aspect of ≠Gao!na, the one closer to and not quite so forbidding for humans.

Logically, ≠Gao!na is a god not for the entire world, but only of the Bushmen. As their Habitat, he is all about and alive. But as the same Habitat/habitat, he may also be dead, for in his death throes, as we learn from a Gikwe Bushman story, "his thrashing and writhing limbs gouged out the *omubaras* (dry water courses), the putrefaction of his body became the rivers, and his back hair became the rain clouds" (ibid., p. 236). Yet he is also a person who walks about the veld, gathering up the souls of the dead to take them to his house in the east and to treat them with smoke, converting them into spirits of the dead. He encompasses—but does not create!—not only himself, but also the water holes and the water in it, the metal and the sky, the rain, the sun, and the winds, medicine to renew himself, as well as the plants and the animals. Neither did he create the people.

His presence is so imbued with power that not even the medicine men can tolerate being near him. Yet he is neither omniscient nor omnipotent, and his namesake may even disagree with him. As habitat, he may give or withhold food, and many prayers are directed to him on this account. But these prayers represent a "talking to"; no special posture or address is required, although the third person of address is often employed, being a mark of respect.

For the Tiwi, living as they do on islands and surrounded by water, the woman Pukwi represents the habitat. She made creeks while she walked over the earth; she made the land, the sea, and the islands, but not the people. When some hunters killed her, her urine made the sea salty.

On the Australian mainland, a number of different beings stand for the habitat in the alternate reality. The reason is easy to see. Historically, the Australians did not interact with the entire continent as one habitat. They were intimately involved with only a single section, their "country," but aware from their wanderings also of a number of adjoining ones. So there are "heroes," spirit animals who "in the Dreamtime" left, for example, a particular stone behind as a storehouse of kangaroo life or spirits; or a sky hero, who led the various bands of original inhabitants to their present home and formed its natural features. He lives in the sky and owns fresh water as well as quartz crystals, which can cure people and turn a postulant into a medicine man. The features of the land that have a connection with such alternate-reality entities must be approached with caution, and simply coming close to them may induce a trance.

The Andamanese are islanders, just as the Tiwi are, but their habitat has a special feature: It is subject to the oscillating cycles of the monsoons. From December to the middle of February, the monsoon blows from the northeast. The weather is cold, and there is little rain. Then it turns hot from the middle of February until the middle of May. During this period, roots and fruit are plentiful, and in the hot season, there is an abundance of honey. Land animals, however, are in poor condition. From May to November, the monsoon comes in from the southwest. Vegetable food is scarce, but jungle animals and fish are abundant. Until the end of September, the weather remains rather even, wet and predictable. But in October and November the storms come up, often of terrible force, frequently churning up water spouts and culminating in killer cyclones. Paralleling this habitat, there are two entities of the alternate reality, Biliku, thought to be female, and Tarai, the First Man, who sprang from a bamboo joint. He in turn created a wife for himself and made people from clay. His children are the sky, the wind, the storm, and the foam on a rough sea. The frightening, stormy interlude between the two seasons is called *kilim*. It not only is the interface between the seasons of the northeast and the southwest monsoons, but with its unpredictable fury it also marks the boundary between the ordinary and the alternate reality.

Everywhere on the island there are spots where either Biliku or Tarai used to live, marking them as habitat essences, as Habitat. Biliku threw rocks into the sea, which can still be seen. She made the sun and the moon, as well as the earth (meaning the islands), discovered fire, found the edible roots, and invented all manner of useful things. Her ordinary-reality correspondent is the most striking tree of the Andaman Islands, a redwood. Looking at its flowers will make people giddy, mad, or even "dead." In other words, going near that tree will induce a trance.

Some Navajo data from North America will further illustrate the relationship of the habitat to the alternate reality. Gladys Reichard quotes a singer as saying, "These mountains are our father and mother. We came from them; we depend on them. . . . Each mountain is a person, the water courses are their veins and arteries. The water in them is their life as our blood is to our bodies" (1950: 19). And from another source, very eloquently,

> This peak [the San Francisco Peaks] was made by the holy people in the begin-
> ning. At that time when it was made it was made only by the holy people, not
> by the white people or any Indians, it was made just by the holy people and
> this thing here, this San Francisco Peak is prayers, is a prayer and it is sitting
> there with prayers and it has white shell beads and turquoise and Apache tear-
> drops and abalone and that is what it is sitting there with and also plants of life,
> sitting there with life. (Zolbrod, 1984: 345–346)

And we are very much in the presence of the Navajos' hunter-gatherer past when we hear that the sons of Changing Woman (a deity) overcame the monsters who were killing the people. The remnants of their unburied bodies litter the Navajo countryside in the form of rocks; the mountains are their heads, and in the lava flows their coagulated blood.

Much more abstractly, however, and again true to hunter-gatherer tradition, Navajo religious philosophy recognizes the Habitat as an all-encompassing spiritual essence and calls the unnamable *nitch'i*. As James K. McNeley explains in his outstanding work on *Holy Wind in Navajo Philosophy*, "The term . . . has been translated in this book as 'wind' (consistent with established usage), although this clearly does not adequately convey the sense of the Navajo word. *Nitch'i* refers to the air or atmosphere in its entirety, including such air when in motion, conceived as having a holy quality and powers that are not ac-knowledged in Western culture." Farther down, McNeley continues,

> Suffusing all nature, Holy Wind gives life, thought, speech, and the power of
> motion to all living things and serves as the means of communication between
> all elements of the living world. As such it is central to Navajo philosophy and
> world view. . . . The central thesis is that by this concept the Navajo Soul is
> linked to the immanent powers of the universe. (1981: 1)

Obviously, if a non-Western religion appears simple, this merely indicates that not enough research has been done on it. As is made clear here, Holy

Wind is not a Judeo-Christian creator god, imputed to the hunter-gatherers by Father Schmidt. Stories about the beginning of things, which these societies of course equally possess, should properly be called emergence or origin tales, not creation myths, which suggests the postulation of a single creator god, believed to be the "ultimate cause." As we have seen above, the hunter-gatherers instead conceive of the earth as preexisting, with a multitude of different beings already in place as the first day dawns, and the first humans, wide-eyed as children, arriving on the scene and looking about in a new and marvelous world. No wonder that Marshall found, "I could discover no formulated myth of creation which everybody knew or anything which told how ≠Gao!na created himself. People simply said that they did not know" (1962: 234).

The spirits of the dead. According to the view of all the hunter-gatherer societies discussed here, the spirits of the dead live in a well-ordered world, similar to the one surrounding them in their earthly existence. They do not beget children, but the men have wives, and the women are seen with children. The deceased are welcomed to their new home by their dead kin. The only reason the spirits of the dead might become dangerous to the living is that a lonesome spirit may desire one or the other of them as a spouse, and so may cause them to die. The boundary between the two realities is quite fluid, and so in face-to-face interaction, people sometimes need to make sure that they are talking with someone of the ordinary reality, and not with the other aspect of a living person or possibly with a dead one. In fact, the two worlds are so intertwined that death holds little terror. "People return to the Forest" is what the songs of the Pygmies tell when a death occurs.

The view of the Bushmen is nearly identical. They tell also that the spirits of the dead travel on invisible, fine cords stretched out over the sky. When there is a medicine dance, they cluster around just out of sight. They are neither good nor bad, but may cause mischief by sending a hunter out needlessly by giving him the wrong message in a dream. On occasion, however, they may lead him to game, or to honey. Mainly, however, they act as messengers of ≠Gao!na, bearing fortune, misfortune, illness, or even death at the god's whim. Medicine men can see them—sometimes they appear in their dreams—and anybody can talk to them, exhort them, and make them go away. As they have everything that humans have, they are given no offerings and no thanks for their help.

The Tiwi see life as progressing through three stages, that of the unborn, the *pitapitui*, that of the ordinary one, and that of death. Death is final, and a person does not pass through these stages again. When a person dies and the proper rituals have been completed, a *mobuditi*, or spirit of the dead, arises. In fact, the rituals at the grave are designed to introduce the deceased into *mobuditi* society, which is very much like the ordinary one. The dead live in their own country, for their society is organized on a local basis. The system

is quite explicit: A man, for instance, belongs to his own matrilineage in ordinary life, but as an unborn or as a *mobuditi*, he is a member of his father's
matrilineal kin group. Death, in this respect, is the obverse of life. *Mobuditi*
not only like to be around when there is a ceremony, but they generally hang
around the campsites. So a child going about at night must have no light, lest
it be carried away by them.

On the Australian mainland, there is the added belief that in order to prevent
the spirits of the dead from following the living, their property must be destroyed, their names are no longer spoken, and the mourners paint themselves
in such a way that they become unrecognizable to the roaming spirit, something also done by the Tiwi. An exceptionally powerful medicine man may
catch such a spirit and use it as his helper. It is thought that young children
and the old die of natural causes, but adults are invariably murdered. By holding
an inquest, a medicine man may be able to discover the murderer's identity.
The spirit will not leave the grave until revenge has been taken (see above,
the *kadaitja* magic).

Although there is geographically a large distance between Africa, Australia,
and the Andaman Islands, they show little variation when it comes to the spirits
of the dead. In agreement with the Tiwi, ceremonies similar to those carried
out during puberty rites initiate the deceased into the society of the dead. The
only divergent trait is that the spirits of the people long dead are respected
as ancestor spirits and are given honorary titles.

Among the Athapaskans of North America, finally, we encounter the additional belief that the dead can be reincarnated, in which case they will shift
family affiliation and will undergo a change in sex. Because they are thought
to bring illness, the Washo fear the spirits of the dead so intensely that the
house of the deceased is burned down or abandoned.

Other beings. Only the Australians have a fully developed society of the
unborn in the alternate reality. According to the Tiwi, the *pitapitui* live the
way ordinary children do. In their "dreams," men see them as small humans.
Woman can even locate them in ordinary reality, where they appear as small
brown birds. According to continental Australian belief, a mother left the spirit
children behind at various locations during the Dreamtime.

There are also some other rather indistinct beings in the alternate reality of
the hunter-gatherers. They could be classed as the other-reality reflection of
neighbors. Only the Pygmies do not share in this complex. For them the
neighbors are close and encroaching, in the form of the Bantu peasants, who
treat them as their slaves.

For the Bushmen, however, the neighbors are part of the other reality, distant
and alien. They are people with no knees, who must always remain standing.
When the sun sets, they catch and kill it. After cooking it, they eat it and throw
its shoulder blade to the east, where it rises once more. The Tiwi speak of
rainbow spirits that are sometimes dangerous, and of the small people whose

families live in anthills. They have weapons, but no fire, and may bring luck to the hunter. The Athapaskans know of spirits of the forest that can be kept away by fire, and of spirits of the sea. The Northern Athapaskans are afraid of brush men who lurk in the bushes and steal children. They form bands and move about invisibly.

Social relations in the alternate reality. In the alternate reality of the hunter-gatherers, all beings are equal; there is no hierarchy. This structure mirrors ordinary social reality, where there is no superordination versus subordination, either, not in the family or in the organization of the bands, and not even as it concerns humans versus animals. The point can be demonstrated linguistically. In Navajo, for instance, there is no overarching category for "animal." Side by side, there are compound words that translate as the "nonspeaking ones," "those that travel by day," "those that travel by night," "those that crawl around on all fours," "those that fly," and, equally casually, of the same order, "the five-fingered ones," the latter meaning humans, which are not set off as masters.

There is evidence of this kind of egalitarianism all across the spectrum of the hunter-gatherers. As Elkin says about the stories told on the Australian continent, "Even if the hero is pictured in the myth as an animal, he acts and speaks most of the time in a personal and human manner" (1964: 199). In a clearly ethnocentric statement, James W. Vanstone, speaking of the Athapaskans (1974: 59), remarks that their distinction between animals and humans appears "blurred." Stones, trees, and animals are "persons" for the Pygmies, the same as humans. They can cross the boundary between ordinary and alternate reality just as humans can. If a hunter misses killing an animal, the reason might be that it was really "from the other side" (Turnbull, Interview). In the folktales of the !Kung, the brother-in-law of the god is a bird, his wives turn into cucumbers, and the little tortoise is a "person." The powerful female spirit of the Tiwi is killed by two hunters using spears, one a large stork, the other a fish. The Andamanese tell of the prawn making fire, the dove (or the kingfisher) stealing it and giving it to the people.

Animals are not that different from people for the Washo, either, and egalitarian notions are dominant equally for the Northern Athapaskans and, as mentioned, the Navajos. The latter tell how shortly after the emergence of the people into the fifth world, they were visited by a Mountain Lion, who looked them over and then chose one of the unmarried women as his bride. And animals even cooperate in feeding humans, deliberately entering the hunter's snare, or letting him kill them, as the deer do, who are holy beings wearing their animal garb out of compassion for the people.

Good fortune, misfortune, and the rituals of divination. In the world view of the hunter-gatherers, good fortune is safeguarded by maintaining a balance between human society and the habitat. Not even the beings of the alternate reality should be immoderate when granting favors. The !Kung tell a story in which ≠Gao!na and his sons kill an eland. On their way home to the werf, they meet a man and give him a gift of some meat. Instead of going home with it, this man hides the gift in a hollow tree, then runs ahead and meets the hunting party again. He asks them for meat, but although the sons remember giving him some, ≠Gao!na does not, and gives him another portion. The scene is repeated five times, until finally the god runs out of meat. Ashamed about not having anything to bring to his wives, he begins hitting his buttocks until his insides fall out, and this is what he takes home. He tries to cook it for his wives, but it proves tough, and although he keeps saying it is really eland meat, no one can eat it, and they all go hungry.

In keeping with egalitarian principles, it is equally reprehensible to attract too much good fortune to oneself. Turnbull (1962: 94) tells of an incident in which some members of the Pygmy band he was with had made a paste from antelope parts, a magic possibly of Bantu origin, and smeared this paste on those going on a hunt. Other members of the band were highly critical of this undertaking, and criticism mounted when one family using it had a long run of good luck with animals always falling into their net, while others had no luck at all. It was decided that this course of events must have been due to the magic paste, and everyone, including the offenders, agreed that the only thing to do was to destroy it. They gave all the horns containing the medicine to a respected elder and promised not to make any such selfish medicine again.

How thoroughly good fortune, concerns of the ordinary and the alternate reality, and the notion of balance can be intertwined, is illustrated by what Elkin tells about love-song cycles, possessed by both men and women in northern Australia. The men sing them, and the women both sing and dance them. But while they are intended by the women to bring new lovers, to make their husbands more ardent, and to bring back absent husbands or lovers, behind all this is "the dreaming mythological basis, similar to that of the great cults. Further [these songs] are their own secret which directly expresses for them the eternal dreamtime" (1964: 194).

Even the famous increase rites of the Australian aborigines are not intended to create an overabundance of a particular species that happens to be an important food source for humans. Rather, as the Australian anthropologist Kenneth Maddock emphasizes,

> [They] were performed . . . to sustain the fertility of the species for which they were performed. In some areas rites specific to the various species were unknown, but men addressed themselves to a power or powers identified with fertility as such, the best known being the All-Mother, the Rainbow Serpent and the *wondjina* spirits. These observances imply harmony between nature and society and exchange between men and vital forces inherent in or hiding behind natural appearances. (1974: 25–26)

Being realists, hunter-gatherers consider most misfortune to be self-inflicted. Only unexplainable accidents and severe illness are attributed to outside agencies and alternate-reality sources. According to the !Kung, for instance, the spirits of the dead may be ordered by the god to kill someone. To accomplish that, they may allow a buffalo to gore him, a lion to maul him, or a snake to bite him. He may fall from a baobab tree, an entirely unintelligible accident, since the Bushmen are remarkably surefooted. Or he may be killed by lightning. These same spirits may be responsible for illness, too, also upon the god's orders. They cause it by shooting miniature arrows into people. These can be felt but not seen, and are usually deadly. But the god can be argued with and cursed, and he may be talked into rescinding his order. This is something for the medicine men to do, who blaspheme him while they are in trance.

Illness, the Pygmies contend, comes to them as a result of magical machinations of the Bantu. It penetrates the body and must be sucked out by the medicine man.

According to the Tiwi, misfortune is usually a person's own fault, not only for being careless but often for having provoked the actions of an angered spirit. The ill will of members of another tribe may also be at fault. They claim that their numbers have dwindled because the white people brought alien tribesmen to the islands, who sang songs of poison, killing them thereby. The spirits of the dead, however, are once more blamed if something goes seriously wrong, either because a person violated a taboo connected with them, or because of their being lonely, which prompts them to kill. These beliefs are materially the same on the Australian mainland.

Careless spirits are the main cause of misfortune for the Andamanese, be they of the water, the forest, or the dead. The latter are greatly feared by the Northern Athapaskans, as well.

In the section about the religious trance, we mentioned the Tiwi concept of *tarni* as a culture-specific illness, which somehow was related to alternate-reality matters, because it could be caused by carelessness during a ritual. Turnbull (Interview, 1977) reports something similar for the Pygmies. They call the condition "forest sickness." Turnbull considers it to be a kind of disjunction between the perception of the ordinary and the alternate reality. If it becomes so severe that it impairs a person's normal functioning in society, a ritual of reversal is performed, a kind of tug-of-war. Turnbull describes it in a later work (1978). The women pull at one end of the rope, the men at the other. Since women and men are equal, it would be unacceptable for either side to win. Therefore, if the men's side is about to lose, a woman will cross over and will in this way "become" a man. If the reverse happens, a man crosses over to the women's side. The ritual terminates with a complete reversal having taken place, with the men's and the women's sides having changed places. The patient, who is a participant in the ritual, is in this manner "reversed," i.e., brought back from oscillating between the two aspects of reality to a recreated stability.

For the Bushmen, the corresponding syndrome is termed "star sickness," a mysterious, magical sickness without tangible symptoms, once more laid at the door of the spirits of the dead. After treatment by the entranced medicine men, it enters their bodies, and they shriek it into the air, back to the spirits who brought it (Marshall Thomas, 1959: 129).

Rituals of divination are widespread among hunters, but given the ambivalent attitudes of Westerners, only one of the authors quoted in this section mentions it at all. That lone exception is Lorna Marshall, although she does not recognize that it involves the switching into trance. She describes a practice of the men using oracle disks. These are five leather disks, about two-and-a-half to three inches in diameter. Depending on the oracle sought, the disks may represent eland bulls and cows, for instance. One disk is the factor of ill fortune. The disks are gathered up and then flung on a kaross on the ground. The way they fall will tell the hunter in what direction to go and what difficulties to expect. Or the disks may represent people, someone who is absent and when to expect him back. Marshall mentions an incident where the diviner correctly foretold the early return of one of her party, who was not expected nearly that soon (1962: 222–223).

Ethics and its relation to religious behavior. Wrongdoings among hunters, as mentioned before, are corrected or avenged not on the basis of an absolute good-evil dichotomy, but by considerations of appropriateness. Murdering a man from another band thought to be responsible for the death of a fellow tribesman, in Australian aboriginal view, is not wrong, it is appropriate, for it redresses an endangered balance. In the same way, dissent, quarreling, or excessive bewailing of the dead is not "evil," it is according to the Pygmies inappropriate because it not only may spoil the hunt, but will also sadden the Forest. Burning bees when gathering honey angers ≠Gao!na, whose wife is the "mother of bees," and he may send sickness to the men responsible. The Washo warn against injuring a pinyon tree, the provider of nuts, which would disturb the harmony between the people and the plants. This kind of morality then reveals itself as part of a larger complex, where human behavior is shaped by considerations of whether it is appropriate principally toward the habitat.

The semantics of "religion." As pointed out in chapter 4, the central column of this composite category indicates that contact in trance with the alternate reality awards power to the hunters. The Bushman term involved is *n/um*, usually translated as "medicine." Upon analysis, similar terms of other hunter-gatherer societies show the same characteristic. The Andaman Islanders, for instance, call the interlude between the two monsoon seasons with its frightening water spouts and fearful cyclones *kimil*. The term also stands for the transition to the alternate reality and for religious trance, and "religion" generally is *Ot-kimil*. And in Australia, I think that the corresponding term is

Dreaming. It has long confounded the ethnographers, one reason being that both the whole category and the various parts of it in English at least bear the same name. So it is only from context that we can decide whether an Australian aborigine means the religious trance, or the alternate, timeless reality, or power, or what we conventionally translate as "religion."

SIX

❧

The Horticulturalists

The history of horticulturalist settlements varies greatly according to geographic location. Judging from the archeological record, it flourished only briefly in Central Europe, and disappeared from the scene well over five thousand years ago. Traces of it can still be found in fairy tales and legends, but the absence of a historical memory of this cultural form contributed to the tragedy of native populations that got in the way of European conquest: It was not agriculture, and therefore it was despised as ignorant and savage. Only around the Mediterranean did some of the central concepts of its religion, especially that of metamorphosis, survive into the time of classical antiquity, as we know from ancient Greece and Egypt. But the ability of humans to change shape and become animals or plants was no longer generally accepted and became the attribute of deities in Greece. Zeus changes into a bull or a swan in order to further his amorous pursuits and seduce beautiful girls. And in Egypt, where many deities appear in a combined human and animal form, the entire metamorphosis complex apparently became part of the esoteric knowledge of the priestly caste. Japanese Shinto, the "Way of the Spirits," is the only example of a large, modern industrial society retaining a horticultural religion. Horticulturalism as a way of life survived into the present in New Guinea, in parts of Southeast Asia, in Africa, and among Amerindian societies in both North and South America.

For the most part, horticulturalists live in small semipermanent villages, with the population usually around 130. Some prefer individual homes, but more often they have communal dwellings, where each family has its own section. There is no chiefly power; only in cases of emergency does some respected man take over command. Even then he can only make suggestions; he cannot order a certain course of action. Men and women have different but equally important roles in religious ritual. Married women are allowed to have lovers, although they are more often victims of male jealousy than with the hunters, and if the group has a war complex, the scales are definitely tipped against them.

What distinguishes the horticulturalists from the hunter-gatherers is the addition of cultivated crops to their subsistence. Their plantings are small, mere gardens; thus the name "horticulture" for this adaptation. Depending on the ecology, the relationship of hunting to gardening varies, favoring either the one or the other type of interaction with the habitat. As could be expected, their religious behavior correlates with this difference, leaning either more toward the hunting side, or more in the direction of agriculture, as the case may be.

The sample. As an example of the religious system of a society with a low utilization of cultigens, we are going to discuss the Akwẽ-Shavante of central Brazil. Examples for a high utilization of cultivated plants will be provided by the Yąnomamö, a society with a war complex, also of Brazil; and the Semai of Malaysia, who emphatically disavow aggression. These three groups, although belonging to one type of adaptation, are sufficiently different to warrant separate discussion within this chapter. This will make it possible to highlight their similarities while also pinpointing their divergence.

The Akwẽ-Shavante use cultigens only as an adjunct to what they can gain from hunting and gathering. They live on the high savannas, on the watershed of the Xingu and the Rio das Mortes rivers. They grow maize (corn), beans, and pumpkins, but little care is lavished on their plantations. Their abundant food base comes mainly from gathering. Hunting, expressing virility, is the favorite occupation of the men. They live in semipermanent villages, which are abandoned only under pressing circumstances. For much of the year they are on trek, exploiting in a yearly round the territory dominated by their respective communities. Their social structure is extremely complex. It is dominated by an overriding dichotomy, namely, that of kin versus affine. All good comes from a person's kin; all danger, but by extension also power, comes from the affines, that is, from those that have married into the line.

The Yąnomamö, by contrast, who occupy sites in the rainforest of Brazil, are much more dependent on their gardens. Like the Akwẽ-Shavante, they equally reside in semipermanent villages and do a great deal of hunting and gathering, but despite the variety of food they obtain from the jungle, they could not exist for any length of time without their cultivated crops. They have institutionalized warfare, with its attendant system of alliances based on trade and the exchange of women. Consequently, women have shifted to a disadvantaged position: They are counters, as it were, in the complicated struggle for power in which the men engage. They can and do have lovers, but at a considerable risk to their personal safety. Neither are they ritually the equals of men, for only the men take hallucinogens, and thus only the men are shamans. The dances that take place during their many feasts are danced only by the men, the women being relegated to a supporting role during the preparatory phase.

While the Yąnomamö consider themselves "fierce," the third group under consideration, the Semai, whose home is in Malaysia, in Southeast Asia, are devoutly nonaggressive. They cultivate mainly foxtail millet and rice. Since the sixteenth century, they have also grown maize, tapioca, and sweet potatoes. In addition, they grow yams, taro, and bananas, all by slash-and-burn tillage. Their protein comes from hunting. Their subsistence pattern is thus similar to that of the Yạnomamö. They do not have any war complex, however, and ritually, women are the equals of men. In fact, women who have ritual power (*halaa'*) are considered more dangerous than men.

A *horticulturalist ritual* (low utilization of cultigens). The following is a description of the *wai'a*, the most important ritual of the Akwẽ-Shavante (Maybury-Lewis, 1974: 255–263). As we shall see, the rituals of horticulturalists who are still predominantly hunters and gatherers are reminiscent of the ceremonies of the latter in their vast sweep of the entirety of the human drama. They also demonstrate, however, the intrusion into the picture of two new, absorbing themes, aggression and metamorphosis.

Only the initiated men are allowed to participate in the *wai'a*. There are actually three different *wai'a*—one held for the sick, one held for the arrows, and the longest and most complete one, always held in conjunction with initiation, the *wai'a* for the masks. It is this third one that will occupy us here. It is strictly forbidden for women and children to witness some parts of the latter two *wai'a*. However, this interdiction is intended more to underline the esoteric nature of the ritual than actually to prevent the women from seeing either the action or the paraphernalia involved.

Summary of the wai'a rite. Using the ritual scheme proposed earlier as a guide (see fig. 5), we are tempted to assume that within the Death Complex, the spirits of the dead are invited to participate at the outset of the rite. But as we shall see, this participation is postponed, to a point where the initiates have become ritually "full grown," and can thus take part as mature adults in the proceedings.

During the introductory sequence, the "welcome" branch of the Birth Complex, the boys are assigned to two different moieties, the woodcutters and the gourd people, that function only during this ceremony, and which are approximately equal in number. The woodcutters are given reddened clubs; the gourd people dance with rattles. It is easily understandable that the group with the clubs, a phallic symbol representing "free-floating generative power," will represent the male initiates, that carrying the rattles, womb-shaped gourds with seeds inside, will be "standing in" for the girls. We will recall that during the *kulama* ceremony of the Tiwi, the men also at one point represented the girl initiates.

The initiates in their role as the unborn in the womb, who do not eat, now embark on a prolonged fast. Repeatedly during the day, the woodcutters dance toward the gourd people, cradling their clubs in their arms. The gourd people, in affirmation of their femaleness, then dance around the woodcutters, as the woman's vagina surrounds the man's penis in intercourse.

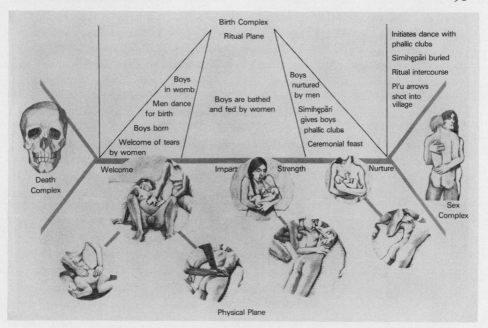

Figure 5. Horticulturalist ritual, low utilization of cultigens: Akē-Shavante.

In the shorthand of the ritual, the initiates at this point represent the promise of new life, hidden away in the mysterious realm of the unborn. But for birth to take place, labor pain needs to ensue, which the men initiate. They have gathered in the jungle singing,[1] and now emerge and dance a furious, stamping, pounding, flailing dance at the collective womb. They go on for days, continually renewing their effort to bring about birth.

Finally, "in the fullness of time," birth is imminent. The womb becomes visible in the shelter that the gourd people erect, enclosing the woodcutters inside. Those that are outside, the gourd people, are ready to be born. The men come from the forest once more and dance around the gourd people; each boy in turn rears up, whirls around, and then falls down, senseless: He is born. The women come into their own. The boy's kinswomen revive him, welcome him with tears, and bathe and feed him. The following day, those that were in the shelter are similarly treated.

With the ritual of bathing and feeding, we have passed through the "impart strength" branch of the Birth Complex. It is now the turn of the men, who under the "nurture" branch guide the newborn into the forest and "grow them up" by investing them with ceremonial arrows. They are instructed to place these arrows beside their mats and to guard them. By sleeping with them, the boys grow into young men by morning. They spend the entire next day dancing with the arrows, shuffling forward a few paces, dragging the arrows toward the center of the village, then shuffling back again. Repeatedly traversing the time-space in this manner, they are fully mature by nightfall, and can now form their own age grade, which they express by going to the men's meeting place and laying their arrows down there in such a way that their points all touch in the center of the circle.

These complex events, however, are only the preliminaries of the *wai'a* proper. With admirable internal logic, it is now that the men call the spirits of the dead to the feast by a special signal, "U, hę, hę, hę ... " repeated after each song. The men, including the new age grade, carry their clubs into the village, the frankly phallic symbols of their sexual maturity. This is emphasized by the dance of the men, a stylized representation of sexual intercourse.

As if for emphasis, the entire ritual sequence is reviewed once more. The "welcome" is acted out by the men pounding on the thatch under which the women are sheltered. "Imparting strength" is performed by a mysterious being called Simihępāri, who, as will become clear later, is actually the habitat. In the forest, he meets two representatives each of the woodcutters and the gourd people. The former receive the phallic emblem of special clubs, the latter a special kind of arrow, of which we hear nothing more. Consonant with their female character, this group typically does not join the dance that mimics intercourse, and remains passive during the rest of the rite.

Within the general structure of the scheme that I am proposing, the ritual should now enter the "nurture" branch. But unexpectedly, it is at this point that a struggle ensues with Simihępāri. Who or what is this Simihępāri? He is fierce, the Shavante say, and they dread meeting him. But meet him they must. Every time the *wai'a* of the masks is celebrated, he appears once more, and they must confront him. There is a vicious struggle, and in the end, he is defeated and falls dead to the ground. The clubs he awarded to the woodcutters are buried—perhaps in his stead—and all return to the village for a feast. The next day, the men go hunting and fishing, procuring the food for the rest of the celebration. So what the rite seems to say is that after he is vanquished and is buried like a seed in the ground, Simihępāri reveals himself to be the essence of the controlled habitat, nurturing those that vanquished him, and turning into fish and game in a grand metamorphosis. In other words, he is the habitat that these horticulturalists are hesitantly, timorously beginning to to conquer. We are reminded of the bullfights of the ancient Mediterranean world, still celebrated today, where a faint glow of priestly aura continues to cling to the torrero. Who knows, in that custom quite possibly our own horticulturalist past may have been kept alive, and the bull once embodied the habitat that needed to be conquered over and over again, so there would be a harvest, much as in the case of Simihępāri of the Shavante Indians.

The lengthy ceremony comes to its end by entering the Sex Complex. This part of the rite centers around beings called *pi'u*. Maybury-Lewis was not able to determine what these *pi'u* were. Their role and actions within the ritual, as well as our scheme, however, indicate that they are the spirits of the unborn, quite similar in nature to the *pitapitui* of the Tiwi, who are waiting in the forest, crying for bodies. In response, the young men prepare special arrows for them out in the wilderness that have humanlike features, two feathers for legs, a shaft clothed in snakeskin for a body, and human hair close to the wooden arrow tips, their heads.

As an invitation to them to take up residence in the village, women representing all three clans are ceremoniously escorted into the forest and there have intercourse with the *wai'a* celebrants. Afterwards, they are painted and decorated as men, and as such dance around the village: They have been to the forest, the alternate reality, and contact with it produces the reversal.

All through the last night, the *pi'u* have been hooting in the forest. At daybreak the men come out to the middle of the village, and wait, tense and expectant, until they hear a whistle signal from outside the village. All at once, the young men shout, "U, hę, hę, hę. . . ." In a complex choreography, the arrows representing the spirits of the unborn are shot into the village; they themselves appear as men painted black from head to toe, and with their dance bring the ritual to a close. The cycle of life is complete, the souls of the unborn have been integrated into the village, and the round of life can begin anew.

The religious trance. Quite generally, the religious trance is extensively utilized by horticulturalists. Many such groups use hallucinogens, although not the Shavante. They also brought to its most intense flowering a complex already used by the hunters for the spirit journey, as mentioned in chapter 5, but that went undetected until our research brought it to light beginning in the late 1970s. As explained before, it involves the use of stereotypical postures, each one mediating a different type of trance experience. Judging from our experiments,[2] there are apparently many horticulturalist postures, for instance for spirit journeys, not only for above the earth, but also into the lower world, for divination, for calling certain spirits, and especially for metamorphosis, a central issue for the horticulturalists (for details, see Goodman, 1986). As evidenced by millennia of native art, the knowledge was shared by horticulturalists around the globe. What we do not know is whether it is still available as a technique today, because anthropological observers were unaware of the existence of the complex. Certainly Maybury-Lewis does not report it among the Shavante.

That awareness of some of the postures has come down to the present in this type of society can be documented; we just do not know if they are still used during trance rituals. In the late 1970s, the Swiss anthropologist Gerhard Baer did fieldwork with the horticulturalist Matsigenka Indians of East Peru. One of their shamans prepared a line drawing for him, showing the spirits and the places he saw during his spirit journeys (pl. 8, from Baer, 1984: 214, fig. 4) The beings directly above the house of the shaman are the *kasankaari*, the pure, fragrant spirits. Their moustache is that of the jaguar, denoting their

Plate 8. Drawing of the alternate reality by a Matsigenka Indian shaman; the large figures in the bottom row above the community dwelling are the "fragrant" spirits. After Baer, 1984: 214; opp. p. 174.

power. The one on the left seems wrapped in a cover, so we cannot tell anything about his posture. But the other three are in postures we are thoroughly familiar with from our research, and which here surprisingly appear as attributes of these important spirits. Going from left to right, the one next to the occulted one is drawn in the posture of the Feathered Serpent, which mediates the experience of death and rebirth; the next one shows the Singing Shaman, a visionary posture loved around the world; and the last one is the tremendously popular healing posture, which we have named the Bear Spirit posture because of its frequent association with that powerful spirit.[3]

Maybury-Lewis's account of the use of trance among the Shavante suffers also from the fact that in many instances, he was not allowed to see certain parts of a particular ritual. During the *wai'a* of the masks, for instance, he was forbidden to witness the events in the forest. He does mention something that could not very well be experienced unless the person in question was in trance, but we are not told any details:

> Shavante . . . seek assistance from the spirits of the dead, particularly dead kin, who are regarded as especially benevolent. Once a soul has established itself in the community of the dead it can come and go with impunity. When it comes back to visit the living, Shavante are not afraid of it, since such souls are generally thought of as having the well-being of their kinsmen at heart. In cases of illness they can sometimes be relied on to 'look over' the patient and make him well again, and they are the source of other minor favours and benefits. (1974: 287)

The spirits of the dead are "invoked," but we do not hear how that is done.

Some of the information given in Maybury-Lewis's account sounds like it might refer to a spirit journey, but again it is not clear how the person in question embarks on it. According to such stories, some men are taken by their guardian spirits on the trail that leads to the village of the dead. But it is a long way, and people always turn back before getting to the "beginning of the sky," for fear that they might not be able to find their way back.

Trance is most certainly also involved in metamorphosis. The Shavante pointed out to the ethnographer that during the rituals, such as the *wai'a,* the impersonators *become* the spirits they represent. Animals may on occasion turn into humans, but according to Shavante belief, only the malevolent spirits of the dead turn into animals.

Controlled dreaming. This type of dreaming is employed extensively by the Shavante. It either happens by chance, or a person so longs to see a particular spirit that he concentrates intensely on it. Eventually it will then appear in a dream. One lineage uses cylinders of polished wood to communicate with the dead. This method is considered to be so important that the respective lineage takes its name from these cylinders. A cylinder is hung either over the grave of a dead kinsman, or over the sleeping mat of its owner. The owner then either visits his dead kin in a dream or receives a visitation from him.

The alternate reality. The habitat. As argued above, for the Shavante the representative of the habitat in the alternate reality is Simihẹpãri. He is not, however, all-encompassing like the Forest of the Pygmies. Neither is he a creator. Just as Lorna Marshall did with the !Kung Bushmen, Maybury-Lewis apparently equally quizzed the Shavante about creation, but to no avail. The world was empty, the Shavante insisted, and then various beings and objects simply began appearing.

The spirits of the dead. The soul leaves the person's body at the moment of his death and starts out on its journey to the village "at the root of the sky," as far east as one could possibly travel. This place is better than the world of the living. It is a place of abundance, where life is easy and food plentiful. The spirits of the dead spend their time singing and dancing. But to get there, the soul needs to escape the aggressive spirits of the affines who lurk along the path, trying to kidnap it. These spirits live at the westernmost end of the sky and are frightening and aggressive. Once in the home village of the dead, the soul is safe from them. "Heaven," says the ethnographer, "is a place where affinity has been exorcized" (Maybury-Lewis, 1974: 290).

Obviously, there are some problems with this scheme, for one person's affine is the other's kin. But we are dealing with alternate-reality geography here. Neither are the aggressive affines *absolutely* evil. They are associated with the dance and with the masks of initiation as the givers of power.

In addition to the spirits of the dead, there are various heroes and other important personages in the alternate reality, such as founders of lineages, but they do not have any effect on the daily life of the Shavante. We learn nothing more about the *pi'u*, although of course they are also part of that other world.

Good fortune, misfortune, and the rituals of divination. Good fortune, as we have seen, originates with the spirits of dead kin. Misfortune, especially in the form of illness, may be caused by contact with the Karajá, a society whose territory the Shavante occasionally visit. They have more dealings with the Brazilians, and may pass infectious diseases on to their visitors. In the view of the Shavante, the Karajá do not use sorcery. They are simply bad and therefore radiate injurious malevolence. True sorcery originates within Shavante society, and is a function of its duality. It is the affines that engage in it against "one's own," causing bad luck, unexplainable illness, and death. The tools of sorcery are certain rituals, such as blowing "bad powder" in the direction of the intended victim, or giving orders to one's earplugs to make a stingray or an alligator attack his adversary. As in the case of affine spirits, the power of the red earplugs is not evil, it is dangerous. But it is also associated with reproductive power. A man will wear his earplugs during intercourse if he intends his wife to conceive.

Divination, as we noted, is done during controlled dreaming. There seems to be no divination ritual used.

Ethics and its relation to religious behavior. It follows from the thorough dichotomization of Shavante society that actions are guided by social appropriateness. For their very survival, people need at all times to apply one set of rules when associating with their kin, and an entirely different set when in contact with their affines.

The semantics of "religion." To his regret, Maybury-Lewis was not able to learn the Shavante language sufficiently well to be able to do any linguistic fieldwork.

Depending on the ecology, as pointed out before, horticulturalists developed a host of different adaptations. The Shavante represent the one extreme in this spectrum, paying little attention to their gardens and a great deal to hunting and gathering. On the other end of the continuum, we find the opposite pattern, with a lot of care lavished on the cultigens, and hunting and gathering deemphasized. In our sample, this pattern is represented on the one hand by the Yąnomamö, who possess a war complex, with raiding the central concern of the men, and on the other hand by the Semai, who are devoutly nonviolent.

The Yąnomamö derive about 85 percent of their subsistence from domesticated crops. Hunting and gathering take second place behind their other interest, raiding. Napoleon Chagnon did fieldwork with these virtually unknown "fierce people" in 1964–66, and again in 1967.

A Yąnomamö ritual. The most important social and ritual occasion for the Yąnomamö is the feast. Feasts are given for a number of occasions: to treat an ally, to lure a group of enemies into a situation where they can be ambushed, for an occasion of endocannibalism, where the ashes of the deceased are mixed with plantain soup and eaten by their relatives, or as a preliminary to a trading undertaking or a raid.

Summary of a feast. (See Chagnon, 1968: 105–113.) Preparation for a feast involves harvesting and hanging up bunches of plantains to ripen, as well as going on a hunt. The young men selected to go hunting sing a special song on the evening when the plantains are hung up to assure themselves of good luck. During the week when they are away, the young women and girls sing and dance in the village to assure their success. The men take food with them, for they are not allowed to eat of the meat to be offered to the guests.

During the feast proper, the ritual structure we used for analysis is only partially activated: The Death Complex and the Sex Complex are absent (fig. 6). The central section is fully represented, albeit in cursory fashion, except for the "nurture" branch. No invitation is issued to the spirits of the ancestors. Its place is taken by a secular activity: A messenger is sent to the guests assembled nearby, formally inviting them to the feast. Meanwhile, the young men of the host group cook huge quantities of ripe plantain for the soup, and green ones to be eaten with the meat. The center of the village is cleared for the dance, and the men of the host group paint themselves in red and black and attach colorful feathers to their hair.

When everything is ready, the men take *ebene,* their hallucinogenic drug. This takes them to the plane of the alternate reality, and there the Birth Complex of the ritual structure is played out in a curiously idiosyncretic manner, almost a negative mirror image of the usually positive content. In *ebene* intoxication, the men chant to the *hekura,* the mountain spirits (welcome branch), sending them to enemy villages to eat the souls of children there (impart strength branch), while enjoining them to prevent their enemies from doing the same to them. Then under the nurture branch, curing is done, with

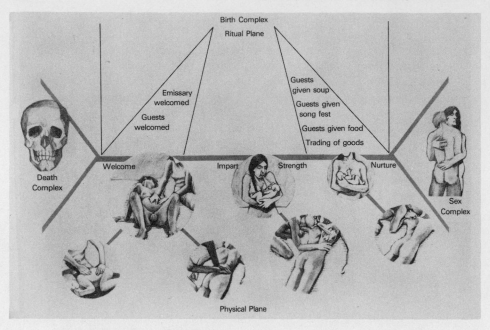

Figure 6. Horticulturalist ritual, high utilization of cultigens: Yąnomamö.

an emphasis again on the negative aspect of the activity, sucking the illness out and vomiting the injurious spirit that caused the sickness.

Returning to ordinary reality, there now follows a rich elaboration of the nurture branch. In midafternoon, a representative of the guest group arrives, entering the village ceremoniously. He marches to the central clearing and strikes a visitor's pose: Motionless, he holds his head high and places his weapons vertically close to his face, the conventional way of indicating peaceful intent. His hosts can now admire him in his paint and feather finery, or shoot him—this does happen occasionally. He then marches to the headman's section of the circular communal building that constitutes the village, and the two men begin chanting with each other, which signifies that the invitation has been accepted. He is fed and given a heavy packet of meat as a gift, which he loads onto his back and takes to his group waiting outside the village. The food is eaten by the visitors while they complete adorning themselves, each member of the party receiving a small portion.

The guests then assemble outside the village in full regalia. The men dance into the village, two at a time, with the young boys, women, and children bringing up the rear, also decorated, but carrying the baggage. When all have entered, the entire group dances several times single-file around the circular inner periphery of the village. In the film Chagnon and his coworker Timothy Ash made of such a feast, the boys carried fresh green plant streamers during this scene, a splendid sight. A highly developed aesthetic sense is evident in all these Amerindian rituals. Maybury-Lewis was asked by the Shavante repeatedly if he thought the dance and costuming of the *wai'a* were beautiful, which they were.

After the completion of the dance, all the visitors gather in the center of the place, forming a tightly packed group. After a few minutes of anxious waiting, the hosts emerge, inviting the guests individually to their respective home sections. The guests go with their hosts and rest in the hosts' hammocks. Even lying down and with their legs crossed, they manage an impressive display of their finery as they stare at the rafters and wait, seemingly unconcerned, for the plantain soup to be brought to them. After the guests have been fed, it is the turn of the host group to dance around the village clearing, showing off their decorations.

The guests usually empty the first large trough of soup while still in the hammocks. They then rise and assemble at a second trough and consume as much soup as possible, next passing on to the third one, for what by now is merely ceremonial consumption, before returning to their hosts' hammocks to rest and regain their appetites.

Shortly after dark, the men of both groups begin an all-night session of chanting. At dawn, the visitors are given baskets of "going-home food," boiled green plantains and smoked meat. The women and children leave, taking the food with them, while the men conduct their business, usually a lengthy trading session.

The religious trance. For the Yąnomamö, religious experience is mediated by *ebene,* extracted from the inner bark of a tree. It is insufflated, in order for the shaman to be able to attract the *hekura* spirits into his breast. These spirits live out in the jungle, but when they enter into the cosmos in the shaman's breast, they become one with him. Together they go flying through the air, visiting faraway places, curing loved ones, or attacking enemies and eating a portion of their souls. This will make their adversaries sicken or die.[4]

The alternate reality. The habitat. The habitat is represented not by a single entity, such as Simihępãri of the Shavante, but by a number of different ones, each with its own function, but all having equal status. There is Waderiwä, for instance, the spirit of the wind. When a strong breeze comes up, the shamans rush to the center of the village and enjoin him to stop blowing the leaves off the roof. "Son of Thunder" stops that portion of the soul that leaves upon death on its way to the village of the spirits of the dead, interrogating it as to the behavior of its owner on earth. No one being is credited with having created the earth and all that it holds. So-called first beings are thought individually to have brought forth some particular plant or object, and even in that case the impression arises that the object preexisted. One of the first men "acquired" plantain, the Yąnomamö staple, and another one stole it from him. The same happened with fire. Until there was fire, the first beings ate dirt and consumed

their meat and insects raw. Alligator knew about fire and kept some of it hidden
in his mouth. A Yąnomamö made him laugh, and a bird snatched the fire out
of his mouth and took it up into a tree. From that day on, eveybody had fire.
There are many other first beings. In ancestral time, Moon descended to earth
and ate the ashes of the deceased Ancestors. One of the Ancestors shot him
in the belly, and his blood spilled on the earth and transformed into the "fierce
people," the Yąnomamö. Their fierceness, then, is preordained; it has its roots
in the alternate reality, in events in the time of the Ancestors.

The cosmos preexisted. It has a top layer, the place of origin of some things.
This layer, however, is empty and has no function today. Three other layers
eventually broke off of this top layer. The topmost of these is called *hedu*. It
is covered with earth and houses the society of the spirits of the dead.

The spirits of the dead. The spirits of the dead live on *hedu* in the same way
as they did on earth: They garden, they engage in witchcraft, they hunt, and
they eat. *Hedu* is a kind of mirror image of what exists on earth. The villages
on *hedu* continually receive new arrivals. The bottom layer of *hedu* is the
visible portion of the sky. The celestial beings are attached to it and move
across it. A piece of *hedu* broke off and formed the surface where people live
today, the jungle and the forest sprinkled with innumerable Yąnomamö
villages.

Finally, there is also a piece of *hedu* underneath the world of people. It is
almost barren and was formed afterwards, when another piece of *hedu* broke
off and crashed through the earth. It took with it a single village of spirit people,
called the Amahiri-teri. Unfortunately, only their *shabono,* their communal
house, and their gardens were carried along; they have no neighborhood in
which to hunt, so they send their spirits up to earth to capture the souls of
children and eat them (from Chagnon, 1977: 44–45).

Good fortune, misfortune, and the rituals of divination. Good fortune, in
the form of cures, may come through the agency of the *hekura.* Misfortune,
on the other hand, especially illness, may be caused by one of the first beings'
turning malevolent. This happened, for instance, with Omawá, one of the hero
Twins. After the great flood, in which many first beings drowned, he became
an enemy of the Yąnomamö, sending them hiccoughs, sickness, and epidemics.
The shamans of enemy villages dispatch their spirits to eat the souls of the
children, so the shamans are continually busy warding off such attacks. Misfortune, clearly, originates from outside one's society.

No ritual of divination is reported by Chagnon.

Ethics and its relation to religious behavior. The Yąnomamö live in a state
of chronic warfare, and to act with social appropriateness is the only way in
which one can assure the validation of one's identity as a truly fierce man, a
Yąnomamö. Killing, lying, treachery are all in this sense "appropriate" actions.
Appropriateness of this nature carries over into the alternate reality. On its
way to the village of the spirits of the dead, the departing soul portion comes

to a fork in the road. There it is stopped by Wadawariwä, the Son of Thunder, and is asked whether in life it was generous or not. "Most of the Yąnomamö I questioned on this asserted that they planned to lie to Wadawariwä," Chagnon tells us (ibid., p. 48). Since this was appropriate under the circumstances, they were all convinced that they would make it safely to the desired destination. Absolute evil does not exist in the Yąnomamö world view. The Amahiri-teri do not eat the souls of the children because they are *absolutely* evil, but because they are hungry and have no place to hunt for game. Neither do the Yąnomamö have any say about their warring ways. That too is appropriate behavior for men descended from the blood of the moon.

The semantics of "religion." Chagnon's report offers no data for the reconstruction of this category.

The Senoi Semai live in the hills and mountains of central Malaysia. Just as in the case of the Akwẽ Shavante and the Yąnomamö, each one of their settlements is politically autonomous. Their subsistence pattern is similar to that of the Yąnomamö, but in contrast to the latter, the Semai do not have a war complex. Yet, as we shall see, despite this fact and although they are half a world away from the Amerindian societies treated above, their religion is quite similar.

A Semai ritual. The central issue of the Shavante ritual we described was initiation. For the Yąnomamö, it was feasting a potential ally. For the Semai, as Robert K. Dentan, their ethnographer, describes it, it is curing. The Semai have a number of curing rituals carried out in the home of the patient. If they remain ineffective, however, a "sing" is held, which usually lasts for two nights. In serious cases, it may be extended to six (fig. 7).

The reason, the Semai explain, that the sings are held at night is that during the day, the *ruai gunig* would be afraid to come. This entity is the soul of a small spirit being that helps with the diagnosis and treatment of disease. For such a sing, the patient is accompanied by his consanguinal kin, and in the traditional settlements, most of the inhabitants come along, some to be cured, others simply to participate and offer support. The women of the audience sit together in a row along the house pole. Each woman brings with her two bamboo tubes, one longer than the other. All through the ritual, they rhythmically pound these tubes against the pole, producing a musical accompaniment to the singing of the healer. The officiating curers, usually men, but sometimes also women, are called the *halaa'*. The patient is placed into a *halaa'* room made of leaves and flowers. Provisions are also made for the *ruai gunig* to be attracted to assist in the cure. It is a spirit perch, a small platform lavishly ornamented with fragrant herbs and flowers. Its precise shape is revealed in a dream, either to the *halaa'* or to someone else. Since the illness may be caused by the absence and roaming of the patient's soul, this perch may also serve to attract that.

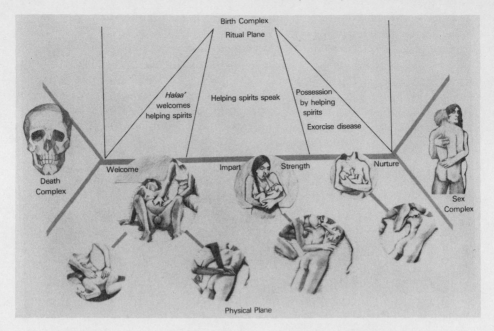

Figure 7. Horticulturalist ritual, high utilization of cultigens: Semai.

Once more, there is no invitation to the spirits of the ancestors, and no involvement with the renewal of the society. Both the Death Complex and the Sex Complex remain vacant, in other words. Only the three branches of the Birth Complex are activated, as was the case with the Yąnomamö, in a pattern common to most horticulturalists with a high utilization of cultigens. The *halaa'* goes into trance and *welcomes* the helping beings into himself. This is considered essential for a cure to take place. They speak through his mouth in a high and squeaky voice, *imparting strength*. The final part of the ritual is then the *nurturing* cure, carried out with the aid of the *gunig*, which provides through the *halaa'* both diagnosis and cure, usually executed as sucking out the illness (after Dentan 1968: 88–89).

The religious trance. As in the case of the Yąnomamö, the Semai *halaa'*, although without the use of drugs, invite spirit beings into their chests, and then expect them to help with some task at hand. The use of the religious trance is considered absolutely necessary if the cure is to succeed. Another utilization of the trance is for a spirit journey of sorts, which Dentan reports for the eastern Semai. The adolescent men, under the supervision of a *halaa'*, dance until they fall senseless to the ground. Their *ruais* are believed to be wandering about, and the young men sometimes need to be restrained, because in trance they may run into the rainforest in order to rejoin their souls.

Controlled dreaming. This sort of dreaming is institutionalized among the

Semai and is reminiscent of the same complex found among the Shavante. The Semai make a distinction between ordinary dreams and "valid" ones. Their thinking on this topic is intricate and sophisticated. According to the Semai, a person's soul is made up of six interlocking processes or entities. Two of these are important for lucid or controlled dreaming, *kəloog* and *ruai*. *Kəloog* can be translated as "life," "will," or "consciousness." When one dreams, the dreamer is unconscious; his *kəloog* is gone, to return when he is awakened. Yet, when he dreams, he also experiences faraway places and other people, or that he is flying. In Semai reasoning, if these experiences are valid, then there must be some part of the dreamer that has left his inert body and is having the experience. This traveling being, which is capable of traversing vast distances, is what the Semai call *ruai*. It is like a human in Semai thinking, because it has the identity of the dreamer, but it is also like a child, for it is easily frightened.

During a valid dream, a person may be given a melody, and this makes him *halaa'*. These melodies, which later are often learned by the entire village, are gifts supplied by the *ruai* or the *kəloog* belonging to another person, to an animal, or to a *nyani'*. *Nyani'* are "evil spirits," or "evil supernatural beasts." The entity giving the melody becomes a *gunig* to the recipient of the gift, a close and enduring relationship, something like that between a father and his child. The possession of a *gunig* makes the owner into a healer. The more *gunig* a person has, the more *halaa'* he/she is, and thus the more effective as a curer. During the "sing," the *halaa'* might sing a song received in a dream. This will attract the *ruai* or the *kəloog*, whom the curer then can quiz as to which *nyani'* is causing the affliction, and thereby obtain important information.

The alternate reality. The habitat. This position is occupied by a number of entities, among whom Thunder and his allies seem to be the most powerful, and as with Simihẹpāri of the Shavante, the Semai struggle against them in a rite intended to stop a thundersquall. In this rite, a person holds a bamboo container under the rain until it is nearly full. He gashes himself and adds his blood to the water, then flings the liquid into the shrieking wind. Thunder and his allies are thought to drink the blood. Omitting the ritual would have dire consequences for the entire village. There is also Wind and Rain, a younger brother of thunder, and a being called Bah Pent ("Shorty"). In Semai stories, the latter suffers gross indignities that make him seem ridiculous. Perhaps by vicariously inflicting humiliation on Bah Pent, the timid Semai are reassuring themselves about their ability to assert control over their habitat.

The Semai do not believe in a village or a society of the spirits of the dead. Upon death, some part of the deceased, perhaps his shadow, might turn into an aggressive alternate-reality being. This malevolent *nyani'* is especially dangerous to the deceased's nearest kin. It is the reverse of humans, having eyes in the back of its head and wearing its backbasket upside-down.

There are, however, some alien societies in the alternate reality of the Semai, such as water spirits, much like neighbors in ordinary life. These "neighbors" are neutral. There are also the *nyani'*, mentioned above, who are not absolutely evil, just powerful. After all, a *nyani'* can, as we have seen, become a *gunig,* a helper and giver of melodies.

The alternate reality of the Semai is populated in an entirely egalitarian fashion. A *ruai* may be that of a river, or a wind, of animals as well as of people. Some exceptionally great healers may be buried, instead of in the ground, on a platform in a tall tree or in a house with a raised floor. If that happens, that *halaa'* might turn into a spirit tiger for the area, looking after the welfare of the people.

Good fortune, misfortune, and the rituals of divination. Good fortune is a gift received from various spirit beings communicating with the living in a dream. Misfortune originates from outside the society. It might be caused by various *nyani'*. It may also arise from inside, though, brought about by violating some taboo, such as those operating against mixing immiscible food categories, but especially in connection with *punan* (see below).

Divination seems to happen mainly in connection with controlled dreaming.

Ethics and its relation to religious behavior. Just as there are no absolutely good or evil beings in the alternate reality of the Semai, there are no good versus bad actions, either. Rather, behavior is governed by a cogent system of behavioral strictures revolving around the basic principle of appropriateness, and called *punan.* "*Punan*," Dentan explains, "is the idea that to make someone unhappy, especially by frustrating his desire, will increase the probability of his having an accident that will injure him physically. The word *punan* refers both to the offending act and the resulting accident proneness" (1968: 55).

Punan is part and parcel of the nonaggressive behavior that distinguishes Semai society. Its rules are not based on any event in the alternate reality, however, or on some interdiction by a spirit being. Rather, it seems dictated by a deep-seated special variant of social appropriateness. Semai would rather run than fight, and when challenged on that, they simply state that that is how they are. "We never get angry," is the often-heard formula. They feel uneasy about killing animals, especially those they raised themselves. They do not curse when unduly provoked, and murders are unheard of. They do not become aggressive when drunk. "Violence," says Dentan, "in fact, seems to terrify the Semai. A Semai does not meet force with force, but with passivity or flight. Yet, he has no institutionalized way of preventing violence—no social controls, no police or courts. Somehow a Semai learns automatically always to keep a tight rein over his aggressive impulses" (1968: 59).

The semantics of "religion." Dentan's material allows the conjecture that for the Semai, the named category in question is *halaa'*. The term is both an adjective and a noun, and also carries the meaning of "religious specialist." It subsumes the religious trance: Singing induces *halaa'* in the curing ritual, as well as the fragrance of herbs placed into the bath water; being *halaa'* attenuates with old age. The individual episode may become very intense, so that young men under *halaa'* will run blindly into the forest. It can be terminated by a sudden sound such as a sneeze, or by sprinkling water on the subject. The experience of *halaa'* provides power for curing, but the true source of this power is in the alternate reality: Success in curing is considered proof of the presence of the *gunig*.

SEVEN

❧

The Agriculturalists

The Agriculturalists as State Societies

The agriculturalist has assured subsistence. All good things come to him, as we read in the *Popol Vuh*, as a blessing from the "House on the Pyramids," from agencies "on high." But in order to have them, he has to work hard, earning his daily bread "by the sweat of his brow." To pay for those good things, all members of the group have to be drafted into a continued and sustained effort. There is no room anymore, as the *Popol Vuh* tells it, for the venturesome and the proud. What the tillers need to inculcate in their young is conscientiousness, compliance, humility, and obedience.

With permanent settlements, agriculturalists can no longer avoid the problems of conflict by picking up and leaving: Conflict resolution, in other words, cannot be brought about by fissioning. Chiefly, authority comes into being as one avenue of solution. There is more personal property, and the concept also intrudes into the position of women. A man wants exclusive rights to his spouse, and his elevated status leads not only to her eventual disenfranchisement, but also to her ritual inferiority.

Viewed historically, this type of relationship, with the habitat and the kind of enculturation of the young needed to make the system work, predisposed this kind of tiller groups to becoming the more or less docile victims of roving predatory warrior bands, or equally predatory bureaucracies or caste rulers, for whom they were then forced to produce and surrender a surplus. Thus, we see agriculturalists as "peasants" in hierarchically organized states. Agriculturalist religious behavior can be found mainly in such states, although at the end of this chapter, I will also describe an independent agriculturalist society for comparison.

First, however, let us examine four agriculturalist societies, all of which arose in focal areas of agricultural evolution. The peasant segment in these cases constitutes a "part society" within the state. It exhibits the effects of a "steady diminution of power, hence of freedom of self-determination, and proportionally an increase in subjection to the whim and will of superiors in the hierarchy," says the American linguist Ethel M. Albert, in speaking of the hierarchically organized kingdom of Burundi in Africa. In such a state, there is a central figure in charge, and tiers of subordinate strata descend toward the peasant at the bottom. "No event," continues Albert, "is predictable, but what actually happens depends on the good pleasure of the determining superior power" (1964: 37).

The states to which these peasants belong are populous; they have cities and well-developed bureaucracies. Those to be treated here are not cleaved by an ethnic line, a feature so prominent in Latin America, where a clear cultural boundary separates the dominant Spanish society from the subordinate Indian peasant. Personal ownership of land is a basic legal principle. Women still have some economic independence, for instance as traders, but their sexual freedom is severely curtailed. While men have access to several women in the form of polygamy, concubinage, or lovers, women no longer have this right. Premarital chastity is demanded and enforced. Marriages are typically arranged, and the economic aspects of this kind of arrangement have considerable importance. Marriages are exogamous, and the residence pattern is patrilocal, further emphasizing male rights. Children get their gratification from the kin group and experience independence and autonomy relatively late.

The sample offered here consists of the following four societies: the Yoruba of Nigeria, the Hindu society of Chhattisgarh in India, a village in mainland China, and an Italian village in Sicily.

The Yoruba constitute the largest ethnic group south of the Sahara, with an estimated ten million or more members. They live in southwestern Nigeria and are the dominant group in Nigeria's elite. Their history has been known in the West only since 1698. They were under British control from 1851 to 1960. On October 1, 1960, Nigeria became independent. Village culture is part of the pattern of the larger Yoruba society of Nigeria.

On their large fields, the Yoruba grow mainly maize, tubers, and beans. They engage in animal husbandry. Village life is hierarchical. There is an established priesthood and an extensive body of orally transmitted sacred texts used mainly for divination (see chap. 4). The material for this discussion is based on an ethnography by William Bascom (1969b), a more sociologically oriented work by N. A. Fadipę, himself a Yoruba (1970), and field observations by Erika Bourguignon (1976) and Olu Makinde (personal communication).

Chhattisgarh, a region in central India, had its own dynastic history and cultural tradition for many centuries before the establishment of British rule in 1818. Subsistence on the village level is dominated by paddy-rice cultivation. The social structure of the village is hierarchical. The religious needs of the village community are taken care of by the *Baiga*, half priest, half curer and diviner. The knowledge of the sacred Hindu texts and the task of guarding their purity is vested in the Brahmins. Religious texts, such as the Ramayana of Tulsidas, are viewed as containing the most abstract substance of the religion,

providing as well the most structured form of ritual behavior. They admit of
no innovation; on the contrary, there is a constant attempt to "Sanskritize," to
keep local observances in line with the general Hindu tradition of India. The
data for this discussion of popular Hinduism in Chhattisgarh derive from the
work of Lawrence A. Babb (1975).

The beginnings of China's venerable history are lost in antiquity. Agriculture
started early, and even today, about 80 percent of the Chinese population lives
in villages. Cultivation involves paddy rice, vegetables, fruit, and tea, with pigs
and fowl the principal domestic animals. The ethnography by Francis L. K. Hsu
(1967) used here reports on fieldwork done before the advent of Communist
rule, which changed much on the village level, too. For convenience, we are,
however, going to present the account in the "ethnographic present." Besides,
China has a way of periodically reverting to ancient patterns. In addition to
agriculture, the rural community in Yunan province that Hsu calls West Town,
has some shop and market activity. The villagers' life is shaped by the religious
style of the larger society. There is a priesthood, conversant with Taoist and
Buddhist sources. Yet the texts of greatest importance are those originating
locally, introducing some variations into the overall scheme.

The ethnography of Milocca, an Italian village in Sicily, was written by Charlotte Gower Chapman before the Second World War, but it was not published
until after the war. Conquered by a succession of foreign intruders since early
antiquity, Sicily has been a part of modern Italy since the nineteenth century.
The peasants have livestock; the principal grain crop is wheat, and they also
grow almonds, broad beans, sumac, grapes, and olives. Their religious life is
dominated by the Catholic church, represented locally by the priest. His most
loyal supporters are the so-called house nuns, women who live in their own
homes but take a vow of chastity and do not marry. Villagers tend to look
down on them not for avoiding domestic responsibilities, but for affecting an
"unnatural" virtue. After all, it is argued, all women have a strong urge to get
married.

A Yoruba ritual. The central issue of all agricultural rituals is the "intaking"
of a substance or essence derived from the alternate reality. Speaking in terms
of the ritual structure proposed earlier, we find that just as in the case of the
horticulturalists with a high utilization of cultigens, the Death Complex and
the Sex Complex remain vacant, and within the Birth Complex, the "nurture"
branch is the most highly elaborated, often to the exclusion of the "welcome"
and "impart strength" sections (fig. 8).

In the case of the Yoruba, this exclusive preoccupation with the intaking
aspect of the "nurture" branch is expressed by a religious behavior termed
"possession," where a being of the alternate reality enters into or straddles the
religious practitioner, the so-called medium. The celebration described below
took place in Haiti, where the Yoruba religion Vodun ("Voodoo") was intro-

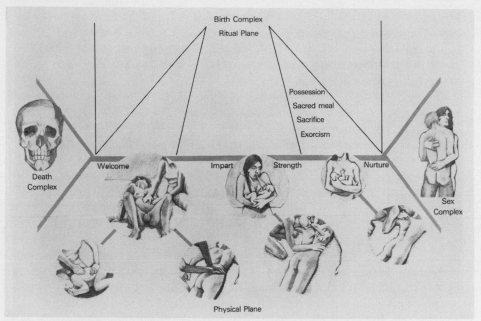

Figure 8. Agriculturalist ritual, an Italian village; opp. p. 200.

duced by African slaves, and where it survives with only minor intrusions from Catholicism.

Essentially, as described by Erika Bourguignon (1976: 18–21), the ritual consists of a sequence of a considerable number of different possession experiences, with the *houngan*, or ritual specialist, merely providing the locale and the necessary supplies, and lending his organizational skills.

Even before the *houngan* officially opened the Vodun dance, and some of the men were drumming, while the *houngan*'s wife was roasting coffee, one man was possessed, announcing that he was *Simbi en dé zeaux*, "Simbi of the two waters," an important *loa* (spirit). More drumming started up, accompanied by the rhythm of a number of different percussion instruments, and some people started singing and dancing. A large fire was lit in the yard, and the assistant of the *houngan* brought out a large, waist-high mortar, two pestles, and a bundle of aromatic herbs. When all was in place, the drumming, singing, and dancing stopped, and the *houngan* drew a chalk design inside the mortar, on the pestles, and on the hands of the men who were going to do the stamping of the herbs in the mortar. Then, squatting beside the mortar and removing their hats, the *houngan* and his assistants recited some Catholic prayers and then the Petro prayer. Before these prayers had ended, another man in the assembled crowd went into trance. He then came forward, completely stiff-limbed, and saluted the drums and then various bystanders. He too was said to be possessed by *Simbi en dé zeaux*.

The men started working the mortar, and their pestles provided a counterpoint to the drumming that had begun once more. Increasingly, possessions began to occur. One woman was possessed by *Maît' Grand Bois*, the master of the forest and of the leaves. The possessing spirit made her climb on top of the mortar, so that the men were obliged to stamp the leaves between her legs. The *houngan*'s niece followed her into possession, also by *Grand Bois*. Some other possessed women rolled on the floor, and there were so many people possessed by now that the drums could not salute all the *loas* appearing, which custom demanded. The aroma of the stamped leaves became intoxicating, and more than a hundred people were tightly packed around the mortar, trying to dance.

Outside of the *houngan*'s courtyard, meanwhile, a large crowd had gathered, with vendors offering cold drinks and snacks. Several of the possessed came out, skirting the fire, jumping across, and disappearing again to the cheers of the crowd. Inside, the drumming and stamping continued. The *houngan*'s brother, a small and deferential man, was possessed by *Papa Loko* and was acting like royalty, full of ceremony.

After several hours of pounding leaves and continuous possessions, the crowd from inside the courtyard began drifting outside. A man with a whip circled a group of women possessed by *Guédé*, beating the air to chase away evil spirits. They were followed by the drums and another group of women, dressed in blue jeans, caps on their heads, their jaws tied as done with corpses. They had wads of cotton in their mouths and nostrils and uttered unearthly groans, indicating possession by *Maît' Cimtiè*, the master of the cemetery. To the rhythm of the drums, they began to dance and to cross the fire. Dancing and singing went on the entire night. Quite a number of the possessions continued into the next day, although the *loas* were supposed to depart at sunrise.

Instead of creating its effect by a broad sweep of the entire canvas of the human drama, as was the case with the hunter-gatherers, this Yoruba possession dance derives its power from endlessly repeating a single segment. The impression one gains is one of single-minded acquisitiveness, almost as if the *loas* were sheaves of grain brought in at harvest time. The theme of "intaking," the importance of feeding or nurture, is illustrated equally by rituals from the other three societies in our sample.

The Hindu ritual of pitar pak. In this Chhattisgarh ritual, in a different elaboration of the "nurture" branch of the ritual structure, it is not the celebrant who takes in something. Instead, he is the one who provides sustenance to his deceased forefathers.

During *pitar pak*, or "fortnight of the fathers" (Babb, 1975: 34–35), the eldest member of a joint family must worship his agnatic ancestors, who are understood to be present in the home at this time. For the members of the farmer caste, the ritual begins with the head of the family going to the village tank for a ritual bath of purification. While in the tank, he makes an offering of water and *dub*, a special grass, to his ancestors.

Meanwhile, his wife and his sons' wives have prepared a festive meal. Upon returning from the bath, the head of the household enters the kitchen, a room of both religious and culinary significance. He carries a plate of food, samples of all the various dishes prepared, together with a smaller dish containing *ghi* (clarified butter) and jaggery, a sugar made from palm juice, as well as a brass pot with water from the bath. One of his sons' wives brings in a piece of burning cow-dung cake, which she deposits at the base of the earthen stove. The father squats in front of it and with his right hand sprinkles some water around it for purification. He places a small amount of sugared *ghi* on the fire, sprinkles water around it, then proceeds the same way with each food item, putting a little of each into the fire. Burning the food makes it accessible to the ancestors. After the last round, he brings his hands to his forehead, palms together, and bows until his hands touch the floor, a gesture known as *pranam*, thereby inviting the ancestral spirits present to partake of the delicacies offered to them. The family then eat their dinner on the veranda. The food consumed after this ceremony is called *prasad*, or sanctified food.

A Chinese ritual of possession. Feeding the forefathers as we saw it in the Hindu ritual is a sacred obligation in this peasant society, and the concept is shared by many other such groups. It follows that neglecting such a duty might have dire consequences. This is an oft-repeated theme in the entire Far East. How to cope with such a situation is demonstrated by a rite well-known in China and on Taiwan. It is actually a combination of a divination and a "nurture" ceremony. The following description is based on a film, *Blood, Bones, and Spirits*, distributed by Far Eastern Visuals (Texas).

It seems that to the sorrow of the family, one of the daughters-in-law is still childless after two years of marriage. A divinatory ritual reveals that the family has an uncle who had no descendants. Consequently, no one tends his grave or burns incense for him.

With the aid of a chair possessed by the spirits of the ancestors, the grave is found, containing a skull and some bone fragments. The skeleton is artistically reconstructed in the form of a bundle, using paper, red ink, and sandalwood incense powder. This figure is placed in an urn, for which a grave is dug under instructions from the spirits possessing the chair.

In the second part of the ceremony, a priest-medium becomes possessed by the Jade Emperor of the Western Heaven. His assistants remove the priest's shirt. He has a sword in his hand, and with quick backward strokes, he draws blood from his own back. With this sword, he marks the spot where the bowl of rice and the spirit money are to be placed on the grave. The urn is covered with a red cloth, and the priest, still possessed, addresses it. He once more draws blood from his back, kneels on the gravesite, and laments the deceased.

How sad is the fate of a man without descendants, he says, how deprived the ghost for whom no one burns incense.

The women of the family have heard that the Emperor of the Western Heaven is possessing the priest. They come running to the cemetery. Bowing before the god in the priest, they ask him to intercede with the ghost, so that the daughter-in-law may conceive. They promise to make yearly offerings to the uncle's ghost. The priest inks a formula on the urn to pacify the ghost and to confine it to the urn. In a renewed deep trance, he gives instructions about the burial and continues to harangue the women. His assistants finally take hold of him from the back, and the god leaves him.

The third part of the ceremony is the burial of the urn, and afterwards there is a festive meal for the family, the guests, and the priest.

A Roman Catholic mass. The mass is also an elaboration of only the "nurture" branch of the Birth Complex. But while in Vodun it is the participants who are possessed by the deities, the *loas*, in the mass it is the bread and the wine. The congregation, by ingesting the divinely possessed substance, shares in this possession. The difference is that usually, no religious trance experience attends the ingestion, so that an alternate-reality event is displaced into ordinary reality.

The Second Ecumenical Council has produced many changes in the external form of the mass, so what Chapman may have seen in Milocca would not have borne much resemblance to a mass in the 1980s. But the core event has, of course, remained unaltered. Chapman does not describe any masses, so here instead is the pivotal section of the mass as observed at the Columbus, Ohio, Newman Center.

A chalice of wine and a basket of unleavened bread are brought to the altar. The priest lifts both high, praying, then replaces them on the altar and prays over them. The bread and wine have now become the body and blood of Christ. He intones the "preface," and the congregation joins him in the closing hymn, "Holy, holy, holy Lord God," and "Hosanna on high," a biblical expression of praise. The priest breaks the bread into small pieces while quoting the biblical passage (Matthew 26:26–28), "During the meal Jesus took bread, blessed it, broke it, and gave it to his disciples. 'Take this and eat it,' he said, 'this is my body.' Then he took a cup, gave thanks, and gave it to them. 'All of you must drink from it,' he said, 'for this is my blood.' "

To the congregation's "Hallelujah" ("Praise the Lord"), the priest once more lifts high the bread and wine. He sets down both, and the congregation sings the Lord's Prayer. Everyone shakes hands or embraces. Once more, the priest holds bread and wine high, and the congregation sings the English version of the Agnus Dei, about their unworthiness to receive the "Lamb of God."

Another priest and some lay helpers each take a small basket and from it hand a piece of bread to those coming to "take communion," saying, "The body of the Lord." The participants, saying "Amen," accept it with their left hands. They put it into their mouth with their right hands, cross themselves, and go back to their seats. The priest takes a sip of the wine. The mass concludes with a song on the theme, "Long have I waited for your coming, come and live in my heart."

The religious trance. As we have seen, the religious trance among agriculturalists is used to mediate the possession experience. In the view of the Yoruba, not every person is capable of experiencing a possession. According to Bascom, those having the ability are recognized because they go through an easily identifiable illness. They wander about in the forest without knowing where they are or what they are doing. They are tormented in dreams and are subject to misfortune. This means that a certain deity wants to claim that person as a worshipper. An Ifa diviner is consulted, and he then determines the identity of the deity. Once this has taken place, the respective individual is initiated into the deity's cult, and the deity will no longer pursue him/her. Members of the cult are regularly possessed by their deity. The deity "mounts" his/her medium, entering through the head and taking control over the body. "The person is spoken of as the horse or the mount of the deity who may speak through him, asking for sacrifices or predicting good or bad fortune" (Bascom, 1969b: 78). Some such beings, such as Xango, the god of thunder, possess only one individual in a given cult group. Others, as we saw in the Vodun ritual, may possess dozens of worshippers at the same time.

The Hindu ritual described above showed no evidence of trance behavior. Actually, however, the religious trance used in the context of possession is an important feature of many celebrations in Chhattisgarh. Babb, for example, mentions a festival of cowherds in a particular village, where he observed how of the throng of cowherds in attendance before the god, several became possessed and were lying on the ground trembling violently. Quite generally, the heat a person experiences during the trance is considered its most outstanding feature and is elaborated accordingly. But instead of cooling the trancers in religious processions, the images of the deities and other ritual paraphernalia are taken to a body of water, where they are vicariously "cooled." This causes the deities to become quiescent and to withdraw from the bodies of the devotees (Babb, 1975: 94).

Conversely, some diseases that are accompanied by high fever are thought to be possession by a deity. Smallpox is a possession by the smallpox deity, as it is also among the Yoruba, and its treatment involves the application of substances that belong to the "cold" or "cooling" category, an important concept in Indian as well as in Mediterranean medicine.

The priestly medium in the Chinese ritual also used the religious trance in order to achieve possession, a ritual behavior well known all over the Far East since antiquity. In his case, possession was by the exalted Jade Emperor of the Western Heaven. But many other deities, as well as spirits of the ancestors, may equally possess such mediums. In a Korean village ritual called *kut*, for instance (Janelli and Janelli, 1982), the mediums are possessed not only by deities, but also by various ancestors, and this part of the ritual is the most important part of every *kut*:

> Ancestors lament their discomforts in the afterlife, complain about their grave locations, or grieve over the mistreatment and neglect they suffered as elders at the hands of their living kin. Playing on the sympathies of their listeners, ancestors plead for a little more money, another cup of wine, or a different grave site. (p. 149)

Apparently since very early times, the Catholic church has excluded religious trance behavior from its services. However, possession continues to make its appearance, often leading to the formation of sects outside of the church. The most important development of this nature in modern times is the Pentecostal movement, which gave rise to a number of large sects and affected also the main-line denominations. This extended even to the Catholic church itself, in what is called the charismatic renewal. Pentecostals experience possession by one aspect of the Trinity, the Holy Spirit, entering them and using their tongues to speak.

In Sicily, however, as everywhere else in Roman Catholic regions, possession is relegated to the unspeakable and unmentionable world of demonic forces. A person so possessed is recognized as being ill, and there is sufficient information to indicate that, indeed, we are dealing with a severe disturbance not only in experience, but also on the neurophysiological level (see Goodman, 1988). All the societies treated here are familiar with the condition of possession by evil forces and have strategies for its cure, termed exorcism. Among the Yoruba, this involves the initiation into the cult of the being causing the illness. In Chhattisgarh, the patient is treated by the village *Baiga*, a low-level religious specialist. He recites his mantras, which are invocations to a long list of deities, both textual and local, ending with pleas to them to cast the affliction out. In this ritual,

> the *Baiga* and his patient squat on the ground facing each other. The *Baiga* then takes a pinch of cowdung ash [a purifying substance] in his right hand and, holding it before his face, begins to intone the mantras. At the conclusion of each stanza he blows the ash unto the patient in such a way that it settles over the patient's body. (Babb, 1975: 207)

Hsu describes no exorcistic rites, but in Korea, the *kut* ritual alluded to above can also serve this purpose. Catholics have an elaborate exorcistic rite, included in the *Rituale Romanum*, a compilation of rituals from the seventeenth century (for details, see Goodman, 1981b). The Chinese, in addition to rites for releasing possessed individuals, have community rites for expelling pesky vagabond spirits: They are offered a suit of (paper) clothing and a spoon of porridge each and are guided to the boundary of West Town. All the societies mentioned here have rituals to expel evil spirits from the premises. In Milocca, for instance, not only are evil spirits expelled when a house is blesssd, but during the Easter celebration, at the moment when the resurrection is symbolically reenacted in the drawing back of the curtain, there is a formula uttered banishing all evil spirits from the community.

Visions, another experience facilitated by the religious trance, are also reported from the agriculturalists. They usually run a distant second to possession, except among Christians. Their various denominations block possession by "good" spiritual beings, demanding blind faith in their existence instead. But the need for experience will not be denied. It may take the form of a lucid dream. Chapman tells of a house nun who saw the baby Jesus floating on the water. She then set up a house altar for him (1971: 159). But usually, visions will take the place of possesssion. The locale of a visionary experience may become a place of pilgrimage, with or without the sanction of the church.

Early mystics relied heavily on visions as an alternative. However, with no autochthonous traditions about induction strategies to guide them, they employed truly heroic methods for producing a trance. This was most assuredly the purpose of flagellation, and the reason for its popularity in the Middle Ages. Heinrich Seuse (ca. 1295–1366), a German mystic better known in the literature by his Latin name, Suso, used to sleep in a tight undergarment, through which nails protruded into his skin, with his arms tied into slings, and his hands stuck into leather gloves with pointed brass tacks pressing inward. For sixteen years, self-torture of this nature rewarded him with intense visions, some of which he described in his *Briefbüchlein* ("Little Book of Letters"):

> One morning in the chapel the Servant [i.e., Suso] lost consciousness. It was then that it seemed to him in a vision that he was being conducted to a choir where the mass was being sung. A large number of the heavenly host was present in that choir, sent by God, where they were to sing a sweet melody of heavenly sound. This they did, and they sang a new and joyous melody which he had never heard before, and it was so sweet that it seemed to him that his soul would dissolve for great joy. Especially they sang the Sanctus so gloriously that he joined in and began to sing also. When in the text they came to the words "benedictus qui venit," they raised their voices exceedingly high, and at the same time, the priest lifted up our Lord. The Servant looked at him with all the humbleness of his own true physical presence, and it seemed to him that a glow of love which no tongue could express streamed toward him, penetrating his soul. Upon that his heart and soul became so filled with flaming desire and an internal light that it drained him of all his strength. It was similar to when one heart is united with the other in reality. And his soul was so exalted that he could find nothing that would compare to it in bodily terms. As he was still without strength and feeling very weak, the heavenly youth who stood beside

him and whom he did not know, laughed at him. And the Servant spoke to him, "Woe, why are you laughing? Don't you see that I am nearly perishing in a faint and with fervent love?" And saying these words, he sank to the ground as a man who died from lack of strength. And in collapsing, he regained consciousness and opened his eyes; they were full of tears, and his soul was filled with the light of grace. (Letter no. 8, from Bihlmeyer's 1906 edition of Suso's complete manuscripts; translation by me)

In addition to possessing a person, an entity or being of the alternate reality is also experienced as possessing an object. Although the role of the religious trance in this experience is not at all clear, it is such a frequently encountered phenomenon that it should be briefly included here. Thus, Fadipę mentions a Yoruba ritual in which the practitioner makes a small clay doll called *sigidi*. This little figure can go on errands for its master at night to kill his enemies, after which it will return to him. This sounds like a variant of a spirit journey. Divination carried out in the Chinese ritual described above involves a small chair, which is possessed by the spirits of the ancestors. In the film, the chair is held by one of the participants, and it begins to jerk quite impressively as the questions are being posed. In that case, we might assume a "single-limb trance" (see Goodman, 1971), affecting only one arm. The same behavior may be involved in an elaborate ritual described by Hsu. A temple in West Town, Hsu tells, possesses a "recorder," which consists of a tray filled with fine sand, a stylus of willow wood, and a smoother.

> The stylus is held by two officers sitting opposite each other, with its point touching the surface of the sand. After the proper rituals of invocation have been performed by the priests, the stylus moves as if "automatically." The spirit or god invoked uses it to convey a message. The stylus writes one word at a time. The reporter pronounces it and the recording officers write it down in a book. All spiritual messages are obtained in this way. (1967: 170)

Not only individual messages, but also lengthy texts are recorded in a similar manner. Hsu refers to a compilation entitled *A Precious Bell for Awakening the Ignorant*, recorded in the above manner in West Town in 1927 and used for decades as a devotional text. It contains messages from the gods, particularly from the judges of the "lower world of spirits," which give advice about the right way to live. In addition, in what seems like a vestige of a spirit journey, the reader can enjoy "a systematic description of the mediums in their journeys through the spiritual world day by day for a period of two weeks and what they saw" (ibid., p. 137).

In another case of object possession, Babb gives details of a Hindu ritual called *Saptashati path*. It involves the ceremonial recitation of the *Shri Durga Saptashati*, a lengthy Sanskrit text of Puranic derivation. It lasts for nine days, during which the goddess Durga is elaborately praised and given a large variety of festive foods in hopes of obtaining her aid in some pressing matter. After initial purification and other rites, there comes the most important act of this lengthy ritual. It is the placing of the *kalash*, a device that serves as the material location of the deity during the ceremony.

> The *kalash* . . . consisted of a small brass pot containing water, curds, and *ghi*. Five mango leaves had been placed around the lip, and a coconut was set on top of the whole. The *kalash* is the most important item among all the physical paraphernalia of ritual. It represents, a priest explained, "the infinite in the finite," that is, a tangible form of the deity during a ritual. (1975: 42)

Object possession is also present, as described above, during the mass, when "transsubstantiation" takes place. According to this Roman Catholic doctrine, the whole substance of the bread and wine is converted into the body and blood of Christ in the Eucharist.

The alternate reality. The habitat. In the alternate reality of the agriculturalist, the central position is assigned to the radiating power center, the supreme God. This deity seems no longer a representative of the habitat. Rather, the strength of the position now comes from a combining of two factors: the older habitat and a newer one, namely, society.

How to structure the relationship within this duality of forces, the habitat and society, is a problem solved somewhat differently by the various societies treated here. For the Yoruba, Olorun, the impersonation of the habitat, assigns the job of creation, as a social task, to one of his sons. The data from Chhattisgarh indicate no such clear division of labor. Philosophically, the Chinese see the position of the habitat as superseding that of society, at least if we consider what Laotsu says in the Tao Te Ching:

> Heaven and earth last forever.
> Why do heaven and earth last forever?
> They are unborn,
> So ever living.

However, their ruler of heaven is definitely a representative of society. And the distant, indistinct Holy Spirit of the Christians, the once-female spirit that floated above the waters, is the habitat relegated to a peripheral position.

To give some examples, in Yoruba beliefs, the central position in the alternate reality is occupied by Olorun. Westerners, among them Bascom, translate his name as "Sky God." Fadipẹ, however, points out that a better rendition would be "Owner of Heaven," which translation emphasizes his social aspect. Olorun as habitat is not the object of any formal worship. No sacrifice is offered to him. He has no priests, symbols, images, or temples. Olorun as a social force, as society, however, appears in many guises:

The average Yoruba uses the name often in proverbs, in prayers and wishes, in promises, in planning for the future, in attempts to clear himself of accusations, in reminding his opponent of his duty to speak the truth ... for all general purposes it is more natural to invoke the name of Olorun than that of [some other sacred being]. (Fadipẹ, 1970: 282)

For Chhattisgarh, the same position in the alternate reality is filled by the historically older Rama, benevolent but quite distant, and by the somewhat later Vishnu, again very benevolent and powerful. The latter's derivation from the habitat is still indicated by the fact that he goes to sleep during the rainy season, making it possible for malignant forces to take over. A cult of Rama, known in various parts of India today, is of relatively recent origin. In Chhattisgarh it is not Rama who is worshipped, but rather Hanuman, his devoted servant, a god of overpowering strength and goodness, and, most important, one always available to human supplicants. Borrowing from Lévi-Straussian structuralism, we might see him as the perfect mediating term tying together the habitat and society, that is, the habitat alive in his monkey face and society in his heavily muscled, human male body.

For China, there is the Jade Emperor, the supreme ruler of heaven, the "Western World of Happiness." All final *social* authority flows from him. Yet Chinese ideas about this ruler are quite vague, according to Hsu, and there are no temples to the Jade Emperor in West Town.

Theoretically, we would expect that in Milocca the Trinity should occupy the position of the radiating power center. However, the Trinity as such is not recognized in Sicilian Catholicism. For one, the Holy Spirit plays no role at all. As a stand-in for the habitat, it has no anthropomorphic traits and is represented by a dove. It has a rather tenuous relationship to the Father, the creator and peak of the social pyramid. And even the Father is only a theologically propagated, shadowy figure. The godhead is Jesus, and only he, a trait found in other Roman Catholic cultures also, especially in Latin America. "The identification of the Son and the Father is complete," remarks Chapman. Punishment for sins comes largely from him, but again no votive offerings are given to him in Milocca. Feasts in his honor, principally Christmas and Easter, are financed from church funds, rather than coming from the coffers of individuals or citizens' organizations.

Agriculturalists ascribe creation to the radiating power center, a feature not encountered in the types of societies discussed earlier. As Maybury-Lewis remarks about the horticulturalist Akwẽ-Shavante, "The problem of creation out of nothing, which exercises such a perennial fascination in many religions and philosophical schemes, does not concern the Shavante" (1974: 285).

For "creation out of nothing" to become thinkable, humans had to be creators themselves first, and they had to conceive of "nothing." "Nothing" did not appear as a possibility until humans stood before a totally empty field and placed a seed in it. No wonder that the zero, the symbol for nothingness, was invented independently by two agriculturalist societies: first by the Maya and then by the Hindus. It is in their stories that we first hear of attempts to cope with the primal void. The gods originally lived in the sky, the Yoruba tell, and below there was only empty water. And halfway around the world, the ancient Quiché Maya priests, also of an agriculturalist society, taught,

> THIS IS THE ACCOUNT, here it is.
> Now it still ripples, now it still murmurs, ripples, it still sighs, still hums, and it is empty under the sky.
> Here follow the first words, the first eloquence.
> There is not yet one person, one animal, bird, fish, crab, tree, rock, hollow, canyon, meadow, forest. Only the sky alone is there; the face of the earth is not clear. Only the sea alone is pooled under all the sky; there is nothing whatever gathered together. It is at rest; not a single thing stirs. It is held back, kept at rest under the sky. (Tedlock, 1985: 72)

Split off from the radiating power center, there is in the alternate reality of the agriculturalists a profusion of minor beings, saints, deities, demigods, representing both physical features of the habitat and social functions and tasks. In other words, the duality between habitat and society continues into the aura of the power center. The richness of detail that the tillers created bears testimony to the exhilaration born of the fundamentally new experience of interacting intensively and over long periods with individual segments of the habitat, rather than with its entirety. Often each river, mountain, hillock, and dale has its own representation. On the social side, equal enthusiasm abounds about the occupational specialization possible due to greater population density. We need only to think of the many specialized saints of the Catholic church, of those in charge of lost objects, of fire protection, of the traveler, of mothers' milk, of sudden emergencies, and many more. All agriculturalist societies have a similar proliferation on the social side. Since the beings of both aspects are anthropomorphic, the faithful have a plethora of helpers to turn to, while the tip of the pyramid remains distant and blinding.

How did all this specialization come about? The way the Yoruba tell it, the deities used to live in the sky, and under them there was only the vast expanse of water. Olorun, the Owner of Heaven, one day decided to change things. He gave the God of Whiteness, Orishala, a chain, a few crumbs of earth in a snail's shell, and a five-toed chicken. From these he was to fashion the earth. But as Orishala was approaching the gate of heaven, he saw some deities carousing, and so he decided to join the fun. He drank too much palm wine, and drunk, he fell asleep. Odua, his younger brother, took over from him. Odua went to the edge of heaven, together with Chameleon, let himself down on the chain, threw the earth on the water, and put the chicken on it. The chicken began scratching and scattered the earth in all directions. After Chameleon tested the firmness of the earth, Odua stepped on it, too. This was at Idio, and to this day, that is where his sacred grove is located in Ifẹ.

When Orishala woke up and found that the job that was to be his had been completed by his brother, he also went down on earth, and claimed it as his own by right of seniority. His brother would not give up the rule over the earth, and so they started fighting. The other gods soon took sides, and there was a big commotion. When Olorun became aware of it, he ordered the gods to stop and created some order:

> To Odua, Creator of the Earth, he gave the right to own the earth and rule over it, and he became the first King of Ife. To Orishala he gave a special title and the power to mold human bodies, and he became the Creator of Mankind. Olorun then sent them back to earth with Oramfe, the Ife God of Thunder, to keep peace between them, and with Ifa, the God of divination, and Eleshije, the Ife God of Medicine, as his companions. (Bascom, 1969a: 9–10)

The fragmentation of the aura is fully developed in Chhattisgarh, which has its ample share of the "30 million gods" exuberantly glorified in Hindu texts. There are the deities of the texts, and all the uncounted ones associated with families, castes, festivals, activities, diseases, and locales. The texts describe the history of the deities, their distinctive characteristics, their personalities, their attributes, their relationships to other deities. Nontextual beings have a regional and local tradition attached to them. Their traits are part of folklore, or possibly they are known only by their name or by a spot or a festival. One specific elaboration introduced by Hinduism into this complex is a distinction according to sex. As Babb sees it, the female deities represent the active, dynamic component of reality. Goddesses are frightening, sinister, bloodthirsty; only in marriage are they tamed, becoming subservient to their spouses.

Moving on to China, we find that no one actually professes to know how many gods there are under the regime of the Jade Emperor. He has ministers, most important among them the god of war and his sworn brother. Under him there are the heads of the three established religions, Confucius, Buddha, and Laotsu. These are always mentioned together and are considered as having sprung from the same origin. They cannot, however, be addressed when someone is in need. They are thought simply to be present in the alternate reality. Other beings belong to the lower world of spirits. We hear of a goddess of sons and grandsons, of a kitchen god, of the goddess of mercy, of a goddess called Mother Wang, as well as of patrons of local temples and of clans. On the habitat side, there are the gods of heaven and of earth, and the dragon god. This crowd of beings is ranked in the most explicit fashion, an expression of the Chinese way of organizing their huge society.

For Milocca, Jesus is the creator, reflecting the identification of the Father with the Son. His disciples were his helpers in the act of creation, and the saints also pitched in. In other words, the disciples and the saints existed before the world and everything in it came into being. The world created is synonymous with Sicily. In engaging disregard of time sequences, the Holy Family, with the infant Jesus, visited Sicily on their way to Egypt. When Lucifer was expelled from heaven, he fell on the island, and from this terrifying collision arose Mount Etna, the threatening volcano.

The saints in Sicily are in charge of different tasks. They guard the shoemakers, the saddlers, and the smiths; they heal eye ailments or the inflammation of the nursing mother's breast; they are associated with places of pilgrimage and act as patron saints of communities.The town patron is customarily also the weather saint. In larger communities, there is a town patron as well as one for each individual parish. Milocca's patron, for instance, is Saint Joseph. As Chapman relates, "The people are proud of his miracles and of their devotion to him. They do not claim exclusive possession of his favors nor do they neglect other saints in their devotion to their protector. At the same time St. Joseph is peculiarly related to them and is in some way a fellow Milocchese" (1971: 146–147).

The saints are the principal intermediaries between humans and God, that is, Jesus. They are the ones who have cult societies. Promises are made to them in return for aid, and they are the ones who receive offerings. As one informant told Chapman, "Of course, all benefits come from God, but the saints are the friends of God, and they can help us. . . . If we pray to the saints . . . they can more easily obtain grace from God than we can" (1971: 124). Their power is eclipsed only by Mary's, correlating with the special and close relationship in the Mediterranean world between mother and son. "The Virgin Mary, as the mother of God, has power over that of any saint, for she is related to the Omnipotent by the closest ties of kinship. It is said that God refuses nothing to His mother" (p. 158).

The spirits of the dead. The agriculturalist society is represented in the alternate reality by a society of the spirits of the dead. But this society is clearly split into a good and an evil portion. The society of the dead is tied to the living by bonds of mutual obligation. All the societies in our sample show this pattern.

The Yoruba see the realm of the dead as divided into two different areas. In one of these, the air is fresh, and life goes on as it does on earth. People carry on the same occupations, and the same social stratification prevails. The poor are poor, the chiefs are chiefs, and there are villages, and towns, and fields. This is the good heaven. There is also a bad heaven, located in the same part of the world, and it is called the heaven of potsherds. It is hot as peppers are hot, the air is dry, and the sun burns. When a person dies, his ancestral guardian soul, which is associated with him and resides in his head, appears before Olorun and gives a rendering of the person's life on earth. Olorun then decides which heaven the soul is qualified to enter. Upon admittance to the good heaven, the soul becomes an ancestor and an object of worship, an *orisha*, for its descendants. At a certain point in time, it is also possible for this ancestral guardian soul to become reincarnated. It does so by going to kneel before Olorun, who once more grants it the opportunity to choose its own destiny. It is believed to be able to make any choice it wishes, although Olorun may refuse if the requests are not made humbly or if they are unreasonable. Destiny involves a fixed day upon which the soul must return to heaven; and it includes the individual's personality, his occupation, and his luck. When a person is reincarnated in this way, he does not know his destiny. He can, however, learn about it by consulting a *babalawo* (see chap. 4). The *babalawo* can reveal which ancestral soul has been reborn, and thus which "praise name" is appropriate to it. The person in question then bears this praise name in addition to his given one.

To assure the descendants of the services of the ancestral spirit, great care is taken that the deceased's soul remains tied to the compound. Men are buried under the floor of their own room, women in their father's home. If a person dies on a farm, the body is carried home for burial, and "the carriers are preceded by a man holding a live chicken, some of whose feathers are pulled out and are left at every fork in the path. This is to mark the trail so that the soul of the deceased can follow them back to town" (Bascom, 1969b: 66). The funeral rites aim at assuring that there will be an enduring bond between the person who has now become an ancestor and his living descendants. Even during a rite that has as its purpose to release the soul and to sever its bonds with its former body and home, it is summoned to appear before its relatives. Potsherd heaven threatens the soul that refuses to obey. On the other hand, there are rewards: A banana stem is stuck into the ground above the corpse's head, so that when the stem rots, there will be a hole through which the soul of the deceased may be fed the blood of sacrificial animals or cooked food. Every year, the souls of the departed are feasted on a special day.

In Central India, the concepts of what the realm of the dead looks like are very vague. Nonetheless, it exists. The funeral ceremonies are aimed at helping the spirit to free itself from this world and to see it safely and comfortably to the next. Before these rites are performed, the spirit is in a threshold existence. It is half in and half out, an envious menace to the living and a burden to itself. A ritual will transform this spirit, which is potentially a ghost, into a spirit that can safely travel to the other world. The heart of the ritual is the cooling of the remains, that is, submersion of the bones in the water after cremation. Reincarnation happens along the good-evil dichotomy, with a good life being rewarded by a favorable social position in the next earthly life. An evil person may find himself as a leech, or a worm in a dog's stomach. Good persons may pass into heaven, where they will stay until their accumulated merits are used up.

If the realm of the spirits of the dead is only vaguely perceived, there is nothing uncertain about the unbreakable bond between the dead and their descendants. This is evident in the ritual of *pitar pak* described above. The benefit is a deferred one. The ancestors are fed for future protection. There is an astrological event possible, which opens a direct pathway between the abode of the dead, the *pitrilok*, and that of the living. Hungry ancestors could work evil at that time. For the spirits of the dead, which form the base of the Hindu pantheon, are of unmitigated malevolence and jealousy.

It is against this somber picture of life in an agriculturalist society, which holds the individual captive in a continually renewed cycle, without any hope of escape in either this life or the next, that we can understand the emergence and importance of Buddhism. It can be seen as a reaction, as a promise of loosing the ties to "the wheel." The young prince Siddhartha Gautama, on his first excursion into the streets where ordinary humans lived, worked, and died, may have been struck by the suffering, as the legend tells. But what he must have intuited, and what provided the underlying motivation for the religion he founded, was probably something entirely different. It was the vicelike grip in which agricultural society held the individual. What he offered was the hope of liberation from this confinement. Monasticism, so characteristic of agriculturalist societies, has similar roots.

In contrast to popular Hinduism, the Chinese possess in their realm of the spirits a faithful replica of imperial China. When a spirit passes over the line that separates life from death, there is a broad highway which is entered by those who have been widely known for good deeds. It leads to the Higher World of Spirits. Most spirits of the dead, however, travel over the narrower passage, which takes them to the Lower World of Spirits. On this passage, they come to a crossroad with shops and the Gate of Ghosts, which is a castle, just as on earth. In it there is a registration office for the newly dead, as well as a reception room for honored guests. It also houses magistrates, whose duty it is to record the good and bad behavior of the individuals in the districts that they are in charge of. Above the magistrates there are ten judges, each with a specific title. They have assistant judges and recorders under them. Eight of these judges have prisons, containing instruments of torture. Bad people might be confined indefinitely there, or might be detained temporarily waiting for a hearing, for torture, or for transfer to another judge. The judges also have at their disposal guest houses for the deserving. The judges are under the jurisdiction of the Supreme Ruler of the Lower World. The palaces of the ten judges are arranged in a circle, the palace of the ruler being in the middle. The realm coincides with all of China, according to Hsu. Beyond the Lower World of Spirits there are two more worlds, the Higher World of Spirits and the Western World of Happiness, headed by the Jade Emperor. Assiduous reading of scriptures and a behavior based on the implicit desire of becoming a god may in fact lead to just such an existence in the world of the spirits of the dead. There are many stories in West Town about this actually happening. Thus, a local scholar became a god in that realm, acquiring the title of God of Charity, an important official of the spirits. He is a much-sought-after figure in West Town ritual communications with the dead.

The funeral rites at West Town expedite the transition of the spirit from the world of the living to the world of the spirits of the dead. The descendants have the obligation to report the event of a death at their clan temple. It is for this reason that the magistrates in the Gate of Ghosts know what happens on earth in their districts. The prosperity of the descendants depends on the place where the family graveyard is made and how well it is kept up. In addition, there is in every home an ancestral shrine, where daily offerings of incense and simple food and larger periodic sacrifices are made. There are also ceremonies in which the ancestral shrines are taken to a place immediately below this ceremonial room for more elaborate worship. Each family also has a clan temple. The relationship between the living and the dead is one of reciprocity, because by offerings and other rituals the descendants can assure the ancestors of a better position in the world of the dead. The ancestors, in turn, can help the descendants. If a person dies away from home, spirit banners and other implements are used to call the spirit back. The reason for this ritual activity is, of course, that every ancestor is important to the family, and the services of these beings to the living are vitally needed. For example, they sanction marriages, discipline the young, and carry out other important tasks.

For the Sicilians, the spirit abode is as indistinct as it is for the Hindus. The spirits of ordinary persons do not enter paradise directly. All baptized adults go to purgatory first. There is no set time when they might escape this temporary abode. In fact, in Milocca no one ever says that his beloved ones have passed on to paradise, perhaps for fear that there they might no longer be accessible to the living. The funeral rites aim at making it possible for the spirit only to enter into purgatory and to escape the danger of Lucifer's interference, who may attempt to snatch the souls of the dying to take them to his own realm. Once in purgatory, however, the souls may work miracles and spend their time continually praying. The living can benefit them by prayer and their actions, and they in turn can obtain blessings for their friends on earth. At the feast of the souls in purgatory on the first of November, children are given presents, supposedly brought to them by the spirits of the dead, although few children still believe that. There are also stories of people seeing a procession of the spirits of the dead during the night preceding the feast day. As this description shows, the Milocca veneration of and interaction with the spirits in purgatory marks the latter as the beneficent spirits of the ancestors. The complex is a characteristic trait of all agricultural societies, and Catholic Sicily is no exception.

Not even reincarnation is absent, although it is not thought of in these terms. Reincarnation is postponed, not rescinded. Humans have to wait for the final

Judgment Day, when those found good on the basis of their performance on earth will rise in body and live once more as they had before, with the evil half of humanity exorcized, however.

It is interesting in this context to ask what happens to suicides. Persons who take their own lives do, after all, exempt themselves from further service to society. This is an intolerable act in the view of the agriculturalist: No one should be allowed to extricate himself from the shackles of obligations. To the suicide, the agriculturalist says, "You wanted out, so stay out." They are banished forever. They do not even get to potsherd heaven, the Yoruba say, but forever roam the earth, lost, clinging to the treetops like bats. The same fate awaits them in Chhattisgarh, as well as in China. In Milocca, a suicide cannot be buried in consecrated ground. This denies the spirits access to purgatory. Their ghosts haunt the spots where they died and may harm passersby.

Even Yoruba children who die are punished, as they refuse to stay home and become serving adults. The Yoruba believe that if several children of one mother die in succession, it is because they are incarnations of an *abiku*, a child spirit, not exactly evil but certainly mischievous, who needs to be frightened into staying on earth. This is done by punishing the dead child's body. Only persons who innocently come to a tragic end are exempted: Their souls may become ghosts, but not evil spirits. They go to another town and can even marry there and have children. After living out their allotted life span, they will be allowed to go to the good heaven and be reincarnated. The message is clear: The life span once granted must be lived, the service must be completed.

The theme is even more emphatically expressed in Chhattisgarh. Any person recently dead may give rise to a potentially malevolent ghost. That is, dying is itself a violation of the obligation to society. Dying in childbirth magnifies this sin enormously, for no longer will the woman continue providing new members for service. Such women turn into evil kinds of ghosts. Their composite is the demoness Churalin, who sucks the blood of attractive and unprotected children.

The overriding need for successive generations of workers makes the heirless person nearly as reprehensible as a suicide in the eyes of traditional Chinese. His spirit becomes a vagabond ghost crushed by poverty and misery, entirely dependent on charity. This may even happen to one who is executed, for his useful life is cut off. However, since his death came to pass through no fault of his own, priests can be hired who by prayers and scripture reading may help to transfer the ghost to the world of the spirits of the dead.

Good fortune, misfortune, and the rituals of divination. Good fortune rains down capriciously from an all-powerful central deity. Well-cared-for forebears or other intermediaries can improve one's chances, even in Milocca. Neglected ones can cause misfortune, and it is through divination that their identity, as well as appropriate remedies, can be discovered. For the Yoruba (see chap.

4), divinatory rituals are central to religious life. Babb reports no divination in Chhattisgarh, but in China, as we saw, divination is an important part of religious observances. In Sicily, probing the reasons for God's visitations is blocked by Old Testament injunctions against "necromancy," and divination is thus relegated to socially decried agencies as possibly gypsies (not mentioned by Chapman), or to the shadowy world of witchcraft.

Witches are to be found in all agriculturalist societies.[1] As to our sample, the Yoruba think of them mainly as old women, fearing those that make a habit of demanding things belonging to other people, or watching greedily when others eat. Such women, Fadipę tells us, are sometimes the recipients of forced hospitality. They are thought to have the evil eye, causing harm by simply looking. They can also make injurious use of their breath, a soullike substance all people possess in addition to their ancestral guardian spirit. The witches, however, can send their breath out to trap the breath of another person, which is wandering about during dreaming. Once the breath is in this way prevented from returning to its owner, that person dies. Bloodsucking witches are especially feared, as they may cause difficulties in childbirth.

In Chhattisgarh, the witch complex equally focuses on women and children, but the tone is shriller than among the Yoruba, in agreement with the strong emphasis Hindus place on the threatening aspect of everything female. Old women, according to Babb, may be suspected of witchcraft if they are observed to pay special attention to some attractive child and the child subsequently sickens. Actual accusations are rare, however. Witches appear ordinary by day, but at night they go out and drink human blood. They are devotees of the goddess Kali and function as her demonesses.

As to China, Hsu tells us little of interest from West Town concerning this topic. Either the "Fox Woman," a witchlike Chinese being, is not known there, or Hsu was not privy to such peasant beliefs. Illness in children is sometimes attributed to witchcraft. People quarreling in a house not their own may bring misfortune to its owner. In that case, the owner may take recourse to witchcraft in order to take revenge.

In Sicily, specifically in Milocca, Chapman finds that women having the reputation of being witches are thought to have the evil eye and are also sought out to prepare love potions, to carry out a *fattura*. She gives no details, but we know from other sources (e.g., Risso and Böker, 1964) how richly this complex is elaborated all over southern Italy. A *fattura* may make a man fall in love, cause him to forget transgressions by a woman, force him into marriage, or help discover if he is faithful. The *fattura* does not produce real love, only fatal, irresistible attraction to a woman, something dreaded by men, who think of women as being mysterious and powerful. There is also a *fattura a morte*, intended to kill its victim. The borderline between the two is indistinct—their symptoms coincide to some extent—and even a ritual intended to induce love, a *fattura d'amore*, may lead to the death of the bewitched man. Chapman reports from Milocca that there is no use appealing to God or the saints against witchcraft. Only other witches can effect a cure.

Ethics and its relation to religious behavior. With the agriculturalists, a new ethical principle makes its appearance, namely, the cleavage between good and evil. Why it might have arisen is a matter of anthropological and philosophical speculation. The tiller is in constant conflict with undesirable, "bad" plants and animals that try to intrude into his fields and barns. He has an intense feeling of protection within his permanent settlements and struggles to keep the "outside," that which is alien and dangerous, both human and alternate-reality agencies, from penetrating. It is a precarious situation, and the mythology of our sample societies does not agree on where to attach the blame. The Yoruba think of quarrels between the gods. In Hindu mythology (O'Flaherty, 1980), there is the concept of the sinful deity, which explains the origin of evil as a result of the malevolence of gods toward men. The biblical story of the Fall puts the shoe on the other foot and forever burdens womankind. The split is carried over into the alternate reality, with the good in the afterlife being rewarded, and the bad forever damned. The Yoruba, as we saw, have a "good" heaven, and another one where the air burns like pepper. The Hindus are reincarnated in accordance with how they behaved. They may stay in heaven only long enough to consume the merits they accumulated by ritual acts, fasting, worship, and charity to Brahmins and mendicants. Somewhat misanthropically, the Chinese have weighted their afterlife heavily on the side of punishment. After all, eight of the ten judges handling the spirits' cases upon arrival have prisons! And beyond purgatory, heaven or hell awaits the Milocchese.

The semantics of "religion." The villagers within the hierarchically organized state live a life of perpetual dependency. Sometimes they are favored by those in power, most of the time they are trampled underfoot, and nearly always they are exploited. The power center is distant, invisible, and capricious. It needs to be approached via intermediaries, cajoled, adored, mollified. With luck, sometimes, a blessing will then come raining down. It is understandable that with thousands of years of experience of this kind, the villagers' concept of what religion is will incorporate this hoped-for, prayed-for gift, in addition to the experience of the religious trance and the contact with the alternate reality.

To illustrate, the Yoruba have a named category called *oogun*. Conventionally, this is translated into English as "medicine." It is, however, a medicine of special properties, not only an attribute of quartz crystals, herbs, and roots of trees as objects of the ordinary world, but also their essence, their representation in the alternate reality. Indeed, *oogun* derives from the latter; it is a gift handed down by spirit beings. "Every *orisha* has his bush," is a Yoruba saying. In other words, every deity, but not the ancestral guardian spirits, which are placed lower in the sacred hierarchy, possesses the essence of some object or substance, which can be conferred on a supplicant. *Oogun* can produce, or perhaps in fact is, the religious trance, as when a man becomes invulnerable after reciting the proper *oogun* formula, since the trance tightens the muscles and prevents bleeding. At least, that is the interpretation suggested by Fadipę's report that during the annual feast of Ogun, *orisha* of iron and war, organized orgies of knife slashing were allowed to continue year after year without tragic incidents.

Oogun, it seems to me, can be considered the category "religion" of the Yoruba, with a strong emphasis on the essentially undeserved and capriciously awarded blessing that results when in trance a believer touches the alternate reality. What that category may be in the various Sanskrit languages I do not know, but a similar world view may be at work in Hinduism, leading to the fear of pollution, given such wide berth in discussions about Indian religious behavior. There is continuous and overriding anxiety that the flow of that all-important grace, the blessing from above, might in some way be impeded. Therefore, the Brahmin, in charge of religious observances, needs to obey cumbersome rules to protect him from pollution.

Hsu provides no help in discovering the category in West Town, but the central issue of blessing, in the form of grace, is also evident in Milocca. During baptism, we learn from Chapman, the spiritual grace given to the infant by applying holy water, salt, and oil is believed to manifest itself physically in wealth, strength, and beauty. Saints obtain grace from God for their supplicants. Believers often make large offerings to their patron saint in return for blessings obtained. Grace, it is thought, may also devolve on the believer by kissing the feet of the statue of the Madonna, or by rubbing a handkerchief against her robe. Grace enters into the food that has been blessed, making it beneficial for the person who consumes it. A "mystic state" may be experienced as one approaches the shrine on a pilgrimage.

Agriculturalists without a State

Agriculturalists that are entirely separate culturally from the state in which they live, are quite rare. One such society, described in detail by Louis C. Faron, is that of the Mapuche Indians of Chile. These agriculturalists never made the transition to a hierarchically organized state. Comparing the religious behavior of the Mapuche to that of other agriculturalists might give us a few hints about what the contribution of the state as a social form might be to religious evolution.

The Mapuche, about 250,000 strong, have throughout their history successfully eluded cultural incorporation into a state until the sixties of this century, when the Chilean state embarked on a concerted effort to wipe them out as a community by eroding their land base through legislative maneuvers. Before white contact, they were apparently not the victims of the cycles of conquest prevalent in their region. They were situated in such a way that whenever threatened, they could withdraw into the impregnable reaches of the Andes and revert from large-scale, open-field tillage to horticultural cultivation. There is historical evidence that this is how they defied the Inkas. These efficient conquerors, mauled by the skilled and experienced Mapuche guerilla warriors, were forced to skirt their territory and overran instead the more docile populations in the valleys. Their techniques of ambush and evasion served them well also against the Spaniards, who kept losing garrisons and even entire towns to them. They were not subdued militarily until the beginning of this century, long after the demise of the Spanish Empire. In the course of their struggle, the northern and southern portions of their nation wasted away, but their center persisted. They now occupy a large, albeit fragmented, area across the middle of Chile, south of the Bio-Bio river. That is where Faron did fieldwork with the Mapuche from 1952 to 1954.

The Mapuche have no "king," no authority beyond the lineage chief. There is, however, a clear perception of the greater ethnic unity, and large communal rites, such as the funeral ceremonies, bring together crowds from all over Mapuche territory. The lineages—people, that is, who are related to each other by blood because of being descended from a known line of ancestors—are patrilineal, which means that descent is counted through the father's line. These ancestors are kept favorably inclined toward the living by the proper rites, and are the source of moral strength. Men and women have equal rights sexually before marriage, each having free access to any partner considered marriageable under the incest rules. Women are also the equals of men ritually. The men are in charge of the large communal gatherings of the funeral and fertility rites, while the women are the mediums (*machi*). There is no historical evidence that the Mapuche ever had any male mediums.

A Mapuche ritual. The most important ceremony of the Mapuche is the funeral (Faron, 1968: 91–98). It expresses the durable link that the Mapuche feel exists between the living and the dead, and that gives cohesion to their society. And although death is involved, not birth and initiation, we see an acting out of the entire ritual structure, except for the Sex Complex, which quite logically remains vacant. The Death Complex of the ritual structure is activated; in fact, it is even expanded. For when a man (or a woman) dies, not only are the lineal ancestors, mainly males of social prominence, invited to the wake, as well as the mythical ancestors, who are potentially on their way to becoming regional deities, but an invitation is issued also to the lesser gods, such as the god and goddess of the south wind, the god and goddess of thunder, the god and goddess of the sea, etc., and to the Supreme Being Ñenechen, who is thought to preside over all matters of life and death. Passing to the "welcome" branch, the human guests invited include representatives of the patrilineal descent groups most closely related to the deceased by blood ties or marriage; they are primarily responsible for looking after the well-being

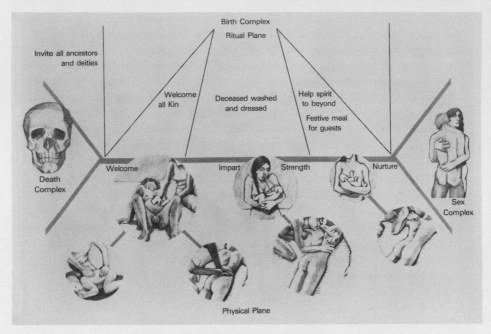

Figure 9. Agriculturalist ritual, Mapuche Indians.

of the dead person's spirit during the wake. They also bring their wives along. Affinal relatives, that is, those related by marriage to the deceased, must attend in order to ward off the suspicion that they might have brought about the death of the person whose funeral is being conducted.

Passing on to the "impart strength" branch, attention switches to the deceased, who is washed, dressed in his best clothes, and placed into a coffin. During the wake, the evil spirits lurk around the house, and the mourners have the task of driving them away. The spirit of the deceased is also still present and needs to be speeded toward the afterworld. This is a time of grave danger for this spirit, for it might become contaminated by evil, or it could be kidnapped by a witch, the *kalku*. If the rituals, which represent the "nurture" of the departing soul, are carried out properly, it will arrive successfully at *nomelafken*, far from Mapucheland, to live contentedly with his kinsmen.

After the four days of the wake, the coffin is taken out of the house and is borne to a bier in the center of a field at some distance from the dwelling. Members of the funeral assemblage congregate there and express their regard to the deceased, further continuing with "nurture" and richly elaborating on it. This is done by formal orations held by lineage elders or other well-informed Mapuche, called *weupin*, which is a dialogue between the living and the dead. Some are brief eulogies. Others last an hour or more and are delivered by the lineage elders, who are familiar with the genealogies and are best able to link the deceased with branch lines of his own and the affinal lines. Care is taken to emphasize those links of the dead person to living kin and ancestral spirits that have general importance to the reservation community and to Mapuche society as a whole. A sumptuous meal is prepared for the assemblage by the members of the household of the deceased, with many contributions of food and labor from the closest patrilineal kin. Guests arriving must be greeted by a patrilineal kinsman of the dead person, and everyone, even a nonrelative, is addressed with a kinship term. Women wail and tear their hair. Close relatives and friends deposit coins, articles of clothing, personal trinkets, and other gifts in the coffin before it is closed. Although the spirit of the dead still lingers close, it is now less endangered by evil forces than before.

When all the *weupin* have been spoken, the coffin is taken to the cemetery. Libations are poured over the grave as it is being filled in, and more wine is drunk by the few close kinsmen who accompany the deceased. Now begins the lifelong responsibility of all close kin to propitiate this particular ancestral spirit by bringing offerings to it along with all the other "hawks of the sun." Put differently, the Mapuche share with other agriculturalists societies the belief that the living need to care for the ancestors, who in turn are obligated to aid and support their descendants.

The religious trance. The trance is used to experience possession. Mapuche mediums, the *machi*, are possessed by spirits, which are often inherited matrilineally. During such possession, they can handle hot coals and pass their arms through fire. They speak in a secret language, which needs to be interpreted in ceremonies conducted to heal a patient whose illness is thought to have causes rooted in the alternate reality.

The *machi* considers possession dangerous. She is afraid that her spirit familiar, while on its way to her, might be captured by a *kalku* (witch), and then turn against her. Or her own roving soul may suffer the same fate while her familiar possesses her, thus turning her into an evil person. Evil spirits that cause illness can be exorcized by sucking them out. They can be chased away from around the house or the ceremonial field by circling the area on foot or on horseback.

Also, objects can be possessed by an essence deriving from the alternate reality. Thus, the *machi* has a notched pole standing outside her home with steps carved into it, which she climbs during ceremonial occasions. It is thought that the pole contains power transmitted to it by Ñenechen, and also by her spirit familiar.

The alternate reality. The habitat. In agreement with other agriculturalists, the alternate reality of the Mapuche contains a radiating power center. It is occupied by Ñenechen, who is the father of Mapuche society. He has other, subordinate personages associated with him, said by some informants to be nothing more than names for his various attributes. It was Ñenechen who created the world. After he had accomplished that, there was a struggle between the forces of good and evil, in which mankind, that is, the Mapuche, emerged in control of the world. It is obvious that he is not all-powerful, not the center from which all power emanates. He is surrounded by an aura of specialists. Some of these represent the habitat: thunder, the volcanoes, the south winds. Others mirror the social sphere: There is a deity who is the maker of people, and another one who creates abundance.

The spirits of the dead. Mapuche society is represented in considerable detail in the alternate reality as a society of the spirits of the dead. The spirits live in a shadow world; they perform the same work as they did on earth, except that they do not have to work very hard, and everything they undertake is successful. They even carry on wars against the Spaniards and the Chileans. A person's soul usually proceeds directly to this realm after death. Should there be signs that the spirit is tarrying, there is a ceremony to tell it to be on its way. Once arrived, the soul becomes an ancestor, a glittering bluefly if later seen by mortals, a butterfly, or a "hawk of the sun," an ancestor forever obligated to watch over, guide, and protect its kin. For hawks of the sun are eternally tethered to specific unilineal kin groups, Faron tells us. This bond can be destroyed only if through negligence of the heirs, or because of some infraction of the moral code, a hawk of the sun is exposed to the wiles of a *kalku*, who then might ensnare it and force it to perform evil at night. The *kalku* is part of the evil force that has existed from the beginning and is continually replenished by such activities as the kidnapping of souls. Suicides equally add to the stock of evil, and are thought to lose personal identity by their action.

The hierarchy in the alternate reality is entirely explicit. There are the ancestors, in the ranking of bluefly, butterfly, and hawk of the sun. Above them are the deities of the lineage, the deities of the region, and the ethnic deities. Ñenechen, at the peak of the pyramid, can be approached directly, but usually the lineal ancestors, especially dead chiefs, are asked to intercede. The latter are quite exalted and walk the earth, watching over the Mapuche in the company of celestially conceived sons of the gods. These personages are impervious to attacks by *kalkus*.

Other beings. Neighbors in the alternate reality are the enemies against whom the Mapuche have fought in historical times. The struggle against them continues in the realm of the spirits of the dead, and the guns of the Spaniards can be heard in thunder.

Good fortune, misfortune, and the rituals of divination. While good fortune is a gift obtained through intervention by the ancestors, things can go wrong as a consequence of the wiles of the wives of the gods. They are thought not to be wholly reliable, since they are inmarried, as all wives in observance of the incest rules are, that is, they come from outside the lineage. However, the most fearsome source of misfortune is the *kalku*. *Kalkus* are usually women and, of course, Mapuche. "Every house has its *kalku*," is a Mapuche saying. As inmarried women, they are often left out of genealogies. Their power comes to them in dreams or visions. It may also be inherited from ancestors who were themselves *kalkus*. A young woman recruited into witchcraft requires many years of maturation and becomes a powerful *kalku* only upon reaching old age. It is the old women who bear the brunt of witchcraft accusations and who are therefore sometimes driven off the reservation. Propitiating ancestral spirits is good protection against witches. Amulets and homespun and woven belts with a magical design are also useful.

Kalkus can extract and use the "evil essence" of plants and animals. They can also perform various injurious activities. One of these is a rite called *koftun*, a vengeful act which a female client is thought to be able to cause to be performed against a former lover who left her pregnant. If she can provide the dead body of the male child she has borne as a result, his testicles are slowly roasted. It is believed that this will dry up the semen of the father. With their power, *kalkus* can also capture free-floating evil spirits or the spirit of some ordinary person and send these out to do evil deeds, even to commit murder.

If it is suspected that a death is due to machinations by a *kalku*, divination by autopsy is sometimes carried out by the *machi* or her helper. The stomach, the liver, the appendix, or the bones are examined for irregularities that indicate that a *kalku* was at work. A simpler method is to place a bowl of flour near the head of the corpse. If by the following morning some of the flour is gone, it is assumed that the spirit is hungry and well and not in the hands of a *kalku*.

Ethics and its relation to religious behavior. Mapuche see behavior as being either good or bad. "The eternal struggle between good and evil . . . engages the ethereal ancestors and their descendants, and is reenacted daily in Mapucheland," remarks Faron.

Comments. As demonstrated by the Mapuche material, there is no complete overlap between the agriculturalists who have their own state and this society that does not. Their principal ritual, the funeral, utilizes the entire ritual structure except for the Sex Complex, which is different, although the "nurture" branch of the Birth Complex is intensely elaborated, as in all agriculturalist societies. The altered state is used to achieve possession, but the religious specialists are all female, and women are the equals of men, not subordinate or their property. Representing the dark side of the female, there is abundant witchcraft activity, with witches being members of the society. The principal position in the alternate reality is occupied by a being that is a male creator, but he is not omnipotent. Compared to an African, Hindu, Chinese, or Christian central deity, he is not the same absolute monarch, not the peak "from which all blessings flow." In addition, he has features both of the habitat and of society in a more balanced distribution than seen with state societies, a trait found also with the aura of specialists surrounding him. On the other hand, the social structure of the alternate reality is strongly hierarchical. Behavior is judged as being either good or evil, and the alternate reality follows this line of cleavage.

Because we treated only one example of an agricultural society that does not have a state, it is difficult to tell whether it is the organizational form of the state that is responsible for the obvious differences between it and those agriculturalists that live in hierarchically ordered states. We may also be seeing instead strong Indian ethnic traits that survived into the agricultural adaptation.

EIGHT

⮑❧⮐

The Nomadic Pastoralists

The adaptation of nomadic pastoralism arose so gradually within a number of different ecological conditions that it is difficult to make any general statements concerning its time of origin. Some forms antedate agriculture; others arose as an adjunct to it. At any rate, once an adaptation developed, it remained impressively stable. Take, for instance, the Evenk (Tungus), to be discussed later in this chapter. Archeologists have found traces of their way of life going back as far as the Neolithic, about 8000–9000 B.C., not too far from where they make their home today in eastern Siberia, in the region of Lake Baikal.

Comparing the subsistence activity of nomadic pastoralists, we can distinguish three subtypes:

1) those who combine pastoralism with hunting and gathering;

2) those who have ties to and obtain part of their subsistence in trade relations with agriculturalists; and

3) those who by virtue of a sexual division of labor are partially horticulturalists, a task that has fallen to the women, and partially pastoralists, the lifeway of the men.

The sample. The societies to be discussed for the above three adaptations are the Evenks (or Tungus) of Siberia, the Tuareg of East Africa and the Basseri of Iran, and the Dodoth of sub-Saharan Africa. Because of their obvious diversity, we will proceed as we did with the horticulturalists and will treat each of the three subtypes independently.

Pastoralists Who Are Also Hunters

In all likelihood, this kind of nomadic pastoralism arose by hunters' attaching themselves to existing herds, such as reindeer, or creating herds out of psychologically suitable stock, such as horses. As an example for the subtype, I have chosen a Siberian society, that of the Evenks, also known as the Tungus. They are the largest society among the various ethnic groups inhabiting eastern Siberia. The Evenks fall into two main segments. There are, on the one hand, the horse and cattle pastoralists and, on the other, the much more numerous reindeer breeders, for whom hunting has remained the preferred occupation into the twentieth century. Our discussion will center on the latter.

The reindeer-herding Evenks live in the taiga, a vast mountainous region with dense forests and fast streams. In the forest, larch predominates. Grass can be found only in the valleys. The reindeer herd provides the principal subsistence, but depending on the season, bands follow the wildlife, going on extended treks and taking the herds with them. The streams abound in fish. During the brief summer season, the women collect berries, field onions, and wild garlic.

Like all nomadic pastoralists, the Evenks are organized into patrilineal clans. In theory, the father of a tent group has absolute power over his family, especially the women, and is the sole provider. The significance of the woman for the survival of the group is deemphasized. In practice, however, the woman plays an important role economically, but this fact is not socially recognized. Before marriage, her activities benefit her father and brothers, and after marriage, her husband and sons. The clans are exogamous, and this makes the woman the stranger, the intruder in the clan of her husband.

The religious specialist of the Evenks and similar Siberian and Central Asian societies is called a shaman, which is an Evenk word. (See Eliade, 1964.) Shamans have great power: They can command many spirits, they divine, go on spirit journeys, guide the souls of the deceased to the realm of the dead, and especially, they heal. Both men and women can become shamans, but great ambivalence is attached to the woman as shamaness in these societies. R. Hamayon (1984: 307–318) reviews material on the topic. Although he discusses mainly the Buryat, another nomadic pastoralist society from Siberia, the situation is materially the same for the Evenks.

According to Hamayon, the right to claim the shamanic function, i.e., the "essence," is hereditary in these societies, and the clan owns it. But before becoming a shaman, the individual in a clan owning an essence needs to prove his personal capability. The shamanic essence can be inherited equally by boys and girls, so it should be possible for a woman to become a shaman as easily as a man if she shows personal capability, but this is not so. The problem with respect to women arises out of their position in a patrilineal society such as these pastoralists. No woman remains unmarried, but according to the patrilineal rule, only a man is a full member of his clan. A wife may not attend the clan sacrifices, which shows that she is not considered a member of her husband's clan.

In shamanic families, according to tradition, which certainly has some basis in history, extreme measures are taken to assure that the shamanic essence does not pass to another clan by way of marriage. There are stories of parents' burying their daughters alive, or brothers' doing the same thing to their sisters, so as not to lose the essence.

Since an essence that is not represented on earth by a shaman may be dangerous to its living owners, an essence-owning lineage will always try to avoid the situation of having no living shaman. But severe conflicts arise if there is no boy, or none with the requisite capabilities, and a girl needs to be initiated as a shaman, because when she gets married, the essence will leave her father's clan and pass on to her husband's. In her husband's clan, however, she is not welcome as a shamaness. She is often prevented from exercising her call and may be driven to suicide as a result. On the other hand, if she is the only living holder of her essence, she may be initiated into her husband's clan and operate for its benefit, and may then even work at shamanizing with her husband. Such cases, however, are the exception and not the rule.

Female shamans wear the same dress and own the same paraphernalia as their male counterparts. But they are not allowed to kill animals for sacrifice, as healers they usually heal only themselves, and their single ritual activity of significance for their clan is that of divining (see below). They become shamans later in life than the men, and really come into their own only after death. While in life, a shamaness is not allowed to ascend sacred mountains, she is often buried there, she may be glorified as an ancestor, and she may have collective sacrifices addressed to her as a spiritual protector.

An Evenk ritual. The shamanistic rituals of nomadic pastoralists of this type are often concerned with healing. The exceptionally colorful and detailed decription summarized below is from a lengthy article by the Russian ethnographer Arkadiy Fedorovich Anisimov, a specialist on the history of religious beliefs among the Evenks, who did fieldwork among them in the 1920s and 1930s. He observed the ceremony in the Podkamennaya Tunguska Basin in 1931.

For this shamanistic ritual (see fig. 10), the round tent erected by the helpers of the shaman is the middle world. A spirit river, originating in the upper world, flows through it. In the course of the ritual, the shaman's soul floats down on it to the lower world, with the drum his boat and the drumstick his pedal. The upper world is shown in some wooden figures opposite the east entrance to the tent. They are "giant reindeer," the most powerful spirit helpers of the shaman and herd leaders of all his other animal spirits. To the southeast of the upper world, a pole is set up with sacrifices hanging on it, colored fabric and skins of sacrificed animals. This is the road to the upper deities. The sun and the moon, and an assemblage of deities called collectively "bear," are represented in the same area. Opposite the west entrance of the round tent is another group of wooden figures, the representatives of the lower world. The central figure is a spirit elk, flanked by Siberian spirit stags. Anthropomorphic figurines of the shaman's watch spirits guard the lower world from the back, preventing the spirits of enemy shamans from entering.

A tall young larch tree is placed in the center of the tent, with its top drawn

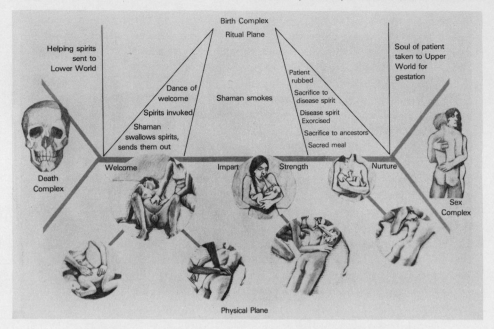

Figure 10. Nomadic pastoralist ritual, Evenk reindeer herders.

through the smoke hole. On this "tree of the world" the shaman travels to the upper world, and during intervals in the ritual, his spirit helpers rest in it, gathering strength.

After the men have assembled, the entrance of the tent is closed by small planks, the spirit watchmen. A fire is lit in the middle, and the men who came along with the patient sit down along the sides. The shaman sits opposite the entrance, his face pale and twitching, his hands trembling. At a sign by him, his assistant dresses him in his shamanistic robes and places an iron crown on his head with iron reindeer horns on it. He warms the drum at the fire. The shaman sits down on a small wooden platform representing fish spirits. Holding the drum in his left hand, he places it on his left knee and strikes its rim with the drumstick. The conversation breaks off: The ceremony is about to begin.

As the ritual enters the Death Complex, the fire is damped. Swaying slowly from side to side in time to his drum beat and in a quiet, melodious voice, the shaman begins the invocatory song to the spirits. After each verse, those present sing a rhythmical refrain. In the song, the shaman calls on the spirits to help him in his struggle against the disease spirit. Addressing each of his spirits in turn, the shaman vividly describes its form, listing its services to the clan and the characteristics of its power. He relates where the spirit is at the time, what it is doing, and whether it is obeying the summons. Finally, he tells how each spirit is leaving its own ranges and is coming to the tent. The song ceases, the sound of the drum is muffled, changing into a short roll. In the ensuing silence, the spirits begin to announce their presence: There is a snorting of beasts, bird calls, the whirring of wings. As each one appears, the shaman yawns deeply and with it, takes the spirit into himself, then calls to the next one to the incessant rolling of the drum, until he has gathered all of them into himself.

The shaman now issues orders to the spirit assemblage inside him. Some are to guard the tent, others all the various pathways. Under heavy spirit guard, he then dispatches his *khargi*, his chief spirit helper, to the lower world to learn the cause of the clansman's illness. While the sound of the drum becomes thunderous, the song of the shaman more agitated, the *khargi* and his body-guards pass to the lower world by way of the world tree. In a dramatic and often comic dialogue, wild screams and noises from the mouth of the shaman, the audience hears how the *khargi* seeks out the chief ancestor spirit of the shaman and consults with him. The tempo of the song accelerates ever more; the drum moans, dying down in peals and rolls under the swift, nervous hands of the shaman. After a few deafening beats, the shaman suddenly leaps from his place. Swaying from side to side, bending in a half-circle to the ground and smoothly straightening up again, he looses such a torrent of sound on the audience that it seems that everything is humming—the poles of the tent, even the buttons on the clothing of those present. Screaming a few parting words to the spirits, the shaman reches the peak of his ecstasy. He throws the drum into the hands of his assistant, seizes the thongs attached to the tent pole, and begins to dance a pantomime, illustrating how the *khargi* with his guards rushes further on his dangerous journey.

The shaman's assistant beats out a furious roll. The snorting of the beasts is heard once more; the ecstasy spreads to all those present. The shaman leaps into the air, whirls while still holding on to the thongs, demonstrating the running and the furious flight of his spirits, then with foam at his mouth collapses on a rug. The "death" of the shaman concludes the sojourn in the Death Complex of the ritual.

The assistant fans the fire and bends over the lifeless body of the shaman, who at this point is the *khargi* in the lower world. The assistant tries to persuade him to return to the middle world, initiating the entrance into the "welcome branch" of the Birth Complex. Finally the shaman begins to stir. A weak babble can be heard, the barely audible voices of the spirits announcing their coming. The assistant bends down, puts his ear to the shaman's lips, and reports what the shaman says is happening during this return of the *khargi* and its entourage. The shaman's voice becomes stronger; he utters a loud mutter, then disjointed sentences and loud cries. The assistant gets hold of the drum once more, warms it over the fire, and, starting to beat it, entreats the shaman not to get lost on the road, to look more fixedly at the fire, to listen more closely to the sound of the drum. He beats the drum louder and faster, and the shaman's outcries become clearer. This leads the shaman into renewed ecstasy; he leaps up and starts dancing the return of the *khargi* and its attendant spirits.

Now the shaman's dance becomes subdued; his tempo slows; he sways from side to side on the thongs; the dance has ended. In a recitative, he tells the audience of the *khargi*'s journey to the other world and all its adventures. Letting go of the thongs, he returns to his place. He is given the drum, and in a song, he tells of the advice of the ancestor spirits about how to fight the disease spirit. He puts the drum aside and enters the "impart strength" branch of the rite; one of the men present offers him a lit pipe, and, pale and exhausted, he smokes it, signaling the end of the first section of the ritual.

After this brief rest, it is time for the shaman to proceed into the third branch, that of the exorcism proper. He picks up the drum and begins the attempt to expel the disease spirit. He starts negotiating with it, trying to talk it into leaving the patient's body voluntarily. The spirit refuses. The shaman becomes irritated because the discussion drags on. He bursts into expressions of anger, cries, and threats. The sound of the drum gathers strength. Once more he hands it to his assistant and, leaping from his place, grabs hold of the thongs. He goes into a furious whirling dance beside the patient, but to no avail. Tired and powerless, he takes the drum from his assistant, returns to his seat, and in a song asks his spirit helpers about what to do next. Upon the advice from his *khargi*, he begins to try and expel the disease by fanning and rubbing the spot where the disease is located in the body of the patient by using some hair from the neck of a reindeer, a piece of skin from the nose of a Siberian stag, the antler of a wild deer, the skin from the forehead of a wolf, and eagle feathers. Again he is unsuccessful.

Furious, the shaman denounces all manner of disease spirits; he sits down, beats his drum indignantly for a long time, then passes into the former melody once more to consult with his spirit helpers about what to do next. Following the advice of the *khargi*, he now proposes that the disease spirit pass into a sacrificed reindeer. A long dialogue develops between the shaman and the disease spirit. The shaman praises the flavor of the reindeer's meat, of the different parts of its body, and speaks disparagingly about the body of the patient. It is obvious from the disease spirit's answers that he does not share the shaman's opinion. Finally, however, it does agree to accept the reindeer as a substitute for the patient. The reindeer is brought into the tent; a rope is fastened around its neck, and the loose end is placed in the patient's hand. To the sound of the drum, the patient twists the rope, making it shorter, until the reindeer's head is close to his own. At that moment, one of the men standing next to the reindeer kills it with a blow from his knife. The reindeer is skinned, and the skin is suspended on the pole as a sacrifice to the supreme deity. The shaman is handed the heart, which now supposedly holds the disease spirit. He bites a piece off of it, spits it into a hole in one of the spirit figurines, stoppers it, and carries it to the representation of the lower world west of the tent. There he orders his spirit helpers to throw the captured evildoer into the abyss of the lower world.

Unfortunately, however, the disease spirit has fooled the shaman and has remained in the patient's body. The shaman, extremely annoyed, once more throws himself on his drum. Playing it loudly, he shouts invectives, abuse, and threats at the offending spirit. He orders his spirit helpers to surround it and to start attacking it, and begins an account of the ensuing battle. It seems that the disease spirit has now hidden itself in the patient's stomach. The goose, the most cunning of the shaman's spirits, pushes its beak into the patient's stomach and catches the disease spirit. To the ringing sounds of the drum, the shaman and his spirits celebrate the victory, and the clansmen present sigh with relief.

The joy, unfortunately, proves premature. The disease spirit tears itself loose from the goose's beak and throws itself at the onlookers, who are stunned with horror. However, another of the shaman's helping spirits, the splintered pole, a stand-in for the tree of life, manages to catch it, squeezing it into its wooden body, and together with two other wood spirits, takes it in front of the shaman.

The shaman's spirits surround the captured disease spirit and begin battering it with malicious jokes, profanity, ridicule, and threats. They pinch and bite it, and pull its legs; the most outraged of them even defecates and urinates on it. The tent rings with the sound of the drum, the shaman's wild cries imitating the voices of his helpers, until the frenzy reaches a peak, and once more the shaman seizes the thongs and switches into a frantic dance. The assistant works the drum; it groans and then dies in a thunder of beats. Wild screams, the snorting of beasts, and the calls of birds fill the tent. The spirit reaches the fire, and coals, brands, and ashes fly about. The audience also gets into the act, trying to help the shaman with their shouts. Then, as the bedlam can go no higher, the shaman and his helpers drag the disease spirit to the lower world. On its brink, in the exact reversal of the birth act, the loon spirit swallows it, flies over the abyss, and there expels it through its anus. On their way back to the middle world, the party barricades all the passages. Upon arrival, the shaman's dance ends. He returns to his seat, and to the accompaniment of his drum, he recounts all the details of the expulsion. Then there is a pause, so that the shaman and his spirit helpers can get some rest.

The shaman now reports that his *khargi* has learned from the ancestor spirits who sent the disease spirit to the clan. Amid exclamations of indignation and threats, the clan spirits, a group of zoomorphic monsters, are sent out under the leadership of the *khargi* to avenge the deed.

In the concluding part of the curing rite, the action switches into the positive opposite of the exorcism. A reindeer is offered in sacrifice to the gods of the above. The skin is hung on a larch outside the tent, and the meat is eaten by the participants in the ritual. In a special song addressed to the gods, the shaman thanks the protectors of the clan for their help. He then performs a special dance, his journey to the upper world, which he reports reaching by way of the larch. In the actions that now follow, the shaman has reached the Sex Complex. When he reaches the upper world, he walks over its earth until he gets to *Amaka sheveki*, Grandfather Spirit, and leaves in his keeping the soul of the patient (conception), in the form of a small wooden figure of a man attached to the tip of the larch. *Amaka sheveki* returns the soul into his care (gestation). A final, ecstatic dance celebrates the return of the shaman to the middle world, and with that the rebirth of the patient to renewed health. The tent is left to the elements afterwards; only its reindeer-skin covering is removed.

The religious trance. One cannot but deeply admire the trance performance of this shaman. He sustains the changed state of perception for hours on end, using principally the spirit journey, although with the swallowing of the spirits in a yawn, and subsequently their voices sounding from his mouth, he also switches into a form of possession. Both these possibilities of trance utilization are expertly intertwined in the masterful performance of this religious specialist.

The alternate reality. The habitat. According to Anisimov, the Evenks think of the upper world as divided into several levels. *Amaka sheveki* lives on the topmost of these. He is in charge of the societal aspect of the Evenk world. On the lower level of the upper world, there are a number of aspects of the habitat. This is where the supreme lord of the animals, birds, fish, and plants lives. It is also the abode of the spirits of the sun, the moon, thunder, the stars, the clouds, the sunset, and daybreak. In addition, the upper world has a storehouse for unborn souls. It is guarded by watchmen whose generic name is "bear." This ties the Evenks into the circumpolar culture complex that shares the veneration of the bear as the healer and giver of life. The hierarchical organization of the realm is unmistakable.

The spirits of the dead. The spirits of the dead live in the lower world, which is equally hierarchically organized. Admission to it is handled by the clan mother, who is the mistress of that realm. The shaman has the task of guiding the departing soul to her and requesting permission for it to enter. The people live in camps there, as they do on earth, the middle world. Its exits are guarded by watchmen such as spirit eelpouts, who gulp down any spirit inhabitant of the lower world that might attempt to cross its boundary and trespass into the middle world of people, causing them harm. Other watchmen guard the mouth of the spirit river to prevent the spirits of hostile shamans from entering the territory of the clan through the lower world. Disease spirits are banished to it, and all manner of pernicious spirits, assuming the form of ermines or stoats, also live there.

Other beings. The neighbors of Evenk society are equally represented in its alternate reality. In Anisimov's words, "A very special category of spirits was comprised of the ruling spirits of waters, mountains, forests, various species of beasts, and others. There were whole tribes of these in Evenk thought"

(1963: 108). The different species of animals that Evenks hunt are thought to be the tame herds of these spirits, which have the same social structure as that of the Evenks. The Evenks have cordial relationships with these "neighbors." Since they have tame herds of what to the Evenks are wild animals that they need for subsistence, a kind of food exchange is set up between them and the Evenks in the form of sacrifices to these spirit beings.

Good fortune, misfortune, and the rituals of divination. Good fortune comes from keeping intact the reciprocal relations with the many important spirits of the alternate reality, especially by way of regular sacrifices. Misfortune, especially disease, is on occasion caused by a spirit of the dead, which eludes the watchmen and penetrates into the middle world, with dire consequences for the living. The principal source, however, is outside, in the form of an attack by the spirit of the shaman of an enemy clan. To ward off such attacks, the shaman surrounds the territory of his clan with a spirit stockade. On dry land, the stockade is a fence of wood spirits. It extends, invisibly, across the taiga, from one ridge to the next, from rivulet to rivulet, from mountain to mountain. Day and night, the spirit watchmen of the shaman guard this fence. In the air, they are supported by bird spirits, in the river by fish spirits. If the spirit of an enemy shaman does break through, it is the task of the shaman to repair the damage in the stockade. This may lead to a fierce struggle between shamans. Shamans always die by being murdered in the alternate reality by other shamans. Upon a shaman's death, the stockade disappears, and it is imperative for a new shaman to reconstruct it.

Divination is an extremely important ritual for reindeer herders. It is always the first act of a shaman, an indispensable preliminary to all rites. When in the above curing rite the shaman sends his *khargi* to the lower world to learn the cause of the clansman's illness, he is performing a divinatory rite. A more extensive divination concludes the curing ceremony. In this case, the shaman uses his drumstick by throwing it up into the air, and from the way it falls, he determines whether or not the desires expressed by the various clansmen will be fulfilled. He then takes the shoulder blade of the sacrificed reindeer, lays hot coals on it, and blows on them, and according to the direction and character of the cracks in the bone, he predicts what awaits his clansmen in the future.

Divination may also be performed by female shamans; in fact, as we have seen, it is their only public shamanizing task (see Hamayon, 1984: 312–313). Shamanesses are frequently asked to divine in connection with healing, thwarting deceit and fraud, discovering lost animals, and finding out whether the animal killed in sacrifice has been accepted by the spirit for which it was intended.

Ethics and its relation to religious behavior. As demonstrated in the curing rite, there is no division between good and bad. The disease spirit is reviled and banished to the lower world, but if the shaman has the chance, he will send it to an enemy clan. Each shaman protects his own and is aggressive against other clans. Evil, in other words, is not absolute, it is relative, and actions are judged on their social merit. Murder can be acceptable if appropriate—in order, for instance, to prevent a daughter from taking the shamanic essence to an enemy clan.

(Anisimov provides no material for a semantic analysis of the category "religion" of the Evenks.)

Nomadic Pastoralists with Ties to Agriculture

In a number of regions around the world, nomadic pastoralism did not, it is thought, grow out of hunting adaptation directly, but as an adjunct to agriculture. Animals capable of domestication began congregating around plantings, according to prehistorians, becoming first the pets of humans and then an important subsistence source. When, for various reasons, the human population began increasing, part of this increase could no longer be accommodated and was pushed out into adjoining regions not suited for agricultural exploitation, but still capable of sustaining herds of domestic animals.

Nomadic pastoral societies of this type can be found in many parts of the world. The two societies to be described here, the Tuareg and the Basseri, located in East Africa and Iran respectively, interact intensely with the cultivators that work the regions adjoining theirs. Most of the time, they are also of the same religious persuasion. The above two societies, for instance, profess Islam. These religious affiliations, however, provide no more than the customary idiom for religious expression. Pastoralists are usually lax to indifferent to their "official" faith. The Arabs say about the Tuareg, for instance, that they are negligent Muslims who do not carry out the ritually prescribed washings or prayers, do not fast, do not enforce the premarital chastity of the women, and even allow women to speak freely to men. The attitudes reflected in this judgment can easily be generalized to the entire societal type, and they are not likely to evoke admiration in the religious practitioners of the sedentary peoples with whom the nomads have to have contact. Frequently also nomadic pastoralists incorporate idiosyncretic features into their nominal faiths, a process aided by the fact that they rarely have religious practitioners of their own who would insist on religious orthodoxy. In any event, the effect of varying faiths, as well as differences in ecology, types and size of herds, etc., is minor, outweighed in large measure by the many traits nomadic pastoralists have in common. Briefly summarizing the literature (see, e.g., Spooner, 1973), we find that these societies share the following characteristics.

The subsistence of the group derives only in part from the herds, but other foodstuffs, of agricultural origin, although of considerable importance, are ideologically deemphasized. They do not actively modify their natural environment, but exploit it by interposing their animals. The size and subsistence of the herd dictates the composition of the social herding unit, which may be anywhere from one married couple to a group of families forming a camp. The herding unit is unstable because its composition needs to be adjusted from day to day to the fluctuations of the herd.

Herding demands enormous physical exertion on the part of the men, who are intensely competitive, emphasizing the "strong man" image. As they are also in exclusive possession of herding technology, it is understandable that all decisions are made by the male heads of the respective herding unit; the women are divested of power beyond the domestic sphere. This does not necessarily lead to a double sexual standard, however, for while the Basseri, for example, try to enforce premarital chastity in the girls, such is not the case with the Tuareg. In addition, this powerlessness of the women is balanced out in the ritual sphere, for instance in the case of the Tuareg, where possessed women are the center of festive exorcistic rituals (see below).

The pastoral nomad is continually prompted by considerations for the safety and well-being of his herd to gather information from the whole of his territory. This makes him acutely aware of the unitary aspect of the area he views as his own, the arena in which he structures his cyclical migrations. Within it, however, there is usually one particular region, outstanding possibly because of lush pasture, an exceptionally reliable source of water, or some other features, which the respective society considers more essentially homeland than all others traversed during the year. A number of these societies also possess places of pilgrimage, valued as politically neutral territory.

With respect to kinship structure, the native model is most commonly genealogical, invariably based on agnation, that is, patrilineal descent. This model, which leads to a view of the social universe as encompassing the entire nomadic population, lends stability in daily interaction, which takes place in continually shifting local groupings. It also makes it possible to manage these fluctuations with the aid of a second social principle, namely, that of an (implicit) contract. The core of the group is permanent; other persons join it or separate themselves from it on the basis of contractual arrangements, the rules of which everybody knows and takes for granted.

A number of nomadic pastoral societies have tribal chieftains, either because they are needed to administer the flow of migration through difficult terrain, or to facilitate and mediate the relations with the surrounding sedentary society, perhaps because of taxation, or in case of legal disputes. The contact between the chieftain and the nomadic population is always direct, without a bureaucratic structure intervening, and orders are usually transmitted by messengers who do not have any power themselves.

There is for the most part little material in modern ethnographies about the religious behavior of these societies. A notable exception is the report of the Danish anthropologist Johannes Nicolaisen, who did fieldwork with the Tuareg in East Africa in the 1950s and wrote a lengthy essay on their "religion and magic." Some scanty remarks gleaned from a monograph about the Basseri provide a sketchy basis for comparison. It was written by the Swedish soci-

ologist Fredrick Barth, who observed the Basseri in South Persia (Iran) during
the same decade. Both these societies are nominally Islamic. Nicolaisen goes
to some lengths trying to isolate religious traits that antedate the conversion
to Islam of the Tuareg. On some points, the separation clearly cannot be made,
given the fact that Islam, like the Hebraic tradition, has strong roots in the
ancient lifeways of nomadic pastoralism.

A *Tuareg women's ritual.* Men and women tend toward different lifestyles,
and so they have different rituals, too, with the women experiencing possession
and the men in charge of sacrifice. The women's rite described here is summarized from Nicolaisen (1961: 126–129). The possessing spirits that appear
in the ritual are the Kel Asouf, the exponents, it would seem, of pre-Islamic
Tuareg religion.

As is familiar from agriculturalist possession, e.g., Vodun (see chap. 7), these
women's rites elaborate only the "nurture" branch of the ritual structure, in
both its form of possession and its obverse, the exorcism. As is the case with
the *loa* of Vodun, the Kel Asouf spirits are not invited. Their arrival simply
happens. Women are possessed by them not only if the spirit enters into them,
but also if one of them happens to get too close.

Possession by the Kel Asouf manifests itself by an attack of "ecstatic con-
vulsion," which takes hold of women during certain songs and dances that are
accompanied by a rhythm beaten out on the tambourine. These songs and
dances are the standard features of marriage and naming feasts, of the celebration of Islamic holy days, and of many other occasions. At the conclusion
of such feasts, it often happens that one or more women collapse in what
appears to be spasmodic hiccoughs. The attack may be so severe that the
women will remain lying on the ground unconscious, foaming at the mouth.
When this happens, steps are immediately taken to expel the Kel Asouf spirits
from the possessed, usually by means of an object made of iron. A man draws
his sword and moves it over and around the prostrate woman. If she then rises
and starts running around in a confused manner, with her hands cramped and
folded, he will try to separate them with his sword. However, the most efficacious method of exorcism is to induce in the possessed three successive
ecstatic attacks by means of the rhythms of the drums and the songs. After
that, it is thought, the Kel Asouf will leave on their own.

In preparation for such an ecstatic experience, the woman is helped to a
sitting position on two large leather cushions. Her head is swathed in cotton
bands, applied so tightly that she cannot see. One woman begins beating the
drum, while all the other women of the group mark the rhythm with singing
and clapping. The particular beat is used exclusively for this rite. During the
music and the singing, the possessed woman rocks from side to side on her
pillow, marking the rhythm, sighing, murmuring, or whistling, as is customary
during the trance. Eventually, she falls unconscious once more. The women
revive her with water, and the entire procedure begins anew, until it happens
a third time. Some women accomplish the three falls with ease. Others find it

very difficult. In that case, several evenings of singing and dancing may pass before the third fall is brought about. In the interim, the possessed woman remains in her tent during the day, occasionally drinking some water, but not eating anything. Such Kel Asouf rituals are not considered dangerous. Rather, they are most usually the extension of the feast at which the first attack occurred, and there is much laughter and merrymaking accompanying the event.

A Tuareg men's ritual. The men's ritual usually takes place with the co-operation of a *marabout*, an Islamic holy man. The ritual quoted below is part of a name-giving feast, and is celebrated seven days after the birth of a child. Its aspect of sharing food with a being or beings of the alternate reality marks it once more as an elaboration on the "nurture" branch of the ritual scheme.

> A marabout, that is a Tuareg of the Ineslemen class, and the father of the child stand close together with their faces toward Mecca, while the animal to be sacrificed is held to the ground. The marabout cuts the animal's throat and while doing so cries out the name to be given to the child, and this name is thereupon repeated by the child's father. (Nicolaisen, 1963: 231)

Men offer sacrifices also to the Kel Asouf, which the women do not do, and during such rites, there is usually some divining. The latter, however, is not a male prerogative.

The religious trance. The women employ the religious trance in order to experience possession. Whether men experience a trance during sacrifice is not known, but repeated reports of visions during sacrifice suggest that this may indeed be the case. In many instances, the religious trance of the pastoral nomads may go unreported because of its subtle nature and its induction by context. This may be the underlying process in the following observation reported by Barth for the Basseri.

Troubled by the fact that he was unable to record any religious rituals for the Basseri, Barth stipulated that the migratory cycle itself might be classed as such. He noted that there was a clear increase in tension and general excitement as the tent group that he was traveling with slowly approached the high plain of Mansurabad, the area of congregation before the large spring migration. In order to have something to measure, he began recording the times of awakening, packing, and departure of the camp. The resulting data revealed some clear and regular features. Tension, he found, built up progressively within shorter cycles of three to six days, broken by a day or two of camping and rest, and followed once more by a new cycle of buildup. "When we topped the last pass," he says, "and saw before us the mountains for which we had been heading, all the women of the caravan broke out in song, for the first and only time during the whole trip" (1961: 152).

The alternate reality. The habitat. As we noted above, the individual in this type of nomadic pastoralist society is in continuous, intense daily interaction with the entirety of the region where the society's migratory cycle takes place.

This experience correlates with their monotheism. God is this habitat; not anthropomorphic, he is everywhere, an abstract, absolute force, present in everything and everywhere. The social power of this entity is mainly punitive, again agreeing with the harshness of the habitat. It might be argued that the features of the monotheism are the result of the nomads' association with Islam. But that is putting the cart before the horse. After all, Mohammed spent his formative years herding sheep in the desert. His monotheism was shaped by the world view of the Bedouins, not the other way around.

The spirits of the dead. These spirits do not live in structured communities or groups, but roam the alternate reality as individuals. The Tuareg fear them, for they can bring illness. The only contact they maintain with them is by the sacrifice of a goat or sheep on the anniversary of the father's or the mother's death. The Basseri reserve this kind of attention only to those of their kin who died under especially tragic circumstances. In such cases, small groups of mourners may assemble for a visit to the grave. "Often, they will knock at the stone slabs of the grave with pebbles, to call the attention of the dead to their laments; before leaving, they distribute sweets to the village children" (Barth, 1961: 143–144). This small ritual may be interpreted as feeding, that is, bringing a sacrifice to the spirits of the deceased.

Other beings. The alternate reality of these nomads also houses an unstructured assemblage of spirits, in the sense that the central power does not rule over them as a king would, they are not ranked as higher or lower, and they do not obey anyone.

The spirits of the Tuareg can be divided into three categories: 1) There are the angels, who carry messages, also reported from other nomadic pastoralists, and who are often identified with lightning; 2) there are the saints, disciples or more often descendants of the Prophet's son-in-law, who have a great deal of *baraka,* to be discussed later; and 3) there are the Kel Asouf.

References to the Kel Asouf lace the entire discussion of Tuareg religion given by Nicolaisen. They are clearly pre-Islamic. When sacrifices are offered to them, the name of Allah is not mentioned, for instance. In fact, they are known to the Prophet and referred to as *djenoun* or *djin.* In the Koran, they are often confused with Satan, the Iblis of the Tuareg (see below). However, for the Tuareg, there is no confusion, especially also grammatically: The Kel Asouf are always referred to in the plural, while Iblis is not.

If we assemble all the scattered material that Nicolaisen recorded about the Kel Asouf, a complex emerges so similar to the spirits of the Evenks that the agreements simply cannot be overlooked. One gets the impression that the Tuareg had preserved a more archaic form of this belief complex, before the respective spirits became attached to the shamans. This may be indicative of some ancient and no longer traceable connection of the Tuareg to Asia. Other pastoralists of the present type, such as the Basseri or the Bedouins, have nothing even vaguely resembling this type of spirit.

Let us first consider the obvious differences. The Tuareg have no shamans; instead, the Kel Asouf complex belongs predominantly to the women. If a man has anything to do with Kel Asouf spirits, the contact awards him power. The spirits attach themselves to his hair, and he can then divine or locate lost objects.

Evenk spirits belong to a particular clan, but the Kel Asouf spirits do not appertain to any particular class, a prominent feature of Tuareg social organization. Rather, they are "people of the solitude," of the desert, the earth, or the night, that is, of the habitat. Logically, they have their own regions, which need to be avoided. They are also attached to prehistoric or pre-Islamic graves. In other words, whatever they may do to people, they do on their own; they are not sent by an enemy shaman, they do not represent any aspect of society.

Everything else said about the Kel Asouf has its own sometimes very close parallel in Evenk, and thus also in other Siberian belief systems. The Kel Asouf, in fact, have nearly all the characteristics of the spirit helpers of the Evenk shamans. Even the fact that they are attached to particular regions reminds us of the spirits of a shaman being located in the territory of a particular clan. Kel Asouf may assume either anthropomorphic or animal shape. They have a strong affinity to wild game. In the former case, they are somewhat "peculiar," beings of elongated shape, having only four fingers on each hand, eyes with a vertical slit, their faces on the back of their heads. But as "people," they are of both sexes; they reproduce and die, and they have their own "spirit" language. Anisimov mentions that the Evenk shaman sometimes speaks in an unintelligible idiom when possessed by one of his spirits. They may hide in blowing sand, in stones or trees, and in the sources and the flow of rivers. When water suddenly rises, threatening the people bathing or the animals, that is the doing of the Kel Asouf.

Not only do we see here an affinity of the Kel Asouf with a river, but they also have their favorite tree, the *agar* (*Maerua crassifolia*), as demonstrated by the following example. According to Islamic law, a woman may not remarry or have sexual contact for three months after the dissolution of her marriage. She can free herself of this burdensome rule by going to an agar tree, preferably to one standing alone. She asks the tree to lift the prohibition. At the same time, she deposits kohl (a cosmetic) and perfume, and especially a length of cotton cloth. She then strikes the tree with a stick or an ax. The tree is, just as in the case of the Evenks, an avenue for contact with the beings of the alternate reality, a kind of tree of the world.

Contact with the Kel Asouf is dangerous and may well result in illness. They are responsible for mental illness, fever, and any kind of "invisible" malady, such as rheumatism, and they can kill people or animals, too. They can hide in a patient's intestines, and can be lured out of the patient's body by the blood of a sacrificial animal spilled over him.

However, people, either men or women, can make a compact with the Kel

Asouf, and in that case they will be their helpers. Such friends of the spirits, incipient shamans, as it were, can carry several Kel Asouf with them, talking with them in their special language and sending them on errands. When sent out this way, they will travel fast and very far, locating a lost camel, for example. The friends of the Kel Asouf can also give advice in the case of an accident or an illness bearing the earmarks of having been caused by other Kel Asouf.

Finally, Kel Asouf will do battle with each other. A friend of the Kel Asouf related that one day he saw his own Kel Asouf fighting with those of a woman, who was also one of their friends. "As a result of this struggle, two Kel Asouf died on one side, and one on the other side. The friend of the Kel Asouf who reported this is still alive, but he no longer has any Kel Asouf, he says. They all died" (Nicolaisen, 1961: 130).

The Kel Asouf cannot be considered the representation of neighbors in the alternate reality. Those are present, also, but they are the spirits of the saints, originating with Islamic, agriculturalist societies surrounding the Tuareg. The Tuareg hold that they roam the earth, bringing *baraka* to those who come in contact with them. The Basseri hold similar beliefs.

Good fortune, misfortune, and the rituals of divination. Good fortune is tied in with a complex category called *baraka*, which Islamic pastoralists share with sedentary Islamic societies. For the Tuareg, according to Nicolaisen, *baraka* is contained in everything and everybody having a close relationship to God. It therefore follows that Mohammed, God's prophet, had the greatest share ever, and that his descendants are favored in proportion to their nearness to him. His first disciples, whose spirits still roam the earth, also received it from him. As to objects, the Koran contains it in largest measure. Amulets of quotations from the Koran are efficacious for this reason. *Marabouts* derive their *baraka* from the Koran, and a person can receive a share of it by kissing their shoulders or their hands. When they die, they become closer to God, and this translates itself into a great deal of *baraka* being concentrated in the earth and the stones of their graves. By putting a bit of earth or a stone from these graves on one's head or in one's mouth, it is possible to receive some of this *baraka*. However, the horns of sacrificed animals also contain *baraka*, and there is a special kind of *baraka* in the shoulder blades of sacrificed or hunted animals, making these parts suitable for divination. The moon is good and full of *baraka*, and by extending one's open palms toward it in prayer, one may obtain a share of it. *Baraka* has important relationships to fertility, and it is in life-giving rain, in good pasture, in date palms, and in domestic animals, not, however, in dogs or asses.

Baraka can be hurt or dissipated by contact between pure and impure objects or persons. Thus, menstruating women or soil, that is, earth, both considered impure, must not come in contact with such pure substances as milk, or objects containing *baraka*, such as the shoulder blades of sacrificed animals, or the Koran.

The question, then, is, What exactly is *baraka*? Nicolaisen calls it a "notion of benediction," or a "mystical force." Geertz, a long-time student of Islam, is more explicit. He says,

> Literally, "baraka" means blessing, in the sense of divine favor. But spreading out from that nuclear meaning, specifying and delimiting it, it encloses a whole range of linked ideas: material prosperity, physical well-being, bodily satisfaction, completion, luck, plenitude, and, the aspect most stressed by Western writers anxious to force it into a pigeonhole with mana, magical power. In broadest terms, "baraka" is not, as it has so often been presented, a paraphysical force, a kind of spiritual electricity—a view which, though not entirely without basis, simplifies it beyond recognition. Like the notion of the exemplary center, it is a conception of the node in which the divine reaches into the world. Implicit, uncriticized, and far from systematic, it too is a doctrine. (1968: 44)

Geertz is speaking here of *baraka* as he observed it in Islam. But the concept is older than this faith. In Judaic tradition, the cognate *beraka* is mainly reproductive power, tying it in with the Tuareg notion that there is an important connection between *baraka* and fertility. And we can go even further afield. According to Pertti J. Pelto (personal communication), the Skolt Lapp, nomadic herders with whom he did fieldwork, have a notion called *tuuri*. *Tuuri* is present in luck during a card game. It may be expressed in good weather, and it is working when a reindeer thought lost shows up.

A bit of linguistic detective work may be interesting here. The Lapp or Saami speak a Uralic language, while the language of the Evenks belongs to the Tungus family. Both these languages, however, belong to the larger unit of the Altaic phylum. The Evenk cognate of the Lapp word *tuuri* is *turu*, according to Anisimov meaning "support," "stay," "prop," or "pillar." It refers to or stands for the larch, which, as we saw in the Evenk ritual, is thought of as the "tree of the world," on which the shaman can travel from the middle world to the upper one. Over the world tree, the generative power lodged in the alternate reality can reach the human world, bringing its manifold blessings. We might posit that the Altaic word refers to the pathway of the life force, the Islamic and Judaic one to what is being conducted, namely, good fortune in the widest sense of the word.

Misfortune can result for these societies not so much from a spirit agency as from malfunctioning social relations within the group. Both the Tuareg and the Basseri agree that what brings about misfortune is unconscious envy between close associates. The Tuareg speak of both "evil eye" and "evil mouth" to conceptualize this. Neither has any long-distance effect. The Tuareg expressly avoid praising themselves or others, their animals, or their children, for fear of precipitating either attack. And the Basseri emphasize that "only friends, acquaintances, and relatives, 'one's own people' can cast the evil eye, while declared enemies are impotent to do so" (Barth, 1961: 145). The deleterious action is not due to any volition, but to the envious quality of unconscious thoughts which have an automatic effect.

Much more sinister than either evil eye or evil mouth is black magic, which, according to the Tuareg, can take effect over long distances and is used intentionally. In every way, this complex is identical to the *fachera* of southern Italy, even down to the ingredients of the maleficent concoctions, and its involvement with male-female relationships. With it, the Tuareg participate in an area-wide culture complex ringing the Mediterranean.

Divination is important to all nomadic pastoralists. That it involves the switching into religious trance, for instance, among the Tuareg may be gathered from the report that men can divine if they have "Kel Asouf attached to their hair." For the Tuareg, Nicolaisen (1963: 171–172) describes a system known as sand cutting, familiar in a number of variants to all societies of northern Africa.

For this ritual, the diviner presses his thumb or forefinger into the sand and quickly makes two parallel rows of holes. He is not aware of how many holes he has made. He then counts them in each row and and makes a special sign in the sand for even and uneven numbers. There are four possibilities: There may be an uneven number of holes in both rows, or an even number in both rows; the number of holes may be even in the right row but uneven in the left row, or uneven in the right row but even in the left one. The diviner goes through the procedure six times. His divination depends on the combination and the relative position of the signs to each other.

Ethics and its relation to religious behavior. Nomadic pastoralists are generally cited for their generosity and hospitality, which is determined by social appropriateness. The ethnographic works consulted for this section give only a general impression of this aspect of the life of such societies, so I consulted material on other nomadic societies of the same type, such as the books by Robert B. Ekvall on the Tibetan high-altitude yak herders, the "aBrog Pa." I also talked with anthropologists who published reports about such societies but treated topics other than religious behavior, and who generously shared their impressions with me. These were William G. Irons, who was with the Yomut Turkmen in the 1960s in northern Iran; Robert Paine, who did fieldwork off and on for two years between the middle 1950s and the middle 1960s with two Norwegian Lapp groups, the Karasjok and the Kautokeino; and Pertti J. Pelto, mentioned before, who observed the Skolt Lapps of Sevettijarvi in northeastern Finnish Lapland in 1959.

Getting one's animals stolen, for instance, the single most important hazard in the life of nomadic pastoralists, is usually grounds for retribution. If a man gets killed during such a raid, this may even lead to blood feuds. However, it is not considered an absolutely evil deed. As Ekvall found among the aBrog Pa, community consensus about such actions is colored by the feeling that in case of real need, such as actual destitution and hunger, the act may be justified, life obviously being more important than considerations of property. The Lapps add traveling to destitution or hunger as another justification for stealing or poaching. The assumption is that you will later return what you took, or negotiate about it, and there is considerable tolerance in cases where restitution might have been forgotten. Paine adds an interesting elaboration from the Lapps he worked with in the Finmark of Norway. A theft may actually be institutional, a sort of term in a code. Suppose an individual has trespassed into another's pasture. This entitles the offended party to steal a yearling—but not, for instance, a cow—from the herd of the guilty party. The theft in this situation acts as a warning as well as compensation. Other offenses carry different theft signals. "The Norwegians," says Paine, "are continually mystified by these Lappish attitudes. After all, a theft is a theft." The only thief bracketed out of the code is the heinous one who takes without good reason, and who will then be subject to ostracism.

Even murder is similarly evaluated. It is the result of circumstance, and not an offense against a good/bad moral order. The Turkmen, Irons relates, feel that murder, while it will certainly be offensive to the kin of the victim, may not appear that way to others. Restitution then is a matter up for arbitration between the injured kin and the guilty party.

The evaluation of the Kel Asouf by the Tuareg is another case in point. They are dangerous, not evil. The same may be said of Iblis, often called Satan in Western descriptions of the Tuareg. To be sure, Iblis, according to Nicolaisen, is thought to be God's adversary. However, here his similarity to Satan stops. He can be present anywhere; he is associated with finger- and toenails and can be found in any man, including the *marabouts*, for without Iblis there is no generative power. The Tuareg believe that fecundity and germination and similar processes are good because of *baraka*, and that nothing is born without the will of God. But it is Iblis who provokes the desire and the force for procreation. Once, a man caught Iblis and tied him to a stone. This freed him of all evil associated with Iblis. But neither did he or his woman have any desire to make love. It is said that if a man is overactive sexually, the reason is that he has too much of Iblis in him. Iblis is also associated with feasts of music and dancing, for these may provide an occasion for amorous encounters. Iblis is in various musical instruments. Because of this association, a man may not pronounce the name of such an instrument in the presence of his father or an older relative, just as any allusion to sexual matters is forbidden between individuals belonging to different generations. There is an essence of Iblis in anything that is strong, in any form of excitation. Anger is due to Iblis, and there is something of Iblis in tobacco.

The semantics of "religion." It could be argued that the composite named category designating "religion" for these nomadic pastoralists is exemplified by *baraka*. It subsumes the trance, without which there is no religious experience. It has numerous strands to the alternate reality, and it touches the ordinary one in manifold ways, as outlined by Geertz.

Pastoralists Whose Women Are Cultivators

As an example of nomadic pastoralists whose women are cultivators, we will discuss an African society called the Dodoth. They were studied in the 1950s by Elizabeth Marshall Thomas.

The Dodoth are Central Nilo Hamites, living in Uganda. The men are nomadic pastoralists, ranging during the dry season to the far corners of Dodoth, to the northern mountains by the Sudan border, and west toward the plains of Acholiland. They live in large, polygamous households. Their life revolves around cattle. The women cultivate corn, millet, sorghum, pumpkins and gourds, and many types of beans and squashes on small fields or in gardens. Premarital sexual freedom is taken for granted by both sexes. The men are not only herders but also warriors, for periodically, they are raided by neighbors, especially by the Turkana.

The Dodoth call their religious specialists *ngimurok*, the plural of *emuron*; the female form is *amuron*. As we hear from Marshall Thomas,

> Great *ngimurok* appear from time to time like comets, rise to fame, change matters in Dodoth a bit and die. Long after they are gone, the world remembers them.... Their job is ... to serve as God's oracles, and though they do cause wonder, it is not by contrivance. By their prophesies, [*sic*], great *ngimurok* make rain or cause dry weather, or bring health, disease, or locusts, or avert disasters to the nation such as raids. (1972: 162, 166)

A Dodoth women's ritual. Marshall Thomas describes a ritual designed to cure her earache and carried out by the *amuron* Nadolupe. It took place at the *amuron*'s home in the women's compound of the polygamous household. Nadolupe had told her that her trouble had been caused by a witch who had watched her eating. The ritual was a simple "sucking-out" of the illness-causing substance. When Nadolupe threw the six tiny pellets she had retrieved across the fence, they simply fell down, which prompted the healer to explain that the spell must have been cast in another part of the country or perhaps in the ethnographer's homeland. "When I throw away a spell that a Dodoth witch made, the spell flies off like a bird" (1972: 164–165).

A men's ritual. There had been numerous raids against the Dodoth, creating a great deal of tension. So the men decided to hold a sacrifice to rally themselves, foresee the future, and avert the raid, if it was coming, before it began. As in the case of agricultural rituals, all the action of the ritual centers on the "nurture" branch of the Birth Complex. It is a divinatory ritual which consists of the sacrifice, the ritual meal, and its obverse, the exorcism of the enemy (summarized from Marshall Thomas, 1972: 138–148).

At midmorning, men began to gather at the ceremonial ground. This was on a high bluff above a bend in the river, where the sacred trees stood, hundreds of years old. Men kept arriving through the morning in twos and threes. They settled by the rockslide above the river, in a thicket of spears, watching the cattle that were taking turns at the trough below, by the river bed. They were waiting for an ox to appear that would be suitable for sacrifice. It was to be a red ox, its coloring foreseen in the intestines of a previous sacrifice. When the red ox was killed, its intestines, in turn, would reveal the coloring of the next sacrifice, in a chain of divination that reached back through time.

Around the bend of the river came a large herd, including a red ox. The men began a discussion with the owner's father, for the ox belonged to the herdboy. When a man's ox is sacrificed, he is reimbursed with a heifer. When an agreement had been reached, and the herd had finished drinking, the men called down to the herdboy to let the herd go but to keep the red ox and one of its companions in the river bed. An ox will not let itself be driven alone. The boy began to cry, but no one paid the slightest attention to him. A few young men took up their spears and scrambled down to the river bed. There they drove the red ox away from the white ox, its companion, and threw a spear into its side. The ox tried to escape to its herd, and in so doing, it ran more than a mile in a huge circle north of the river. It was supposed to die under the sacred trees, but it would not go alone. Someone drove its white companion to it; it leaned its head against the white ox's side, and the white ox supported it until it was under the fig tree, where it groaned, knelt, and rolled over, dead.

The ox's death was the signal for the start of the ceremony. The mood changed and took on a formal, passionless quality, like that of an important church service. The men, numbering about ninety by then, plumed and carrying spears, divided according to their age sets and sat down under the trees, the uninitiated on one side, the initiated on the other, ranked according to seniority.

Butchering must be done by a member of the clan who owns the sacred place, and is carried out according to age-old, precise rules. The ox must not be skinned; it must be cut only with a spear. The front legs and adjoining ribs are lifted from the chest, so bowls will form in which the blood is caught; and the white integument and rumen must be carried to a bed of leaves. The sacred joined hind legs and hips are severed from the body, and the sacred fatty fold between the anus and the withered testes is removed to be eaten by the old men. The hind legs must be divided with a spear, using the severed front leg as a club to batter them apart. The meat must all be eaten. It is roasted on a fire for which the wood is carried in a circle around the ox.

When the ribs and front legs had been removed, the elders came one by one to kneel and drink from the blood in the abdomen. As each man finished, he wiped his lips on the hairy hump, because the Dodoth say, "There is fighting there." The younger men came also and drank from the chest cavity. Blood gives men courage and strength.

The integument had dried in the meantime and had begun to constrict

around the edge. One of the elders, Uri, poured some water on it and began
the divining. The integument can be read "like a page in a book," the Dodoth
say. What Uri saw was a fire on Dodoth soil, a streak, the path of a bullet, and
a mottled brown ox, the next sacrifice. In a hollow between two lumps, a pass
between two mountains, were tiny black dots that meant a raiding party of
Turkana were entering, and beyond the dots, tiny threadlike capillaries showed
the people whom the Turkana had killed. After the men had discussed the
findings, they returned to the sacrifice.

The ritual continued with a speech denouncing the Turkana and exhorting
those present to stand firm against them and to support each other. An old
man led an invocation and response:

> Our cattle will drink in peace
> They will
> The disease of the cattle will go
> It will
> The disease of the calves will go
> It will
> The disease that weakens their legs will go
> It will
> It will
> It will
> And all bad things will be destroyed
> They will.

After many more sermons, the first speaker called on the young men to
stand. They formed two columns and sang a somber, rolling hymn, "The Bel-
lowing of Calves." At a signal from the speaker, the song stopped; the men
broke ranks and, brandishing their spears, charged at the watching crowd in
a show of force. They then formed their lines again, sang: "A Man Is a Man in
Cattle," and were sent to wait for the Turkana at the pass.

The ceremony concluded with another prayer and the response from the
crowd:

> They will all die!
> They will!
> Our spears will stop them!
> They will!
> Rain! It will come!
> It will!
> Will it stop?
> No!

The religious trance. The Dodoth experience possession, which is connected
with illness. Water spirits may possess people and make them ill, for instance.

But the most important way in which one may come in contact with the alternate reality is controlled dreaming, familiar to both men and women. As Nadolupe tells Marshall Thomas, "We dream. God can slaughter you in a dream, or take you to play in the water, where you do bad things" (1972: 164). Great *ngimurok*, for instance Lomotin, whom Elizabeth Marshall Thomas came to know quite well, engaged extensively in dreaming:

> Lomotin had a stool on which he sat when he rested by day, but used as a pillow by night. The stool was beautifully carved and had a special power to make his dreams come. He dreamed of ways to heal the sick, and his cures had an eerie, dreamlike quality. He would tell a patient, for instance, to sacrifice an ox, a dog, and a bird. On the stool, he dreamed his prophesies [*sic*], which, like messages, were literal. He would see it raining in a dream, then see a red ox being sacrificed, and he would know, when he awoke, that the sacrifice of such an ox would bring the rain. He was uncannily right. Whenever such a prophesy [*sic*] would rise from the depths of his mind to form itself into a dream, the result of the dream would leave the world astonished and increase his reputation. (1972: 173)

The alternate reality. The habitat. The Dodoth have one god, and his name is Akui. He is vague and remote, and little is known about him, except that he inhabits the air and sometimes settles on treetops. The alternate reality of the Dodoth shows no hierarchical ranking: Akui sends his messages to an undifferentiated laiety. He communicates with people in dreams. He uses the sacred trees of the groves as channels. The sacrificed ox is another channel. It is identified with a shooting star, which is a message from God and points to where a disease or a raid may come from.

The spirits of the dead. The dead survive as individuals, although not in any kind of heaven. Some elders return in the shape of snakes. They wear white plumes like the plumes of a headdress, and visit the sacred groves.

Other beings. The water spirits form a society and may be interpreted as neighbors. They have human form and are transparent like water, with billowing rust-colored hair. They are seen in lightning and can also float in air like mist. Sometimes they roam the earth, following rivers or appearing over wet places. They keep cattle below the rivers, marry, have children, and die. If a water spirit dies, his family moves away, and the pool where they lived dries up. They must be treated with respect, or they will possess people and cause illness or death. If that happens, an *emuron* has to paint that person with clay stripes like the stripes of a rainbow. He then persuades the water spirit to enter a goat, leads the goat around a tree, and the water spirit will climb the tree. The goat is then sacrificed.

Good fortune, misfortune, and the rituals of divination. Cattle are synonymous with good fortune, and threats to them of the nonordinary kind, that is, not, for instance, raiding, arise from within the society. A poor man is rarely visited, because his envy is considered to be dangerous to humans and cattle. The greatest danger to humans and cattle, however, comes from witches. Their ability is inherited in families. Witches betray themselves by day through extraordinary behavior, such as fixed staring or pointing, but principally, they are discovered at night, and if caught, they are put to death. The witch rides on the back of a hyena. When he nears a dwelling, he dismounts and begins to circle it in a curious stumbling or rolling motion. When he has cast his spell, he leaves.

In addition to the elaborate divination performed in connection with the sacrifice of an ox, Dodoth also use another, less formal strategy. If a man is on a journey and wants to know what is going on at home, he will sit down, remove his sandals, and drop them over and over again. The position in which they fall will give him the information he is seeking.

Ethics and its relation to religious behavior. Rules of conduct are based on social appropriateness. For instance, a man who foolishly incurs the enmity of a powerful *emuron* knows that the latter has a perfect right to cast a deadly spell as a retribution for socially inappropriate behavior.

Overview of the religious behavior of nomadic pastoralists. Despite the fact that the nomadic pastoralists discussed in this section represented three subtypes, their religious systems still had a great deal in common:

—Ritual showed a division into ceremonies for men and for women. Within the ritual structure, the "nurture" branch showed the greatest elaboration, with its shared meal and its obverse, the ritual of exorcism.

—The spirit journey was encountered principally with those herders who were also hunters. Even with them, the experience of possession assumed increased importance. Controlled dreaming was a skill especially in Africa.

—The central position in the alternate reality was occupied by a number of different beings. If herding was associated with hunting, the habitat was still present in the alternate reality, but it was split into many different aspects, and the central spot belonged to society. The habitat became diffuse, unclear, as agriculture was paired with herding, with the power representing society becoming remote and autocratic.

—As to the spirits of the dead, only the hunter-herders thought of them as living in a society that mirrored that of the living. Misfortune originated from within the society, except in the case of the hunter-herders.

—Behavior was governed by social appropriateness, and as a result of the contact with the alternate reality by way of the religious trance, there was a suffusion of a beneficial life force, neither power nor grace.

NINE

~❧~

The City Dwellers

Humans have lived in cities almost as long as they have in villages. But cities have probably been different from villages from the start. Since this point may not be generally accepted, and since what happens with respect to religious behavior in the city as the last of the human adaptations to emerge is of special interest to us as urbanites, I will include some references to ancient cities here as well. The difficulty is, of course, that no outsider, such as a foreign anthropologist, did any participant observation in the cities of ancient Mesopotamia, and what written records we have are for the most part boastings of the rulers, so I cannot quote any ethnographic material. But historians have made some educated guesses, which might be at least of some value within a comparative framework. We are better off with ancient Rome, where we have a wealth of manuscripts, political speeches, essays, personal letters, and literary creations that give us a pretty good idea about those topics that interest us here.

Let us first look at the city as a form of adaptation. We will disregard here that agriculturalists in many instances also live there and concentrate on those inhabitants who incorporate traits that set them off from other adaptations. Cities or towns need energy to function, and for the largest part of their history, this was food. However, city dwellers, ancient and modern, do not work the land. They work at many specialized tasks instead, and although the tillers that feed them make use of their services, it still means that urbanites are divorced from the habitat. With the advent of agribusiness, for whom fields are merely a commodity, this process has accelerated and has led to dangerous degradation of the land. The peasantry that supplied food to the preindustrial cities was forced to produce a surplus by means that varied through history from naked force, enslavement as in the case of serfdom, taxation, expropriation of land and rents, and other measures. In many areas of the world, some of these conditions still prevail, and "land reform" has fueled many a revolution.

Both psychologically and physiologically, the city is a burdensome place. As the sociologist Kevin Lynch summarizes it (1968: 193), cities pose a continuous perceptual stress by subjecting the city dweller to unceasing symbolic and acoustic noise; they have an uncomfortable and polluted climate; they lack diversity and flexibility; they are incoherent and repetitious; and they are not legible, in that they do not form a readable system of signs.

As far as the position of women in the city is concerned, it takes its form from the traditional religion dominant in the culture from which its inhabitants originated. In the case of those cities that we will discuss here, that substrate is agriculture, where the woman is subservient to the male head of the household. Premarital chastity continued to be enforced in the city, and married women were strictly supervised to assure that their reproductive capabilities and sexual services would remain the exclusive property of their husbands. Under such conditions, male sexual adventure became a commodity. It may be assumed that the emergence of prostitution, initially located in the temples and religiously motivated, coincided with that of the city. A contributing factor to prostitution continuing into the present is certainly also a structural one, namely, that cities represent mobile systems with shifting residence patterns, where men will seek casual alliances, easily contracted and just as easily dissolved.

However, in the course of the growth of the city, women began to loosen these bonds. Roman writers, all male, bemoaned the demise of the "moral" family, where the *pater familias* ruled and women obeyed unquestioningly and tended to their proper female duties. They heaped scorn on those women who engaged in various sports, properly the domain of men, and even demanded equal property rights in marriage. They especially decried the development that women were demanding to learn how to read and write and to study grammar. Juvenal cautioned a friend, "Let not the wife of your bosom possess a style of her own.... Let her not know all history; let there be some things in her reading which she does not understand" (Carcopino, 1971: 103). With the decay of large metropolitan centers such as Rome, the woman's position once more reverted to earlier patterns, and the struggle for secular and ritual equality waxed and waned until the present.

The city dweller is impoverished not only with respect to interaction with the habitat, but also in regard to the strength, resilience, and extensiveness of his social network. In its absence, city dwellers make use of shifting associations, and need somehow to manage the resulting insecurity. One strategy is to establish friendships. Jacobson describes it for townsmen in Uganda, but it is equally well known in other cities, also. The more mobile the social environment, the more rapidly such ties shift, and the more protracted becomes the time required for someone to be called a close friend. From these ephemeral friendships, a stable network is produced, which remains intact, although the people involved in it may change. These networks act like "little worlds"; the overall membership is permanent, so that there is always a chance to encounter one another again.

City dwellers bring to their new environments the faiths they held before and pass these on to their children. Sometimes easily, sometimes over several generations, these systems weaken and become meaningless; they become secularized. The same process was also operating in antiquity. "One obtains the impression—confirmed by other indications," writes the American historian A. Leo Oppenheim, "that the influence of religion on the individual as well as on the community as a whole was unimportant in Mesopotamia" (1964: 176). The French historian Jérôme Carcopino speaks in similar terms about the role of traditional religion in classical Rome. Quoting from the works of various writers, he shows how instead of offering experience, the traditional religion demanded belief, and that these urbanites could no longer muster. He quotes, for instance, the poet Juvenal, writing, "That there are such things as Manes and kingdoms below ground, and punt holes, and Stygian pools black with frogs, and all those thousands crossing over in a single bark—these things not even boys believe, except such as are not yet old enough to have paid their penny bath" (1971: 140).

Much conflict between the generations in the cities arises from the fact that the older generation cleaves to the faith of its fathers, and the younger generation finds the same faith irrelevant to its life and experience. So the city dwellers are often subjected to heavy-handed missionizing from traditional faiths, be that from electronic evangelists in this country or from Islamic mullahs in the cities of Iran. But despite a few apparent successes, such effort is usually short-lived. You might as well talk a river into flowing upstream. As the psychiatrist Roland Laing says, "We live in a secular world. To adapt to this world, the child abdicates its ecstasy. . . . Having lost our experience of the spirit, we are expected to have faith. But this faith comes to be a belief in a reality that is not evident" (1967: 144).

In this intellectual climate, religious observances become a social routine. Carcopino shows this to be true of the great public sacrifices, as well as of other religious observances in imperial Rome, and it is the same story in modern Tokyo. As the anthropologist tells of the inhabitants of Shitayama-cho, a Tokyo ward, the upkeep of the local shrine is for them simply a matter of fulfilling the duty of a good citizen, on much the same level as paying taxes. Individuals visit such shrines on average fewer than ten times a year. Joining a congregation for social gain is a familiar strategy in the city. In this vein, an American father told the sociologist studying Levittown, "I don't quite believe the teachings . . . but it's good for the kids to have the background. Also, it's because I bought a house, and for becoming part of the community."

Yet in the long run, the absence of religious experience, what might be called trance deprivation, cannot be supported. This accounts for the fact that eventually all cities, past as well as present, will show the appearance of cults or movements answering to this need. It happened in Rome, where "chappels," groups of philosophical sects, appeared, as well as brotherhoods committed to various Oriental mysteries, all making available trance-mediated religious experiences. In a familiar pattern, they were ridiculed; Juvenal attacked the supposedly shameless exploitation they practiced, claiming that their rituals were injurious to health and even obscene. Yet they endured. One of them was the infant Christian movement.

The sample. The five ethnographies used in this chapter for comparison all deal with modern industrial cities. They describe itinerant townsmen of Uganda (Africa), a Tokyo ward, the South American city of São Paulo, Brazil, Levittown, New York, and black street-corner men in Washington, D.C.

A city ritual. Because of the diversity encountered in the city, it is difficult to find a ritual that would be more or less characteristic throughout this cultural adaptation. Typically, the one that comes to mind is not a religious but a secular ritual, namely, certain sporting events. These are the events in which instead of demonstrating skill—the fastest runner or the best swimmer—the purpose is to eliminate an opponent and, where the contestants can easily switch roles, to be either winners or losers. As I will argue, they are actually giant exorcisms, an elaboration of the "nurture" branch of the Birth Complex. Rome had its circus; in the modern world, there is football in America, sumo wrestling in Japan, and soccer in the rest of the world. They bring out crowds and arouse passions. A spectator described a soccer game in Mexico City in the following way:

> When you watch a soccer game, it is like good and evil being played out. You believe in your own team, it can do nothing wrong. The bad guys are the other team. You go to a game because everybody goes. But once you are there, everything changes. The flags are waving, and there is a lot of color, a lot of green. Your favorite team is on one side, they look so good in their uniforms. The other team is there too, maybe from Costa Rica, but you don't pay much attention to them. Then they play the national anthem. In school you had to learn it, and probably you didn't care for it. But now it sounds great and everybody sings along. The other team's national anthem is played too, but that doesn't sound impressive at all. They release some white pigeons, and everything is very nice.
>
> When the match starts, you want your team to win, and no matter what they do, everything is always right. Whether they kick a field goal, or just dribble, it doesn't matter. It's so beautiful, you've never seen anything like that before. But when the other team does the same thing, it looks terrible, it doesn't have the same class.
>
> You start shouting and screaming, and you can shout obscenities, nobody knows what it is you're shouting. Everybody does the same thing, and you never realize that you are shouting that much until when the game is over and you calm down, then you realize that your throat is hurting. Maybe two or three days later you still can't talk because your throat is really sore.
>
> At some point you get the feeling that you don't care what happens to you. If there were violence, I could get involved because I don't perceive things clearly anymore. All you know is that you want to do something. If something

were to trigger a riot, I would want to participate. Everyone is one unit, you don't have any responsibility. There was an instance that I remember. I went to a game, it was the Mexican team against Costa Rica, and we were sitting five or six rows away from the front line. We were shouting obscenities, and there were some plain-clothesmen, and one of the guys turned to me and said something like, "Keep it cool," and I was so mad at him. I felt that he was infringing on what I felt. If he would have gotten up and done something to me, I could have slugged him. Nothing happened, but it could easily have turned into a riot. If somebody at that point says something against your team, the team becomes irrelevant, and the confrontation is between you and the others.

You want your team to win so badly that if the Devil were to exist and would arrive at that point and ask you for your soul in exchange for your team winning, you wouldn't give it a second thought. You would say yes, whatever that might mean.

Your body goes into contortions, you want your team to win so badly. Then when it loses, you simply can't stand it. I feel real low, terrible, for days. When it wins, you are happy, but only for a split second. It is hard to describe, it doesn't seem to last. (From my fieldnotes)

The media are used to calling this kind of sporting event a "competition," but that, I think, does not account for the passion unleashed, the feeling of confrontation that switches from vicarious to real, the intense depression as the result of a lost game, and the fleeting sense of jubilation about a win. I suggested above that we are dealing with an exorcism, and in a curious way, we are indeed reminded by this perceptive report of the struggle of the Evenk shaman against the disease-causing agent described in the previous chapter. The question is, What is being exorcized? The Evenk shaman expelled spirits of disease. That is, of course, not the case in this soccer game. Also, unlike a disease spirit, every participant in a soccer game could be a loser and the next time a winner. It seems to be an endless chain that never comes to a satisfying conclusion. Compulsively, the ritual has to be repeated over and over again, a confrontation without end.

The last point may, in fact, hide the clue. It possibly has something to do with how many people a person can tolerate around him, in close contact. Anthropologists know, for instance, that an ideal hunter-gatherer band consists of about 25 members. On occasion, such bands join in larger groups, for a medicine dance, for trading, or for some other reason. Soon, however, fights break out, and the bands drift off, separating again. Among sedentary populations, the ideal village size is about 130. This seems to be something like a biological constant, for when this number is exceeded, be it among the Yąnomamö Indians of the rainforest of tropical South America or the Christian Hutterite Bruderhof settlements in North America, conflicts arise, and the community fissions. Some people move out to found a new village. As we know, of course, the city contains many more people than the ideal 130, and yet

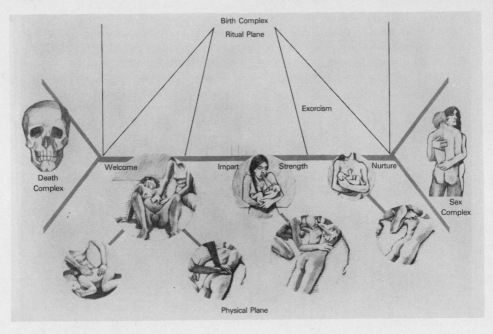

Figure 11. Urban ritual.

there is no way in which it could fission. So how does the urbanite get rid of the terrible burden on the nervous system that he is not programmed for genetically and that the continuous contact with many people subjects him to every day of the week? He exorcizes it on the playing field within the framework of spectator sport, over and over again. (See fig. 11.)

The social history of modern urban societies equally demonstrates that exorcism is the one solution for all ills that is resorted to repeatedly during upheavals in the urban centers. Except as it is wont to happen in the city, the system is displaced toward the ordinary-reality side of life. In the French Revolution, played out in Paris, it was the nobility whose physical extirpation from the body politic was to bring on the millennium. Marxist class struggle and the dreams of anarchists are millennial in character, and in the Russian Marxist revolution, it once more took on an exorcistic character: If all capitalists could be bodily eliminated, nothing would stand in the way of the golden age. Since for inherent structural reasons a new ruling class will once more emerge, the contest continues, and the exorcism is compulsively repeated, just as in the football game.

The religious trance City dwellers are no strangers to the highly aroused ecstasy. They have many cults, as mentioned above, and if we disregard those of Eastern origin with their meditative disciplines, we find that these cults center mainly on possession. This is true of the so-called New Religions of Japan, which spread through most of the large cities of that country after the Second World War. Pentecostalism, with its experience of possession by the Holy Spirit, is a worldwide phenomenon. In Rio de Janeiro, São Paulo, and other cities of Brazil, the mediumistic healing cult Umbanda has millions of adherents. And Spiritualism, another possession cult, which started in the United States more than a hundred years ago, is still a going concern both here and in many urban centers around the world.

Another form of the same change in perception is most assuredly involved in those "flashes of insight" well known from science. Its presence is easily recognized in a description of scientists at work given by the physician Lewis Thomas:

> Scientists at work have the look of creatures following genetic instructions. . . . When they are near an answer, their hair stands on end, they sweat, they are awash in their own adrenalin. . . . There is an almost ungovernable, biological mechanism at work in scientific behavior at its best. . . . It is in the abrupt, unaccountable aggregation of random notions and intuitions, known in science as good ideas, that the high points are attained. (*Science* 179 (1973): 1283)

There are many examples of a similar nature in the biographies of outstanding researchers. Gabor, for instance, the developer of holography, tells that he got the idea that led to his epoch-making idea suddenly one day in 1947, while he was waiting his turn at a tennis court in England. It was a sudden flash of insight that showed him how to create his famous system of lensless three-dimensional photography.

Heisenberg, the originator of modern quantum mechanics, had a similar initial experience that produced one of the major insights of twentieth-century physics:

> I had the feeling that through the surface of atomic phenomena, I was looking at a strangely beautiful interior, and felt almost giddy at the thought that I now had to probe this wealth of mathematical structures nature had so generously spread before me. (*Newsweek*, February 16, 1976)

The alternate reality. The habitat. From his/her nonurban past, the city dweller has carried along various inhabitants of the alternate reality, but usually, with the possible exception of Japan, the central position in the alternate reality is stripped of all aspects of the habitat. It is a purely social entity. Another development is noteworthy at least in Western cities. According to statistical studies carried out early in the 1980s, some urbanites still believe in God: 80

percent of them in this country and in Ireland, although only 31 percent in Germany, but this percentage drops when it comes to hell and the Devil: The figures for hell are 66 percent in the United States, 54 percent in Ireland, and only 14 percent in Germany, and for the Devil, 66 percent in the United States and in Ireland and 18 percent in Germany. It seems that while urbanites have no quarrel with a benevolent deity in the position of dominance in heaven, they are determined to exorcize Satan from their alternate reality.

Many sociologists hold the view that cities are the birthplace of specialization. However, as we saw in chapter 7, the alternate reality of agriculturalists contained a central power source, which was surrounded by an aura of specialists. Specialists also appear in ordinary village life. The impression arises, however, that the urbanites displaced that entire complex into ordinary reality. But in the process the central position became empty. In ordinary reality, then, it was the modern urban centers that in many instances did away with royalty, or completely emasculated it. Architecturally, there are numerous modern cities that have no real center, or urban blight is eroding what was once the heart of the city.

The spirits of the dead. City dwellers accept as absolute dogma that the spirits of the departed live on in the alternate reality. In 1975, an American physician, Raymond A. Moody, published a little book that soon became a best-seller. He called it *Life after Life*, and it contains a collection of first-person reports by people who, clinically speaking, had died and then were brought back to life. A number of other collections have been published since then. For the most part, such persons tell about passing through a dark tunnel and on the other side, entirely in keeping with an empty alternate reality, being met by only a few close relatives and friends.[1]

Other than taking flowers to the grave, which can be thought of as an offering to the spirits of the dead, Western urbanites do not keep up any close contact with these spirits. In Japan, however, ancestor worship is a powerful tradition, and shows no signs of weakening in the cities. All deceased of the family have their names inscribed on tablets, which are kept in the *butsudan*, a family shrine. Food offerings are brought to them, and they are treated as nearly as possible as they were when still alive; the rite is also utilized to produce a meditative state (Dore, 1958: 322). Not all the families in Tokyo's Shitayama-cho had a *butsudan*, reports Dore, especially not if the father of the family was himself a younger son. However, if one of those households lost a wife or a child, the installation of a *butsudan* soon followed. Most of the so-called New Religions of Japan have mediums who during rituals become possessed by the ancestral spirits of their clients, making communication with them possible.

Still another variation can be found in Umbanda. Healing takes place in centers, where trained mediums are possessed by various spirits, who counsel the clients on their problems: health, business, personal relations. Nominally, the spirits are of African origin, but most people who go to the centers think of them as the members of the family they had to leave behind when they came to the city. One of them is the indulgent grandfather, another the stern father, still another a child, or even a friend or a stranger. They represent, as it were, everybody's personal spirits of the dead. What is revealing in this context is the fact that these spirits used to be part of the older Candomblé spirit possession cult: They did not become spirits of the dead until they were adopted into Umbanda, clearly in response to an intensely felt need.

Good fortune, misfortune, and the rituals of divination. In a cult called *Quimbanda*, adherents of Umbanda have a "magical" strategy for the men which serves to ward off evil perpetrated against them by women. But this is the exception. In most cities of the world, changes of fortune are attributed to the actions of impersonal agencies, to chance, luck, and statistical probability, to "being at the right/wrong place at the right/wrong time." For many, astrology provides a welcome explanation for odd or unexpected events, either good or bad, seeking the cause for them in the constellation of the stars. There is nothing anybody can do about the effect of these forces, they cannot be influenced by any ritual or supplication, they cannot be exorcized, and they are not represented in the alternate reality. Humans are the helpless victims of their workings. With all their exuberance, the cities foster an undercurrent of fatalism. This may be one reason why all manner of divinatory practices flourish in the city, from astrology to tarot cards.

Ethics and its relation to religious behavior. Because of the shifting, impermanent relationships in the city that provide little social control for the individual, moral decisions are made on the basis of what serves a person's immediate needs. To ask whether an action is good or evil would in most instances be unrealistic. From his observations in Washington, D.C., Liebow relates the following example, involving a man named Leroy, a frail and ailing homosexual. In return for a place to live, Leroy took care of his girlfriend's children and little brothers.

> During one period, when he had resolved to stop his homosexual practices, he resumed them only on those occasions when there was no money in the house and only long enough to "turn a trick" and get food for the children. When this did not work he raided the Safeway, despite his terror of still another jail sentence. (1967: 37)

Stealing is, of course, morally wrong as far as the religion of the dominant society is concerned. In Leroy's case, however, it served survival, not only his own but also that of the children that he was caring for. In most large cities, in fact, stealing is institutionalized: Employers calculate it in when estimating their probable losses, deducting the estimated value of what will be stolen from the wages they pay and adding it to the prices they charge. In other words, there is a formal, legal system of moral values, and an informal one; frequently the two systems collide, and the informal system of personal appropriateness has to be given preference. It is even built into modern legal systems, which are formulated by urbanites, replacing the older unyielding judgment of "if not good, then evil." It is expressed in the procedure of plea-bargaining, as well as in such principles as "extenuating circumstances."

Expectably, not everyone will agree on what an extenuating circumstance may be in a particular case, and quite generally the principle of individual appropriateness has led to a veritable crisis in city ethics and morality. At a recent (1987) conference on family violence at Ohio State University, one speaker told about a fifteen-year-old girl whom he had asked in counseling if she had ever told anyone that her father had sexually abused her. She said once, when she was ten, she had told two friends. They said that their fathers had done the same thing. Two years later, she told a sixteen-year-old babysitter, who said that her father had molested her, as well. "When I hear this," the speaker added, "I wonder just what the norms are in society."

Just as there seem to be no generally accepted rules about incest, as the above case indicates, urban society is faced daily with questions about ethics for which no one has any answer, because technical and scientific development has long outstripped the ability of this type of society to formulate any relevant moral code. Who is to decide whether it is admissible and proper to release engineered microbes into the environment? Companies worried about protecting sensitive computer data against hackers and other intruders are enjoined to train employees in computer law and to give them a clear statement on ethics, but the company has to find and hire the philosopher first who would be an expert in the field of such ethics. There are problems of a similar nature in medicine, in geriatrics, in fact in every field in both the natural and the behavioral sciences. The same goes for politics, both domestic and international, where the need for ethics and a humane moral code has in many instances not even been recognized yet, or if it has been recognized, nothing is being done about it.

The semantics of "religion." I cannot reconstruct this category from the data I have on Africa, Japan, or Brazil. The respective category for English-speaking city dwellers, I think, is *religion*. I have no doubts about two things: One, it must exist for the others also, simply by internal logic; and two, it must be different from the agriculturalist category of the same geographic area. For the Western urbanite, the contact with the alternate reality in the "mystic state," realized for the most part only in theory, provides not power, grace, or blessing, but "symbols." This makes it possible for the city dweller to think of the religious trance and the ecstatic experience as psychobiological phenomena, to be analyzed, described, and categorized, and the alternate reality not as "reality" but as a symbol for whatever a particular society considers essential or important. This maneuver takes the entire category out of the realm of experience and gives it a communicative, a metalinguistic, character, in agreement with the urgent need of the urbanite to stay in verbal contact with others. The illusion of the city dweller is that this is the "ultimate" truth.[2]

Conclusion

There is much speculation in the literature on whether religion, not as this or that denomination, but as a human behavior as such, will endure. As we saw in our dicussion of urban patterns, there is indeed a great deal of secularization going on, and religion, in the sense in which we use the term here, seems quite impoverished. So if we are truly entering into an era of enormous cities, as some observers predict, where divergent lifestyles will be swallowed up, destroyed, wiped out, then perhaps the question is justified. Not only are large segments of the population of the modern industrial city indifferent to all religious expression, but often they are even actively engaged in attacking it. What they want instead is "objective rationality," which denies the existence of an alternate reality. Religion is to be tolerated only if it is paired with "due restraint." It should relinquish any claim to relevance for ordinary life, resembling more the special behaviors of some exclusive social club. And on the intellectual level, it is to confine itself to issues of history, psychology, sociology, or philosophy. The premise informing such attitudes is, as one social scientist put it,

> that certain kinds of religion—emotionally fervent religion, authoritarian sectarianism, spiritual ecstasy and mysticism—are socially regressive and thus hostile to mankind's deepest aspirations. (Robbins and Anthony, 1982, 29: 3)

Yet at the time these views are propagated, there is in the same cities an eruption of just the kind of religious movements that were identified above as being most objectionable to the world view of the urbanite. (See, e.g., Needleman and Baker, 1978.) The various "new" religions exhibit "emotionality, spiritual ecstasy and mysticism, and strident supernaturalism." These are, of course, the very traits that we found to be the core of religion worldwide. We called them the religious trance and the alternate reality, and found that together they formed the heart piece around which community life could be constructed.

Why should such religions crop up again and again in the urban sphere? Should they not disappear there altogether, since the societal type determines religious behavior? Such a proposition ignores the fact that all behavior has two sources: In addition to our culture, there is also our biology. We are born, like the little lady of Tlatilco (pl. 5), with two faces. To put it into modern terms, we have a biological propensity for experiencing both the ordinary and the alternate reality. In the long run, as I maintained above, humans cannot tolerate ecstasy deprivation. The religious trance is an indestructible part of our genetic heritage. No amount of urban living can change that. If humans were no longer taught any religions, they would, I think, spontaneously create new ones from the content of ecstatic experiences, combined with bits and pieces transmitted by language and folklore. And some day another artist would come along and shape once more a three-eyed lady.

Notes

1. THE RELIGIOUS: CAN IT BE DEFINED?

1. Unless otherwise noted, the authors are American anthropologists.

2. Tylor's minimal definition of religion is the favorite of dictionary writers. The *Random House Dictionary of the English Language* (1971) starts out its definition of religion with, "Concern over what exists beyond the visible world, differentiated from philosophy in that it operates through faith and intuition rather than reason, and generally including the idea of the existence of a single being, a group of beings, an eternal principle, or a transcendent spiritual entity that created the world...."

3. According to Yogic tradition, the human body possesses a number of centers, called chakras, roughly corresponding to Western plexuses, usually seven in ascending order, each one endowed with its own essence.

2. HUMAN EVOLUTION AND THE ORIGINS AND EVOLUTION OF RELIGIOUS BEHAVIOR

1. Some of the arguments in this chapter are based on papers submitted to a conference on "The Origins and Evolution of Language and Speech," held in New York in 1975 and published under the above title as an Annal of the New York Academy of Science, edited by Stevan Harnad, Horst D. Steklis, and Jane Lancaster.

2. In an attempt to discover at what point in time humans might have started to speak, Philip Lieberman (1975) reconstructed the soft tissue on Neanderthal skulls. He came to the conclusion that they could not have had speech. Skeptical fellow paleontologists joked that not only would the creature have had difficulty talking, but it could not have eaten, either.

3. THE INDEPENDENT VARIABLE: INTERACTION WITH THE HABITAT

1. The discussion summarizes the results of a conference on "Man the Hunter," held in Chicago in April, 1966. The book that brings together the papers presented at that meeting was edited by Richard B. Lee and Irvin DeVore.

2. Charles A. Reed, ed., *Origin of Agriculture*, Papers from a conference, 1973 (The Hague: Mouton, 1978).

3. I have used the Spanish translation of the work by Georges Raynaud, director in the early part of this century of the Section of the Religions of Pre-Columbian America of the Paris Ecole des Hautes Etudes, as well as the excellent study and translation of Dennis Tedlock.

4. DEPENDENT VARIABLES

1. For a review, see, e.g., Erika Bourguignon, *Culture and the Varieties of Consciousness*, Addison-Wesley Module in Anthropology, no. 47 (1974), and her book of 1979, *Psychological Anthropology: An Introduction to Human Nature and Cultural Differences*; Larry G. Peters and Douglas Price-Williams, "A Phenomenological Overview of Trance," *Transcultural Psychiatric Research Review* 20 (1983): 5–39; and Roger Walsh, "The Consciousness Disciplines and the Behavioral Sciences," *American Journal of Psychiatry* 137 (1980): 663–673.

2. A summary of this project is given in the introduction to Erika Bourguignon, ed., *Religion, Altered States of Consciousness, and Social Change* (1973).

3. For further details, see my book of 1972, *Speaking in Tongues: A Cross-Cultural Study of Glossolalia*.

4. On the basis of the work done by Robert Ornstein and others (see Ornstein, 1972, *The Psychology of Consciousness*), it was thought that the religious trance was an activity located in the right hemisphere. This was not confirmed by later research.

5. See Cushing's essay on Zuñi fetishes, in *Zuñi, Selected Writings of Frank Hamilton Cushing* (1979), pp. 194–204.

6. Japanese female mediumship may have been imported from the Asiatic mainland. Both China and Korea, with large peasant populations, have female mediums.

7. Arthur Waley's translation of the I Ching is superior, but in this country, the translation that Cary F. Baynes prepared from Richard Wilhelm's translation of the I Ching into German is better known.

8. I am grateful for this information to Mr. Olu Makinde, artist in residence at Denison University, Granville, Ohio, in the 1976–1977 school year.

9. Jarold Ramsey, ed., *Coyote Was Going There: Indian Literature of the Oregon Country* (Seattle: University of Washington Press 1977); "The Elk, the Hunter, and His Greedy Father," pp. 64–65.

10. Ruth Benedict, ed., *Tales of the Cochiti Indians* (Albuquerque: University of New Mexico Press, 1931); "The Wife Who Was Cast Out by Her Husband," pp. 120–122.

11. Gábor Bereczki, *Földisten lánykérőben: Finnugor mitológiai és történeti énekek* (Budapest: Európa Könyvkiadó, 1982); "Kazán Várost hova építék?" [Where should the City of Kazán Be Built?] pp. 327–331 (translation by me).

12. Grimm Brothers, *Kinder- und Hausmärchen* (Leipzig: R. Becker, n.d.); "Die weisse und die schwarze Braut" [The White Bride and the Black Bride], pp. 506–510 (translation by me).

13. The Marshalls are a well-known family of Africanists. Lorna Marshall's son Peter Marshall's films about the !Kung Bushmen and her daughter Elizabeth Marshall Thomas's book *The Harmless People* (1959) have greatly enriched our knowledge of this society.

5. THE HUNTER-GATHERERS

1. Basic information about the lifeways of the hunter-gatherers can be found in Richard B. Lee and Irvin DeVore, eds., *Man the Hunter* (1968). Unfortunately, the editors carefully skirt any reference to religious behavior.

2. The Bushmen speak a click language; the clicks are sounds that distinguish meaning, and they are represented by such marks as ≠, !, and //. There are also others, of course.

6. THE HORTICULTURALISTS

1. No reference is made to the texts of the various Shavante songs. According to Professor Maybury-Lewis (personal communication), so many archaic terms appear in these songs that modern Shavante no longer understand them.

2. A book about the experiments with the trance postures is in preparation.

3. Professor Baer was unaware of the trance postures at the time of his fieldwork with the Matsigenka.

4. Deeply annoyed by a Protestant missionary who would come shouting into the village and yell recriminations against the Yạnomamös' "filthy spirits" whenever he heard the chanting of the shamans, Napoleon Chagnon decided to participate in the rite himself. He describes the details of his trance experience in the second edition of his ethnography about the Yạnomamö (1977: 157–158).

7. THE AGRICULTURALISTS

1. One of the most frequently quoted works on this topic is E. E. Evans-Pritchard's 1937 work *Witchcraft, Oracles, and Magic among the Azande*. See also my *How about Demons? Possession and Exorcism in the Modern World* (1988).

9. THE CITY DWELLERS

1. In a report on Edith Fiore's work with hypnotic regression (*Fate*, November, 1980, pp. 55–62), she is quoted as saying that she had the distinct impression with regressed subjects that the Beings of Light many of them spoke of were not judges. They were instead compassionate advisers, who guided and counseled the "surviving personality," that is, "the soul between two reincarnations."

2. A few critics of my 1972 book *Speaking in Tongues: A Cross-Cultural Study of Glossolalia* pointed out that I had not devoted sufficient attention to the symbolic significance of the behavior. I found that irritating, because to me it seemed that I had made an important discovery. I had identified a regularly recurring pattern in which there was the religious trance manifesting its effect on the vocalization, on the one hand, and the alternate reality as experienced by the worshippers, on the other hand, both together providing the blessing of the Holy Spirit. It was what the data had suggested, and it was an intellectually satisfying analysis. I saw no need for a superimposed secondary analysis involving symbols. It was not until I had worked out the linguistic analysis of the term *religion* the way I discussed it here that I realized that what was expressed in the repeated discomfort of some of my readers about my neglect of "symbolism" actually demonstrated a cultural difference. I was brought up by East European peasants, and thus both for my agriculturalist informants and for me, the central issue was Grace, not Symbol.

Bibliography

Albert, Ethel M. 1964. "Rhetorics," "Logic," and "Poetics" in Burundi: Culture Patterning of Speech Behavior. *American Anthropologist* 66 (2/6): 35–54.

Andrew, R. J. 1976. Use of Formants in the Grunts of Baboons and Other Nonhuman Primates. In *Origins and Evolution of Language and Speech*, ed. Stevan Harnad, Horst D. Steklis, and Jane Lancaster. New York: Annals of the New York Academy of Science, vol. 280, pp. 673–693.

Anisimov, Arkadiy Federovich. 1963. The Shaman's Tent of the Evenks and the Origin of the Shamanistic Rite. Translated from *Trudy Instituta etnografii Akademii nauk SSSR*, 1952, vol. 18, pp. 199–238. In *Studies in Siberian Shamanism*, ed. Henry N. Michael, pp. 84–123. Toronto: University of Toronto Press.

Arberry, Arthur J. 1950. *Sufism: An Account of the Mystics of Islam*. London: George Allen and Unwin.

Avalon, Arthur (Sir John Woodroffe). 1974 (orig. 1919). *The Serpent Power: The Secrets of Tantric and Shaktic Yoga*. London: Luzac and Co. Reprint. New York: Dover.

Babb, Lawrence A. 1975. *The Divine Hierarchy: Popular Hinduism in Central India*. New York: Columbia University Press.

Baer, Gerhard. 1984. *Die Religion der Matsigenka: Ost-Peru*. Basel: Wepf.

Baroja, Julio Caro. 1964 (Spanish orig. 1961). *The World of the Witches*. Chicago: University of Chicago Press.

Barry, Herbert; I. L. Child; and M. K. Bacon. 1967. Relation of Child Training to Subsistence Economy. In *Cross- Cultural Approaches: Readings in Comparative Research*, ed. C. S. Ford. New Haven: HRAF Press.

Barth, Fredrik. 1961. *Nomads of South Persia: The Basseri Tribe of the Khamseh Confederacy*. Oslo: Oslo University Press. London: George Allen and Unwin.

Bascom, William. 1969a. *Ifa Divination: Communication between Gods and Men in West Africa*. Bloomington: Indiana University Press.

————. 1969b. *The Yoruba of Southwestern Nigeria*. New York: Holt, Rinehart, and Winston.

Beattie, John. 1960. *Bunyoro: An African Kingdom*. New York: Holt, Rinehart and Winston.

Benedict, Ruth. 1981 (orig. 1931). *Tales of the Cochiti Indians*. Albuquerque: University of New Mexico Press.

Bereczki, Gábor, ed. 1982. *Földisten lánykérőben: Finnugor mitológiai és történeti énekek*. Budapest: Európai Könyvkiadó.

Bernal, Ignacio. 1969. *The Olmec World*. Berkeley: University of California Press.

Big Jack of Hilibi. 1929. The Orphan and the Origin of Corn. In *Myths and Tales of the Southeastern Indians*, ed. John R. Swanton, pp. 10–15. Washington, D.C.: U.S. Government Printing Office.

Birdwhistell, Ray L. 1952. *Introduction to Kinesics* (orig. pub. Louisville, Ky.: University of Louisville). University Microfilms, a Xerox Company, Ann Arbor, Michigan, 1968.

Birket-Smith, Kaj. 1971 (orig. 1959). *The Eskimos*. New York: Crown Publishers.

Blacker, Carmen. 1975. *The Catalpa Bow: A Study of Shamanistic Practices in Japan*. London: George Allen and Unwin.

Bloomfield, Leonard. 1933. *Language*. New York: Holt, Rinehart and Winston.

Bohannan, Paul. 1973. Rethinking Culture: A Project for Current Anthropologists. *Current Anthropology* 14: 357–372.

Bourguignon, Erika. 1968. *A Cross-Cultural Study of Dissociational States: Final Report*. Columbus, Ohio: Research Foundation.

———. 1970. Hallucination and Trance: An Anthropologist's Perspective. In *Origin and Mechanisms of Hallucination*, ed. Wolfram Keup. New York: Plenum Press.

———. 1972. Dreams and Altered States of Consciousness in Anthropological Research. In *Psychological Anthropology*, new ed., ed. F. L. K. Hsu. Boston: Schenkman.

———. 1973. *Religion, Altered States of Consciousness, and Social Change*. Columbus: Ohio State University Press.

———. 1974. *Culture and the Varieties of Consciousness*. Addison-Wesley Module in Anthropology, no. 47.

———. 1976. *Possession*. San Francisco: Chandler and Sharp.

———. 1979. *Psychological Anthropology: An Introduction to Human Nature and Cultural Differences*. New York: Holt, Rinehart and Winston.

Braidwood, Robert J. 1975. *Prehistoric Men*. 8th ed. Glenview, Ill.: Scott, Foresman, and Co.

Brant, Charles S., ed. 1969. *Jim Whitewolf: The Life of a Kiowa Apache Indian*. New York: Dover.

de Brosses, Ch. R. 1760. *Du Culte des dieux fétiches ou parallèle de l'ancienne religion de l'Egypte avec la religion actuelle de la Nigritie*. Paris.

Burridge, Kenelm. 1960. *Mambu: A Study of Melanesian Cargo Movements and Their Social and Ideological Background*. London: Methuen. (New York: Harper Torchbooks Reprint, 1970).

Butt, Audrey. 1962. Réalité et idéal dans la pratique chamanique. *L'Homme* 2: 5–52.

Campbell, Joseph. 1975 (Dec.). Seven Levels of Consciousness. *Psychology Today*, pp. 77–78.

Cancian, Francesca M. 1975. *What Are Norms? A Study of Beliefs and Action in a Maya Community*. London: Cambridge University Press.

Carcopino, Jérôme. 1971. *Daily Life in Ancient Rome*. New York: Bantam Books.

Cassirer, Ernst. 1944. *An Essay on Man*. New Haven: Yale University Press.

Castaneda, Carlos. 1968. *The Teachings of Don Juan: A Yaqui Way of Knowledge*. Berkeley and Los Angeles: University of California Press.

———. 1971 (Pocket Book ed. 1972). *A Separate Reality: Further Conversations with Don Juan*. New York: Simon and Schuster.

———. 1972. *Journey to Ixtlan: The Lessons of Don Juan*. New York: Simon and Schuster.

———. 1974. *Tales of Power*. New York: Simon and Schuster.

———. 1977. *The Second Ring of Power*. New York: Simon and Schuster.

Cawte, John. 1974. *Medicine Is the Law: Studies in Psychiatric Anthropology of Australian Tribal Societies*. Honolulu: University Press of Hawaii.

Chagnon, Napoleon A. 1968. *Yąnomamö: The Fierce People*. New York: Holt, Rinehart, Winston. (2nd ed. 1977.)

Chapman, Charlotte Gower. 1971. *Milocca: A Sicilian Village*. Cambridge, Mass.: Schenkman.

Chernetsov, V. N. 1963. Concepts of the Soul among the Ob Ugrians. In *Studies in Siberian Shamanism*, ed. Henry Michael. Toronto: University of Toronto Press.

Chomsky, Noam. 1965a. *Aspects of the Theory of Syntax*. Cambridge, Mass.: MIT Press.

———. 1965b. *Syntactic Structures*. The Hague: Mouton.

———. 1972, enl. ed. *Language and Mind*. New York: Harcourt, Brace, Jovanovich.

Christopher, Robert C. 1983. *The Japanese Mind.* New York: Linden Press, Simon and Schuster.

Coe, Ralph T. 1976. *Sacred Circles: Two Thousand Years of North American Indian Art.* N.p.: Arts Council of Great Britain.

Cohen, Mark Nathan. 1977. *The Food Crisis in Prehistory: Overpopulation and the Origins of Agriculture.* New Haven: Yale University Press.

Cushing, Frank Hamilton. 1979. *Zuñi: Selected Writings.* Lincoln: University of Nebraska Press.

Darmadji, Tjiptonu and Wolfgang Pfeiffer. 1969. Kuda Kepang—Ein javanisches Trancespiel. *Selecta*, no. 4.

Das, N. N., and H. Gastaud. 1957. Variations d'activité électrique du cerveau, du coeur et des muscles squelettiques au cours de la méditation et de l'extase yogique. *Clinic. Neurophysiol.* [suppl] 6: 211–219.

David-Neel, Alexandra. 1971 (French orig. 1929). *Magic and Mystery in Tibet.* New York: Dover. (French title: *Mystiques et magiciens du Thibet*).

Davis, Kingsley. 1968. The Urbanization of the Human Population. In *Cities*, ed. Denis Flanagan. New York: Alfred A. Knopf.

Dentan, Robert K. 1968. *The Semai: A Nonviolent People of Malaya.* New York: Holt, Rinehart and Winston.

———. 1970. Labels and Rituals in Semai Classification. *Ethnology* 9: 16–25

DeVos, George. 1974. Psychologically Oriented Studies in Comparative Cultural Behavior. In *Frontiers of Anthropology*, ed. Murray J. Leaf, pp. 189-230. New York: Van Nostrand.

Diószegi, Vilmos. 1958. *A sámánhit emlékei a magyar népi műveltségben.* Budapest: Akadémiai Kiadó.

Dore, R. P. 1958. *City Life in Japan: A Study of a Tokyo Ward.* Berkeley: University of California Press.

Douglas, Mary. 1962. *Purity and Danger: An Analysis of Concepts of Pollution and Taboo.* New York, Washington: Praeger.

Downs, James F. 1966. *The Two Worlds of the Washo: An Indian Tribe of California and Nevada.* New York: Holt, Rinehart, and Winston.

Drucker, Philip. 1963. *Indians of the Northwest Coast.* Garden City, N.Y.: Natural History Press.

———. 1965. *Cultures of the North Pacific Coast.* Scranton, Pa.: Chandler.

Duerr, Hans Peter. 1985. *Dreamtime: Concerning the Boundary between Wilderness and Civilization*, translated by Felicitas Goodman. Oxford: Basil Blackwell.

Durkheim, Emile. 1912 (English 1915). *Les Formes élémentaires de la vie religieuse.* Paris.

Ekvall, Robert B. 1952. *Tibetan Skylines.* New York: Travel Book Club.

———. 1964. *Religious Observances in Tibet: Patterns and Function.* Chicago: University of Chicago Press.

———. 1968. *Fields on the Hoof: Nexus of Tibetan Nomadic Pastoralism.* New York: Holt, Rinehart, and Winston.

Eliade, Mircea. 1964. *Shamanism: Archaic Techniques of Ecstasy.* New York: Pantheon Books.

———. 1969. *Yoga: Immortality and Freedom.* 2d ed. Princeton: Princeton University Press. Bolingen Series LVI.

Elkin, A. P. 1938 (Doubleday Anchor ed. 1964). *The Australian Aborigines.* London: Angus and Robertson.

Emerson, V. F. 1972. Can Belief Systems Influence Neurophysiology? Some Implications of Research on Meditation. *Newsletter-Review*, R. M. Bucke Memorial Soc. 5: 20–32.

Espíndola, Julio Cesar. 1961. A propósito del mesianismo en las tribus guaraní. *América Indígena* 21: 307–325.

Evans-Pritchard, E. E. 1937. *Witchcraft, Oracles, and Magic among the Azande.* Oxford: Clarendon Press.

———. 1956. *Nuer Religion.* London: Oxford University Press.

———. 1965. *Theories of Primitive Religion.* Oxford: Oxford University Press.

———. 1967. *The Morphology and Function of Magic: A Comparative Study of Trobriand and Zande Ritual and Spells.* In *Magic, Witchcraft, and Curing,* ed. John Middleton. Garden City: Natural History Press.

Fadipẹ, N. A. 1970. *The Sociology of the Yoruba.* Ibadan, Nigeria: Ibadan University Press.

Faron, Louis C. 1961. *Mapuche Social Structure: Institutional Reintegration in a Patrilineal Society of Central Chile.* Urbana: University of Illinois Press.

———. 1964. *Hawks of the Sun: Mapuche Morality and Its Ritual Attributes.* Pittsburgh: University of Pittsburgh Press.

———. 1968. *The Mapuche Indians of Chile.* New York: Holt, Rinehart, and Winston.

Fischer, Roland, and Marsha A. Rockey. 1967. A Steady State Concept of Evolution, Learning, Perception, Hallucination, and Dreaming. *International Journal of Neurology* 6: 182–201.

Flanagan, Dennis, ed. 1968. *Cities.* New York: Alfred A. Knopf.

Fox, Robin. 1972. In the Beginning: Aspects of Hominid Behavioral Evolution. In *Perspectives on Human Evolution 2*, ed. S. L. Washburn and Ph. Dolhinow. New York: Holt, Rinehart, and Winston.

Frazer, J. G. 1911–15. *The Golden Bough.* 3d ed. London: Macmillan.

Freuchen, Peter. 1961. *Book of the Eskimos.* Greenwich, Conn.: Fawcett Publications.

Freud, Sigmund. 1913. *Totem und Tabu.* Vienna: Hugo Heller.

———. 1927. *Die Zukunft einer Illusion.* Leipzig: Internat. Psychoanal. Verlag.

Frobenius, Leo. 1937. *Ekade Ektab: Die Felsbilder Fezzans.* Leipzig.

Furst, J. L., and P. T. Furst. 1981. *Mexiko; Die Kunst der Olmeken, Mayas und Azteken.* Munich: Hirmer.

Furst, Peter T., ed. 1972. *Flesh of the Gods: The Ritual Use of Hallucinogens.* New York: Praeger.

Gans, Herbert J. 1967. *The Levittowners: Ways of Life and Politics in a New Surburban Community.* New York: Random House, Vintage Books.

Gardner, R. Allen, and Beatrice T. Gardner. 1969. Teaching Sign Language to a Chimpanzee. *Science* 165: 664–672.

Gazzaniga, Michael S., and Joseph E. LeDoux. 1978. *The Integrated Mind.* New York: Plenum Press.

Geertz, Clifford. 1965. The Transition to Humanity. In *Horizons of Anthropology*, ed. Sol Tax. London: Allen and Unwin.

———. 1966. Religion as a Cultural System. In *Anthropological Approaches to the Study of Religion*, ed. Michael Banton, vol 11, pp. 1–46. London: Tavistock.

———. 1968. *Islam Observed: Religious Development in Morocco and Indonesia.* New Haven: Yale University Press.

Gehrts, Heino. 1967. *Das Märchen und das Opfer: Untersuchungen zum europäischen Brudermärchen.* Munich: H. Bouvier.

Gellhorn, Ernst, and William Kiely. 1972. Mystical States of Consciousness: Neurophysiological and Clinical Aspects. *Journal of Nervous and Mental Disease* 154: 399–405.

Gennep, Arnold van. 1960 (orig. 1909). *The Rites of Passage* [Les rites de passage]. Chicago: University of Chicago Press.

Gilardomi, Virgilio. 1948. *Naissance de l'art.* Paris: Editions de Clairfontaine.

Gimbutas, Marija. 1982. *The Goddesses and Gods of Old Europe: 6500–3500* B.C. Berkeley: University of California Press.

Goffman, Erving. 1967. *Interaction Ritual: Essays on Face-to-Face Behavior*. Garden City, N.Y.: Doubleday.

Goodale, J. C. 1970. An Example of Ritual Change among the Tiwi of Melville Island. In *Diprotodon to Detribalization: Studies of Change among Australian Aborigines*, ed. A. R. Pilling and R. A. Waterman. East Lansing: Michigan State University Press.

———. 1971. *Tiwi Wives*. Seattle: University of Washington Press.

Goodall, Jane. 1971. *In the Shadow of Man*. New York: Dell.

Goodman, Felicitas D. 1971. Glossolalia and Single-Limb Trance: Some Parallels. *Psychotherapy and Psychosomatics* 19: 92–103.

———. 1972. *Speaking in Tongues: A Cross-Cultural Study of Glossolalia*. Chicago: University of Chicago Press.

———. 1973a. Apostolics of Yucatán: A Case Study of a Religious Movement. In *Religion, Altered States of Consciousness, and Social Change*, ed. Erika Bourguignon, pp. 178–218. Columbus: Ohio State University Press.

———. 1973b. Glossolalia and Hallucination in Pentecostal Congregations. *Psychiatria Clinica* 6: 97–103.

———. 1974. Disturbances in the Apostolic Church: A Trance-Based Upheaval in Yucatán. In Felicitas D. Goodman, Jeannette H. Henney, and Esther Pressel, *Trance, Healing, and Hallucination: Three Field Studies in Religious Experience*. New York: Wiley-Interscience.

———. 1976a. Experimental Induction of Altered States of Consciousness. Paper presented to the 85th Annual Meeting of the Ohio Academy of Science, Miami University, Oxford, Ohio, April 23.

———. 1976b. Touching Behavior: The Application of Semantic Theory to a Problem of Anthropological Analysis. *Temple University Working Papers in Culture and Communication* 1: 41–59.

———. 1977. Altered States of Consciousness: A New Classification. Paper presented to the 75th Annual Meeting of the American Anthropological Association, Houston, Texas, December 1.

———. 1980. Triggering of Altered States of Consciousness as Group Events: A New Case from Yucatán. *Confinia Psychiatrica* 23: 26–34.

———. 1981a. States of Consciousness: A Study of Soundtracks. *Journal of Mind and Behavior* 2: 209–219.

———. 1981b. *The Exorcism of Anneliese Michel*. New York: Doubleday. German ed.: *Anneliese Michel und ihre Dämonen: Der Fall Klingenberg in wissenschaftlicher Sicht*. Stein am Rhein: Christiana, 1980.

———. 1986. Body Posture and the Religious Altered State of Consciousness: An Experimental Investigation. *Journal of Humanistic Psychology* 26: 81–118.

———. 1988. *How about Demons? Possession and Exorcism in the Modern World*. Bloomington: Indiana University Press.

Grimm, Brothers, n.d. *Kinder- und Hausmärchen*. Leipzig: R. Becker.

Grinnel, George. 1982. *The Punishment of the Stingy and Other Indian Stories*. Lincoln: University of Nebraska Press.

Grischner, Max. 1912. Die Karolineninsel Namoluk und ihre Bewohner. *Baessler Archiv* 2: 123–215.

Hamayon, R. 1984. Is There a Typically Female Exercise of Shamanism in Patrilinear Societies Such As the Buryat? In *Shamanism in Eurasia*, ed. Mihály Hoppál. Göttingen: Edition Herodot.

Hammond, Dorothy. 1970. Magic: A Problem in Semantics. *American Anthropologist* 72: 1349–1356.

Harnad, Stevan; H. D. Steklis; and J. Lancaster, eds. 1976. *Origins and Evolution of Language and Speech*. New York: Annals of the New York Academy of Science, vol. 280.

Harner, Michael. 1980. *The Way of the Shaman*. Toronto: Bantam Books.

Harris, Marvin. 1968. *The Rise of Anthropological Theory*. New York: Thomas Y. Crowell.

———. 1974. *Cows, Pigs, Wars, and Witches: The Riddle of Culture*. New York: Random House.

Henney, Jeannette H. 1974. Spirit-Possession Belief and Trance Behavior in Two Fundamentalist Groups in St. Vincent. In F. D. Goodman, J. H. Henney, and E. Pressel, *Trance, Healing, and Hallucination: Three Field Studies in Religious Experience*, pp. 1–111. New York: Wiley Interscience.

Hewes, Gordon W. 1976. The Current Status of the Gestural Theory of Language Origin. In *Origins and Evolution of Language and Speech*, ed. Stevan Harnad, Horst D. Steklis, and Jane Lancaster. New York: Annals of the New York Academy of Science, vol. 280, pp. 482–504.

Hillyard, Steven A.; R. F. Hink; V. L. Schwent; and T. W. Picton. 1973. Electrical Signs of Selective Attention in the Human Brain. *Science* 182: 177–179.

Hinsie, Leland E., and Robert J. Campbell. 1970. 4th ed. *Psychiatric Dictionary*. New York: Oxford University Press.

Holloway, Ralph L. 1976. Paleoneurological Evidence for Language Origins. In *Origins and Evolution of Language and Speech*, ed. Stevan Harnad, Horst D. Steklis, and Jane Lancaster. New York: Annals of the New York Academy of Science, vol. 280.

Hsu, Francis L. K. 1967. *Under the Ancestors' Shadow*. Rev. and expanded ed. Garden City, N.Y.: Doubleday Anchor.

Hubert, H., and M. Mauss. 1909. Essai sur la nature et la fonction du sacrifice. *Mélanges d'histoire des religions*, pp. 1–30. Paris.

Huizinga, J. 1939. 3d ed. *Homo Ludens*. Amsterdam: Pantheon Akademische Verlagsanstalt.

I Ching or Book of Changes. 1967 (orig. 1950). Translated from the Chinese into German by Richard Wilhelm, into English by Cary F. Baynes. Princeton: Princeton University Press, Bollingen Series XIX.

Idries Shah. 1964. *The Sufis*. Introduction by Robert Graves. New York: Doubleday.

Issac, Glynn L. 1976. Stages of Cultural Elaboration in the Pleistocene: Possible Archeological Indicators of the Development of Language Capabilities. In *Origins and Evolution of Language and Speech*, ed. Stevan Harnad, Horst D. Steklis, and Jane Lancaster. New York: Annals of the New York Academy of Science, vol. 280, pp. 275–28.

Jacobson, David. 1973. *Itinerant Townsmen: Friendship and Social Order in Urban Uganda*. Menlo Park, Calif.: Cummings.

Janelli, Roger L., and Dawnhee Yin Janelli. 1982. *Ancestor Worship and Korean Society*. Stanford: Stanford University Press.

Jensen, Ad. E. 1960. *Mythos und Kult bei Naturvölkern*. 2d ed. Wiesbaden: Franz Steiner.

Jerison, Harry J. 1973. *Evolution of the Brain and Intelligence*. New York: Academic Press.

———. 1975a. Evolution of the Brain and Intelligence. *Current Anthropology* 16: 403–404.

———. 1975b. Fossil Evidence of the Evolution of the Human Brain. *Annual Review of Anthropology* 4: 27–58.

———. 1976. The Paleoneurology of Language. In *Origins and Evolution of Language and Speech*. ed. Stevan Harnad, Horst D. Steklis, and Jane Lancaster. New York: Annals of the New York Academy of Science, vol. 280, pp. 370–382.

Katz, J. J., and J. A. Fodor. 1964. The Structure of a Semantic Theory. In *The Structure of Language*, ed. Fodor and Katz. Englewood Cliffs, N.J.: Prentice Hall.

Keesing, Roger M., and Felix M. Keesing. 1971. *New Perspectives in Cultural Anthropology*. New York: Holt, Rinehart, and Winston.

Kendon, A. 1975. Gesticulation, Speech, and Gesture Theory of Language Origins. In *Biology and Language*, ed. S. K. Gosh. New York: Academic Press.

Kiefer, C., and J. Cowan. 1976. State/Context Dependence and Theories of Ritual Behavior. Manuscript in preparation, Human Development Program, University of California, San Francisco.

Kluckhohn, Clyde. 1967 (orig. 1944). *Navaho Witchcraft*. Boston: Beacon Press.

———, and Dorothea Leighton. 1961. *The Navaho*. Rev. ed. Garden City, N.Y.: Doubleday.

Kroeber, A. L., and Clyde Kluckhohn. 1952. *Culture: A Critical Review of Concepts and Definitions*. New York: Random House.

La Barre, Weston. 1969 (orig. 1959). *The Peyote Cult*. New York: Schocken.

———. 1970. *The Ghost Dance: The Origins of Religion*. Garden City, N.Y.: Doubleday.

———. 1971. Materials for a History of Studies of Crisis Cults: A Bibliographic Essay. *Current Anthropology* 12: 3–45.

Laing, R. D. 1967. *The Politics of Experience*. New York: Ballantine Books.

Lamendella, John T. 1976. Relations between the Ondogeny and Phylogeny of Language: A NeoRecapitulationist View. In *Origins and Evolution of Language and Speech*, ed. Stevan Harnad, Horst D. Steklis, and Jane Lancaster. New York: Annals of the New York Academy of Science, vol. 280, pp. 396–412.

LaPointe, James. 1976. *Legends of the Lakota*. San Francisco: Indian Historian Press.

Lee, Richard B. 1968. The Sociology of !Kung Bushman Trance Performances. In *Trance and Possession States*, ed. Raymond Prince, pp. 35–54. Montreal: R. M. Bucke Memorial Society.

———, and I. DeVore, eds. 1976. *Kalahari Hunter Gatherers*. Cambridge, Mass.: Harvard University Press.

Lessa, William A. 1959. Divining Knots in the Carolines. *J. Polynesian Soc.* 68 (3): 188–204.

———, and Evon Z. Vogt, eds. 1965. *Reader in Comparative Religion*. 2d ed. New York: Harper and Row.

Levin, M. G., and L. P. Potapov. 1964. *The Peoples of Siberia*. Originally published by the Russian Academy of Science, Moscow, 1956, under the title *Narody Sibiri*. Chicago: University of Chicago Press.

Lévi-Strauss, Claude. 1955. The Structural Study of Myth. *Journal of American Folklore* 47: 428–444; reprinted in *Reader in Comparative Religion: An Anthropological Approach*, ed. William A. Lessa and Evon Z. Vogt, 2d ed, 1965. New York: Harper and Row.

———. 1962 (Eng. trans. 1966). *La pensée sauvage*. Paris: Librairie Plon.

———. 1962. *Totemism*. English translation by Rodney Needham, 1963. Boston: Beacon Press.

Levy, Jerre. 1969. Possible Basis for the Evolution of Lateral Specialization of the Human Brain. *Nature* 224: 614–615.

Lévy-Bruhl, Lucien. 1910 (Eng. trans. 1926). *How Natives Think*. (French title: *Les fonctions mentales dans les sociétés inférieures*.) New York: Washington Square Press.

Lewis, I. M. 1971. *Ecstatic Religion: An Anthropological Study of Spirit Possession and Shamanism*. Baltimore: Penguin.

Lewis, Jackson. 1929. The Origin of Corn. In *Myths and Tales of the Southeastern Indians*, ed. John R. Swanton, pp. 9–10. Washington, D.C.: U.S. Government Printing Office.

Lex, Barbara. 1974a. "Voodoo Death: New Thoughts on an Old Explanation." *American Anthropologist* 76: 818–823.

———. 1974b. The Shaman's Call: Biological Sources of Supernatural Power. Paper presented to the 73d Annual Meeting of the American Anthropological Association, Mexico D.F., November 20.

———. 1975. Physiological Aspects of Ritual Trance. *Journal of Altered States of Consciousness* 2(2): 117–151.

———. 1979. The Neurology of Ritual Trance. In *The Spectrum of Ritual*, ed. d'Aquili et al. New York: Columbia University Press.

Lieberman, Philip. 1975. *On the Origins of Language*. New York: Macmillan.

Liebow, Elliot. 1967. *Tally's Corner: A Study of Negro Streetcorner Men*. Boston: Little, Brown, and Co.

Linton, Ralph. 1924. Totemism and the A.E.F. *American Anthropologist* 26: 296–300.

———. 1943. Nativistic Movements. *American Anthropologist* 45: 230–240.

Lommel, Andreas. 1965. *Die Welt der frühen Jäger: Medizinmänner, Schamanen, Künstler*. Munich: Callwey.

Lovejoy, C. Owen. 1981. The Origin of Man. *Science* 211: 341–350.

Lowie, R. 1920. *Primitive Society*. New York: Boni and Liveright.

Lubbock, J. 1870. *The Origin of Civilization and the Primitive Condition of Man's Mental and Social Condition of Savages*. London: Longmans, Green.

Lynch, Kevin. 1968. The City as Environment. In *Cities*, ed. Denis Flanagan. New York: Alfred A. Knopf.

McHenry, Henry M. 1975. Fossils and the Mosaic Nature of Human Evolution. *Science* 190: 425–431.

McNeley, James Kale. 1981. *Holy Wind in Navajo Philosophy*. Tucson: University of Arizona Press.

Maddock, Kenneth. 1974. *The Australian Aborigines: A Portrait of Their Society*. Harmondsworth, Middlesex, England: Penguin Books.

Mair, Lucy. 1969. *Witchcraft*. New York: McGraw-Hill.

Malinowski, Bronislaw. 1944. *A Scientific Theory of Culture and Other Essays*. Chapel Hill: University of North Carolina Press.

———. 1954 (original articles 1916, 1925, 1926). *Magic, Science, and Religion*. Garden City, N.Y.: Doubleday Anchor.

Man, E. H. 1882. On the Aboriginal Inhabitants of the Andaman Islands. *J. Anthropological Institute* 12.

Marin, Oscar S. M. 1976. Neurobiology of Language: An Overview. In *Origins and Evolution of Language and Speech*, ed. Stevan Harnad, Horst D. Steklis, and Jane Lancaster. New York: Annals of the New York Academy of Science, vol. 280, pp. 900–912.

Marler, Peter. 1976. An Ethological Theory of the Origin of Vocal Learning. In *Origins and Evolution of Language and Speech*, ed. Stevan Harnad, Horst D. Steklis, and Jane Lancaster. New York: Annals of the New York Academy of Science, vol. 280, pp. 386–395.

Marshack, Alexander. 1972. Upper Paleolithic Notation and Symbol. *Science* 178: 817–828.

———. 1976. Implications of the Paleolithic Symbolic Evidence for the Origin of Language. *American Scientist* 64: 136–145.

Marshall, Lorna. 1962. !Kung Bushman Religious Beliefs. *Africa* 32: 221–251.

———. 1969. The Medicine Dance of the !Kung Bushmen. *Africa* 39: 347–381.

Marshall Thomas, Elizabeth. 1959. *The Harmless People*. New York: Alfred A. Knopf.
————. 1972. *Warrior Herdsmen*. New York: Random House.
Maybury-Lewis, David. 1974. *Akwē-Shavante Society*. New York: Oxford University Press.
Meggers, Betty J. 1971. *Amazonia: Man and Culture in a Counterfeit Paradise*. Chicago: Aldine.
Métraux, Alfred. 1928. *La religion des Tupinamba et ses reports avec celle des autres tribus tupi guarani*. Paris.
Michael, Henry N. 1963. *Studies in Siberian Shamanism*. Toronto: University of Toronto Press. Arctic Institute of North America, Anthropology of the North, translations from Russian sources no. 4.
Montagu, Ashley, ed. 1978. *Learning Non-aggression*. New York: Oxford University Press.
Moody, Raymond A. 1975. *Life after Life*. New York: Bantam Books.
Mooney, James. 1896. *The Ghost-Dance Religion and the Sioux Outbreak of 1890*. 14th Annual Report, pt. 2, Bureau of Ethnology to the Smithsonian Institution. Washington, D.C.: Government Printing Office.
Murray, Margaret A. 1960. *The God of the Witches*. New York: Doubleday Anchor.
Naḡm Ad-DIn Al-Kubrā. Ca. 1200. Favā'iḥ Al-Ǧamāl Wa-Fawātiḥ Al-Ǧalāl: Eine Darstellung mystischer Erfahrungen im Islam, ed. Fritz Meier, 1957. Wiesbaden: Franz Steiner Verlag.
Needleman, Jacob, and George Baker, eds. 1978. *Understanding the New Religions*. New York: Seabury Press.
Neihardt, John G. 1961. *Black Elk Speaks*. Lincoln: University of Nebraska Press.
New Testament, Revised Standard Version. 1962. New York: Bantam Books.
Nicolaisen, Johannes. 1961. Essai sur la religion et la magic touaregues. *Folk* 3: 113-162.
————. 1963. *Ecology and Culture of the Pastoral Tuareg*. National Museum of Copenhagen, Nationalmuseets Skrifter, Etnografisk Raekke IX.
Nimuendajú, Curt. 1914. Die Sagen von der Erschaffung und Vernichtung der Welt als Grundlagen der Religion Apapocuva-Guatrani. *Zeitschrift für Ethnologie* 46: 284–403.
Norbeck, Edward. 1961. *Religion in Primitive Society*. New York: Harper and Row.
Noss, John B. 1949. *Man's Religions*. New York: Macmillan.
Nutini, Hugo G. 1971. The Ideological Bases of Lévi-Strauss's Structuralism. *American Anthropoligist* 73: 537–544.
O'Flaherty, Wendy Donigen. 1980. *The Origins of Evil in Hindu Mythology*. Berkeley: University of California Press.
Oppenheim, A. Leo. 1964. *Ancient Mesopotamia: Portrait of a Dead Civilization*. Chicago: University of Chicago Press.
Ornstein, Robert. 1972. *The Psychology of Consciousness*. San Francisco: W. H. Freeman.
————. 1977. Psychological Studies of Consciousness. *Master Lectures on Brain and Behavior Relationship*. Presented at the 85th Annual Convention of the American Psychological Association, San Francisco, August.
Pagano, Robert R.; R. M. Rose; R. M. Stivers; and S. Warrenburg. 1976. Sleep during Transcendental Meditation. *Science* 191: 308–310.
Patañjali. n.d. *The Yoga Aphorisms*. Translated with a new commentary by Swami Prabhavananda and Christopher Isherwood, 1953. New York: New American Library, 1969.
Peters, Larry G., and Douglas Price-Williams. 1983. A Phenomenological Overview of Trance. *Transcultural Psychiatric Research Review* 20: 5–39.

Pfeiffer, Wolfgang M. 1971. *Transkulturelle Psychiatrie*. Stuttgart: Thieme.
Poirier, Frank E. 1974. *In Search of Ourselves*. Minneapolis: Burgess.
Popol Vuh: The Sacred Book of the Ancient Quiché Maya. Translation into Spanish by Adrian Recinos; English version by Delia Goetz and Sylvanus O. Morley, 1950. Norman: University of Oklahoma Press.
Prabhavananda, Swami, and Christopher Isherwood. 1969. *How to Know God: The Yoga Aphorisms of Patañjali*. New York: New American Library, Mentor Books.
Pressel, Esther. 1974. Umbanda Trance and Possession in São Paulo, Brazil. In *Trance, Healing, and Hallucination: Three Field Studies in Religious Experience*, ed. I. I. Zaretsky. New York: Wiley Interscience.
Radcliffe-Brown, A. R. 1939. *Taboo*. Cambridge: Cambridge University Press.
———. 1964 (orig. 1932). *The Andaman Islanders*. New York: Free Press of Glencoe.
Ramsey, Jarold, ed. 1977. *Coyote Was Going There: Indian Literature of the Oregon Country*. Seattle: University of Washington Press.
Rasmussen, Knud. 1930. *Intellectual Culture of the Hudson Bay Eskimos*. Report of the Fifth Thule Expedition, 1921–1924.
Rawson, Philip. 1973. *Tantra: The Indian Cult of Ecstasy*. New York: Avon.
Reichard, Gladys A. 1944. *Prayer: The Compulsive Word*. Monographs of the American Ethnological Society VII.
———. 1950. *Navaho Religion: A Study of Symbolism*. Bollingen Series XVIII. New York: Stratford Press.
Reichel-Dolmatoff, Gerardo. 1971 (Spanish orig. 1968). *Amazonian Cosmos: The Sexual and Religious Symbolism of the Tukano Indians*. Chicago: University of Chicago Press.
Ribeiro, René. 1956. Projective Mechanisms and the Structuralization of Perception in Afro-Brazilian Divination. *Revue Internationale d'Ethnopsychologie Normale et Pathologique* 1 (2): 3–23.
Risso, M., and W. Böker. 1964. Verhexungswahn. *Bibliotheca Psychiatrica et Neurologica*, Additamentum ad Psychiatria et Neurologia. Basel: Karger.
Robbins, Thomas, and Dick Anthony. 1982. Deprogramming, Brainwashing, and the Medicalization of Deviant Religious Groups. *Social Problems* 29, no. 3.
Robinson, Bryan W. 1976. Limbic Influences on Human Speech. In *Origins and Evolution of Language and Speech*, ed. Stevan Harnad, Horst D. Steklis, and Jane Lancaster. New York: Annals of the New York Academy of Science, vol. 280, pp. 761–771.
Runes, Dagobert D. 1960. *Dictionary of Philosophy*. New York: Philosophical Library.
Sagan, Eli. 1974. *Human Aggression, Cannibalism, and Cultural Form*. New York: Harper and Row.
Sahlins, Marshall D. 1972. *Stone Age Economics*. Chicago: Aldine-Atherton.
———. 1976. *Culture and Practical Reason*. Chicago: University of Chicago Press.
Schäden, Egon. 1954. *Aspectos Fundamentais da Cultura Guaraní*. São Paulo.
Schmidt, Wilhelm. 1931. *The Origin and Growth of Religion: Facts and Theories*. New York: Lincoln MacVeagh.
Séjourné, Laurette. 1964. *Pensamiento y Religión en el México Antiguo*. 2d ed. México: Fondo de la Cultura Económica.
Smith, Bradley. 1968. *Mexico: A History in Art*. Garden City, N.Y.: Doubleday.
Spiro, Melford. 1966. Religion: Problems of Definition and Explanation. In *Anthropological Approaches to the Study of Religion*, ed. Michael Banton, pp. 85-126. London: Tavistock.
Spooner, Brian. 1973. *The Cultural Ecology of Pastoral Nomads*. An Addison-Wesley Module in Anthropology, no. 45.
Sreiović, Dragoslav. 1981. *Lepenski Vir*. Bergisch Gladbach: Lubbe.

Stanner, W. E. H. 1965. The Dreaming. In *Reader in Comparative Religion*, 2d ed., ed. William E. Lessa and Evon Z. Vogt, pp. 158–167. New York: Harper and Row.

Steward, J. H., ed. 1946. *Handbook of South American Indians*. Smithsonian Institution, Bureau of American Ethnology, Bulletin, no. 143. Washington, D.C.: U.S. Government Printing Office.

———. 1947. American Culture History in the Light of South America. *Southwestern Journal of Anthropology* 3: 85–107.

Stokoe, William C. 1976. Sign Language Autonomy. In *Origins and Evolution of Language and Speech*, ed. Stevan Harnad, Horst D. Steklis, and Jane Lancaster. New York: Annals of the New York Academy of Science, vol. 280, pp. 505–513.

Swanson, Guy E. 1973. The Search for a Guardian Spirit: A Process of Empowerment in Simpler Societies. *Ethnology* 12: 359–378.

Swanton, John R., 1929. *Myths and Tales of the Southeastern Indians*. Washington, D.C.: Government Printing Office. Bureau of American Ethnology Bulletin, no. 88.

Tart, Charles T., ed. 1969. *Altered States of Consciousness*. Garden City, N.Y.: Doubleday Anchor.

———. 1972. States of Consciousness and State-Specific Sciences. *Science* 176: 1203–1210.

Tedlock, Barbara. 1981. Der Anthropologe und der Wahrsager. In *Der Wissenschaftler und das Irrationale*, ed. Hans Peter Duerr, pp. 154–174. Frankfurt: Syndikat.

———. 1982. *Time and the Highland Maya*. Albuquerque: University of New Mexico Press.

Tedlock, Dennis, trans. 1985. *Popol Vuh*. New York: Simon and Schuster.

Thomas, Keith. 1964. *Religion and the Decline of Magic*. New York: Charles Scribner's Sons.

Thrupp, Sylvia L. 1970. *Millennial Dreams in Action: Studies in Revolutionary Religious Movements*. New York: Schocken Books.

Tonkinson, Robert. 1974. *The Jigalong Mob: Aboriginal Victors of the Desert Crusade*. Menlo Park, Calif.: Cummings.

Trimingham, J. Spencer. 1971. *The Sufi Orders in Islam*. Oxford: Oxford University Press.

Tsunoda, Tadanubo. 1978. *Nipponjin no Noo* [The Japanese Brain]. Tokyo: Taishuukan. Reported by Magorah Naruyama at the 78th Annual Meeting of the American Anthropological Association, Cincinnati, Ohio, 1979.

Turnbull, Colin M. 1962. *The Forest People: A Study of the Pygmies of the Congo*. Garden City, N.Y.: Doubleday Anchor.

———. 1965. *Wayward Servants: The True Worlds of the African Pygmies*. Garden City, N.Y.: Natural History Press.

———. 1978. The Politics of Non-aggression. In *Learning Non-aggression*, ed. Ashley Montagu. New York: Oxford University Press.

Turner, Victor W. 1967. *The Forest of Symbols: Aspects of Ndembu Ritual*. Ithaca, N.Y.: Cornell University Press.

———. 1973. Symbols in African Ritual. *Science* 179: 1100–1105.

Tylor, Edward B. 1871. *Primitive Culture*. London: John Murray.

Underhill, R. M. 1953. *Red Man's America*. Chicago: University of Chicago Press.

———. 1965. *Red Man's Religion*. Chicago: University of Chicago Press.

Vanstone, James W. 1974. *Athapaskan Adaptations*. Chicago: Aldine.

Viski, Károly. 1937. *Hungarian Peasant Customs*. Budapest: Vajna György.

Wagner, Gunter. 1954. The Abaluya of Kavirondo. In *African Worlds: Studies in the Cosmological Values of African Peoples*, ed. Deryl Forde. London: Oxford University Press.

Waley, Arthur. 1933. *The Book of Changes.* Bulletin of the Museum of Far Eastern Antiquities 5: 121–142.

Wallace, Anthony F. C. 1961. *Culture and Personality.* New York: Random House.

———. 1966. *Religion: An Anthropological View.* New York: Random House.

Walsh, Roger. 1980. The Consciousness Disciplines and the Behavioral Sciences: Questions of Comparison and Assessment. *American Journal of Psychology* 137: 663–673.

Warren, Richard M. 1976. Auditory Perception and Speech Evolution. In *Origins and Evolution of Language and Speech*, ed. Stevan Harnad, Horst D. Steklis, and Jane Lancaster. New York: Annals of the New York Academy of Science, vol. 280, pp. 708–717.

Waters, Frank. 1963. *Book of the Hopi.* New York: Viking Press.

Werbner, Richard P. 1973. The Superabundance of Understanding: Kalanga Rhetoric and Domestic Divination. *American Anthropologist* 75: 1414–1440.

White, Leslie A. 1969. Language and Speech. In *Psycholinguistics: An Introduction to the Study of Speech and Personality*, ed. Norman N. Markel, pp. 59-67. Homewood, Ill.: Dorsey Press.

Wilhelm, Richard, and Cary F. Baynes, trans. 1967. *I Ching.* Princeton, N.J.: Princeton University Press, Bollingen Series XIX.

Willett, Frank. 1960. Ifẹ and Its Archeology. *J. African History* 1 (2): 231–248.

———. 1971. A Survey of Recent Results in the Radiocarbon Chronology of Western and Northern Africa. *J. African History* 12 (3): 339–370.

Wolf, Eric C. 1969. *Peasant Wars of the Twentieth Century.* New York: Harper and Row.

Woodburn, James. 1972. An Introduction to Hadza Ecology. In *Man the Hunter*, ed. R. B. Lee and I. DeVore. Chicago: Aldine.

Worsley, Peter. 1968. *The Trumpet Shall Sound.* New York: Schocken.

Wyman, Leland C., ed. 1957. *Beautyway: A Navaho Ceremonial.* Bollingen Series LIII.

———; W. W. Hill; and Iva Osanai. 1942. *Navajo Eschatology.* University of New Mexico Bulletin, no. 377.

———, and Clyde Kluckhohn. 1938. *Navaho Classification of Their Song Ceremonials.* Memoirs of the American Anthropological Association, no. 50.

Yang, Martin C. 1945 (Paper 1965). *A Chinese Village: Taitou, Shantung Province.* New York: Columbia University Press.

Young, Robert W., and William Morgan. 1958. *The Navaho Language.* United States Indian Service. Republished by Salt Lake City: Desert Book Co.

Zolbrod, Paul G. 1984. *Diné bahane': The Navajo Creation Story.* Albuquerque: University of New Mexico Press.

Index

Page numbers in italics indicate an illustration. Page numbers such as "174n.6(4)" should be read as "page 174, note 6 of chapter 4."